THE GOOD BOY
A LIFE RE-EXAMINED

The Good Boy

A life re-examined

TOM DUNNE

CORK cup UNIVERSITY PRESS

First published in 2024 by
Cork University Press
Boole Library
University College Cork
CORK
T12 ND89
Ireland

Library of Congress Control Number: 2024934683
Distribution in the USA: Longleaf Services, Chapel Hill, NC, USA

British Library Cataloguing in Publication Data
A CIP record for this book is available from the British Library.

ISBN: 978-1-78205-593-8

Printed by BZ Graf in Poland
Print origination & design by Carrigboy Typesetting Services
www.carrigboy.co.uk

COVER IMAGE – The author, with the Crawford Art Gallery catalogue of the art of James Barry (2005), which he edited. Taken in the pose adopted by Barry in his late self-portraits. Photographer Fergus Dunne, 2023

www.corkuniversitypress.com

For Clare

The main tension is between two often-contradictory commands: to be faithful to the collective historical experience and to be true to the recognitions of the emerging self.

Seamus Heaney, 'Envies and Identifications: Dante and the modern poet', *Agenda*, vol. 27, no. 1, Spring 1989

Contents

ACKNOWLEDGEMENTS ix

LIST OF FIGURES xi

INTRODUCTION 1

PART ONE. Growing up in Postwar Catholic Ireland

HOME

CHAPTER 1. The Family 14
CHAPTER 2. The Houses 45
CHAPTER 3. The World Outside the Home 62

LIFE WITH THE CHRISTIAN BROTHERS

CHAPTER 4. Training 92
CHAPTER 5. Teaching 121
CHAPTER 6. Leaving 148

PART TWO. Learning to Adapt: The 'Good Boy' in later life

Introduction 155
CHAPTER 7. Personal Life 158
CHAPTER 8. Spiritual Life: From Catholic to humanist 173
CHAPTER 9. Working Life 193
CHAPTER 10. Language and Identity 216
CHAPTER 11. Semi-Retirement 227
CHAPTER 12. Old Age 246

ENVOI 259

INDEX 261

Acknowledgements

After moving house at the beginning of the first Covid-related lockdown I was looking forward to getting back to a book I had half completed, on figures in eighteenth-century Irish landscape paintings. Instead, I found myself immersed in this very different and unforeseen book, a memoir that became *The Good Boy*. Two initial acknowledgements may help to explain why.

Intensive reading in previous years of Michel de Montaigne's essays had made the great French humanist, who died in 1592, a guide and companion in my retirement. He also offered, I became aware, a different way of writing about my life and thought than had been known to me in working on an earlier memoir (*Rebellions*, 2004). That included an account of my time as a teenager in the Irish Christian Brothers, which was read by Joe Veale, a Jesuit and expert on Ignatius Loyola. The idea of *re*-examining my life came initially from him, as he urged me, through a letter to a mutual friend, to rewrite my account of monastic life so as to focus more on the psychological damage it has caused me. The idea stayed at the back of my mind, and was extended over time to re-examining my life and character more generally and radically. The experience of isolation in lockdown may have enabled and encouraged the fusion of those two influences to create this book.

It has been difficult to write, and would not have been completed without the help and encouragement of family and friends. Discussions with my siblings, especially since the death of our mother twenty-five years ago, provided insights into my childhood, which had been interrupted so abruptly at fourteen. I am particularly indebted to them for responses to queries as I wrote this book, for their sourcing of photographs, and critiques of parts of my text. I am particularly grateful to my sister Rosaleen for letting me use her drawing of our childhood home.

I gained valuable insights into my mother's childhood, and particularly the alcoholism of her father, from conversations with my late cousin Bride Roe, and particularly from her typescript based on conversations with her own mother.

My daughters, Fiona and Deirdre, were immensely supportive, sharing memories of their childhood, and reading the account of my marriage to their mother, Mary.

My sons, Oisín and Fergus, were also encouraging, and intrigued, asking their own questions, as appears in my text. Fergus also took the cover photograph.

Friends who read critically the initial drafts gave indispensable support and advice; my thanks to Stefan Collini, John Maguire, Greg Schirmer and, above all, Roy Foster, who has so greatly influenced and encouraged my work through the years. I am grateful to my friend and mentor on art history, Bill Pressly, who read the section on my move to that area of research.

I owe a particular debt to Terry O'Reilly for his sustained interest in the project, even as he coped with motor neurone disease, with great courage and humour, publishing several books, and dying as mine was in production. His unrivalled knowledge of the spirituality of Ignatius Loyola transformed my understanding of the training I received as a novice, and informed my attempt to answer Joe Veale's suggestion. Terry's very deep Christian humanism also helped me to make better sense of my secular version, and I will always be grateful for his friendship.

My memories of childhood were kept alive also by Michael Hanrahan, a great friend from the time we met in kindergarten until he died just before his eightieth birthday earlier this year. He is remembered in these pages.

Likewise, my fellow postulant, novice and junior professed Brother, Leo Wright, assisted greatly in my attempts to remember and understand my time in the Christian Brothers. He sourced photographs and lists, arranged for meetings with old colleagues, and shared many reminiscences, all of which have been important in healing a painful rupture in my life.

I am greatly indebted to the committee of Cork University Press for agreeing to publish this book, to the insightful reader's report they commissioned, and above all to its ever-helpful, prompt and professional managing editor Maria O'Donovan, who has done so much to make the press a byword for quality and innovation.

I am grateful to Stanford University Press for permission to cite from Donald M. Frame, The Complete Essays of Montaigne (1958).

My greatest debt, acknowledged in the dedication, is to my wife and fellow historian Clare O'Halloran. Whatever insights I have gained into my life and my nature have come mainly through talking and living with her. She is the first reader of everything I write, and its most important editor.

List of Figures

1. The author's parents (*his mother on the right*) post-marriage, summer 1942 — 15
2. The author's mother (*second on right, standing*) and friends at Newbawn portal tomb — 16
3. The author's mother, aged four, with her father — 17
4. The author's mother in front of her first shop, Bridge Street, New Ross — 18
5. The author's paternal grandparents — 19
6. Canon Dunne — 20
7. The author's parents on their wedding day — 22
8. The author with his parents, Courtdale, 1943 — 24
9. The author with his parents and sister Mary, by Annie Brophy, Waterford, 1945 — 26
10. The author with his father, Courtdale, 1943 — 28
11. The author's Bradford relations, 1950s — 34
12. The author with his sister Mary on the quay, New Ross, *c.*1945 — 39
13. The author (*on one knee*) with his family in the dunes, Duncannon, 1955 — 41
14. The author (*seated, left*) with his family, by Annie Brophy, Waterford, 1955 — 42
15. Courtdale — 47
16. The house at 14 South Street. A drawing by Rosaleen Dunne, *c.*1966 — 48
17. South Street, New Ross, 1950s, the family shop on the left — 63
18. The Rice family home, Irishtown, New Ross — 64
19. The Tottenham townhouse — 66
20. The Tholsel, New Ross — 67
21. The 1798 monument, New Ross — 68
22. The author's father in Gus O'Kennedy's pub, New Ross, celebrating the visit of President John F. Kennedy to the town in 1963. He is sitting at the bar counter, on the right, wearing glasses. — 74

23. The author's father and the author's uncle John, on holiday in the 1960s 77
24. The Children of Mary in a Corpus Christi procession, New Ross, *c.*1950 79
25. First Communion, 1949 82
26. Sports day, June 1957 84
27. The author (*left*) with Michael Hanrahan, New Ross, 1958 97
28. Novices after taking the habit, St Helen's, Booterstown, 1959. The author is on the extreme left, top row 105
29. The author (*left*) with Danny Brennan, St Helen's, 1959 107
30. The author with his siblings, in front of St Helen's, 1959 109
31. The author with his parents, St Helen's, 1959 110
32. The author (*left*) with Leo Wright in Cork, 11 November 2010 123
33. Staff of Francis Street CBS, waiting to meet Archbishop McQuaid, 1961. The author is in the back row, extreme left. 125
34. The author with the Francis Street CBS athletics team, 1962 132
35. The author, Synge Street, 1961 134
36. A group of young Christian Brothers at 'the Cove', Greystones, 1962. The author is second from right at the back. 135
37. The author's father, Tralee, 1963 138
38. The author's mother, New Ross, 1964 139
39. The industrial school, St Joseph's, Tralee (postcard) 140
40. The author, self-portrait, Youghal, 1963 143

Introduction

Why write a memoir? My life has not been particularly interesting or significant, except perhaps in being representative of my generation in some respects. As such I am in part aware of writing as a historian, now eighty, who has lived through a formative, and already seemingly remote, time in his country's past and wants to share his memory of it. However, I am writing primarily as an individual, attempting to understand myself, and my life's experience.

It is possible also that I have become somewhat addicted to writing about my life, having published a memoir nearly twenty years ago as part of an experimental academic study, focused on a family and local story of 1798 and on the official celebration of the rebellion's bicentenary (*Rebellions: Memoir, memory and 1798* (The Lilliput Press, 2004 [2010])). Responses to that memoir were largely positive but I was struck by those comments that pointed to its limited emotional dimension, particularly its account of the seven years I spent with the Irish Christian Brothers, aged fourteen to twenty-one. Another limitation, obvious to me now, is that it was largely a conventional narrative, with a strong forward momentum, which tends to flatten much of the texture of a life and pay too little attention to its complexity and contradictions.

Now, appreciably older, and far more preoccupied with memory, it seems like a good time to write a more reflective memoir, one that will stand alone, and not be constrained by specific contexts or the conventions of academic history-writing. Having examined my life and background as an aid to understanding my work as a historian, I am now re-visiting it in order to understand myself better. In this effort I have been helped especially by intense reading of Michel de Montaigne's *Essays*, written mainly from his retirement from public life in 1571 to his death twenty-one years later. They have opened up different approaches to understanding my life experience, in terms of the complex evolution of my thinking, and given me a very different way of writing about it, randomly and digressively, rather than simply as narrative.

One of the many paradoxes of old age is that as you become more concerned to remember and understand your past, at the same time you become ever more aware how poor, partial and random your memories are, even of recent events; how unstable they are, how they shimmer and change. Of course, we should not be too fixated on memory loss. Every day, from childhood on, we forget the vast majority of our ongoing experiences. Indeed, without such forgetting, not only the preservation of particular memories, but life itself, saturated in memory overload, would be impossible. Even then, the memories we do preserve are problematic, both in their slow erosion with ageing and in how to understand them.

Like the lawyer and the historian when dealing with memory-based evidence, we learn that memory cannot be relied on to reconstitute a past event accurately, much less to offer solid evidence of fact. Memoirs that are presented un-problematically as sustained transcriptions of remembrance, that purport to recount detailed conversations or to recapture smells, colours and sounds, are more works of the imagination (or re-workings of family stories) than of memory, however sparked by it. Yet, memory is crucial, indeed indispensable, in any attempt to understand our lives, what shaped our formative years, and how we developed as adults. While it cannot be accepted at face value, it can however be stimulated and interrogated, and that, perhaps, is the main challenge in writing a memoir. The point is not to say, 'this is what happened', but 'this is what I remember, and now, in old age, am trying to understand'. Memoir, as attempted here, is not mainly about the past but about coming to terms with what I remember of it today.

Marcel Proust insisted that only 'involuntary' memory, that is, one that emerges unbidden, under a sensory stimulus, is fully authentic, to the point in some instances of being overwhelming. Such for him was the taste of a madeleine dipped in tea that so powerfully evoked a morning visit as a child to the room of his hypochondriac Aunt Leonie; another was the overwhelming scent of hawthorn transporting him back to a favourite childhood walk, and to childhood itself. Many people may occasionally experience such 'involuntary' memory, though few, I imagine, as overwhelmingly as Proust did. Some of my own instances are included in what follows, although I doubt that they can add much to a memoir like mine – as opposed to a novel. Most of what were presented as the unnamed narrator's memories in Proust's great work were not only *voluntary*, that is consciously sought and gathered; they also included the memories of other people, living and dead, all combined in complex patterns to draw out elements of the culture of his time and place, as he understood them. His huge edifice is like the medieval cathedrals that he loved, a harmonious distillation of many elements and skills, but it is not a model for memoir, as usually understood.

However, like Proust, we all at some level develop, and constantly edit and expand, a narrative of our lives, to explain ourselves to ourselves, to those we love or are in dialogue with, at times even to those in authority. The narrative constantly evolves, however subtly; elements are changed or forgotten; newly remembered details are foregrounded. Our memories are many-layered, endlessly reconstructed, and our perspectives on them change with distance and circumstance. This process is not altogether random; subconsciously, and perhaps even consciously, we tend to foreground memories that show us, and those close to us, in a good light, or are otherwise consoling. Conversely, we can suppress memories that are unbearably painful or negative, as I came to learn. Writing about family, as I do especially in Part One, both my original family and later religious one, there is a particular temptation to create a pleasing image. In her rich, complex attempt to 'remember' her scattered family through a century of turmoil, the Russian poet Maria Stepanova discovered a bundle of colourful letters written by her father, then a young man, to his family from remote Kazakhstan, where he was working. They were perfect for her purpose but when she wrote asking his permission to use them, her father refused, declaring them 'fake', written to console and reassure the recipients. Initially upset, she came to wonder whether, 'in place of respectable research, I had been occupied all this time with the Freudian family romance, the sentimentalised past'. An element of sentimentalising may, indeed, be inescapable in memoir-writing, especially for someone of my temperament, but awareness of this may help to avoid its excesses.

Seeing it in terms of layering may also offer a way into understanding memory and engaging with it. Nowadays, the composing and recording of music electronically involves adding layers of sound to a basic melody, combining and transforming their elements to produce a complex synthesis. (This I learn from the hip-hop compositions of my son Oisín, whose passion it is.) What I am attempting in the first section here is such a layered synthesis in text. The basic layer is of memories of my life up to the age of twenty-one. Superimposed on that are important but lightly sketched historical contexts that framed my life and my memories of it; also, elements of texts and music that influenced me and coloured particular times. Of the images that evoke that distant past, the most important are photographs, particularly of myself from infancy, taken at key stages, and in various settings. These can be interrogated, or 'read' (as art historians speak of reading paintings), in order to engage with further layers of memory and understanding that lie below the surface.

These elements of historical context, the use of photographs of key moments of life and the evocation of popular music and texts from childhood, are also employed by Annie Ernaux in one of the most praised and debated of recent memoirs, *The Years* (published in 2008 as *Les Années*). The differences between us may help to clarify my approach further. We are of an age, and she too had been the child of small-town shopkeepers, a teacher and academic. Reading her, I was often dazzled by her insights and unexpected connections, but even more puzzled for most of the book by her avoidance of any sustained narrative, and of the first person – she speaks throughout of 'we', not 'I'. Her memoir features, instead, a seemingly random accumulation of brief, passing references to social and political events, to consumer goods and advertisements, to films and popular songs as a kaleidoscopic framework for discussions at family meals, which remember the past and respond to the events of the day. Only at the end of the book does she explain that she is not writing a personal memoir, but sketching out her daunting range of material for a future communal one. Her ambition, with its Proustian echoes, is daring and remarkable: 'By retrieving the memory of collective memory in an individual memory, she will capture the lived dimension of History.'

This impressionistic approach to the possibility of writing memoir as communal history will seem problematic to most historians. I have no such ambition in this book. I have never kept a diary, and if I had one that recorded the kind of material that Ernaux assembles, I imagine that, overwhelmed by a succession of random 'facts', I would never have attempted to make sense of them. Mine is not a history of any kind, but an attempt to understand such memories of my past as I can access in old age, without much reference to the historical record. This is also true, in part, of Ernaux, whose most productive sources are not her diary or the internet, but a forensic, often painful attempt to recover memory through a range of prompts, mainly photographs. Despite its experimental form, it is intensely personal. Whatever about the formidable intellectual ambition, she acknowledges at the end that, 'more than anything, she would like to capture the light that suffuses faces that can no longer be seen'. All writing, whether it is called history or memoir or, indeed, fiction or poetry, is, as John Berger put it, 'a struggle to give meaning to experience'.

The balance between the attempt in old age to *reconstruct* in memory the world of childhood, and to *reflect* on it is a delicate and shifting one. This will be clear particularly in Part One in the contrast between the early chapters on childhood in my family, and the later chapters on my time with the Christian Brothers, which was both a continuation of childhood and the beginning of my adult experiences. In the former the balance tilts towards reconstruction; in the latter more towards reflection, even analysis. In the former the reflective element is focused mainly on trying to understand myself in my family setting, and especially in relation to my mother; in the latter on understanding my experience as a junior member of a now controversial religious order, and why I left it.

What is unique in any life experience is not the individual story – all share the trajectory from birth to death, and many Irish contemporaries had the same key experiences as I had. What is unique to each is the refraction of such experiences through the particularities of one's background, cultural formation and personality. That is a major element of the loss caused by every death, the unique complexity that only the deceased understood, and then dimly. I hope to recapture, or evoke, some of my experience of that complexity, and also to relate it lightly to some of the remarkable social and cultural changes that, in my memory, have marked my lifetime. So much of what I remember now seems utterly foreign, even fantastical, to my sons, now in their late twenties, and in part I am attempting to reach across generations.

In Vladimir Nabokov's *Speak, Memory*, perhaps the most seductive and plangent of all autobiographies aimed at reconstruction through memory, the impossibly detailed recall of his privileged childhood in pre-Revolutionary Russia is explained by the sudden, radical destruction of the life remembered, indeed of childhood itself. Many people, it seems, feel, as he did, that they are 'in exile' from a lost childhood, but for most this process is slow and piecemeal. I have no sense of that loss as 'exile', but I do share with Nabokov the experience of it as sudden and radical, having left not only my home, but childhood itself, at fourteen to join a religious order; forced to become, in effect, a small adult, returning home only infrequently and for short periods over the next seven years. At the end of that time, my leaving the order, which had become, in very real as well as notional terms, my new family, was also a radical breach, as I was cut adrift, an outcast, without any possibility of continued contact. Part of my hope in writing this memoir is to understand and repair, as far as is possible, the fractures in my sense of self caused by these radical and sudden changes in my early life.

As a child, the eldest of the family, I was always a 'Good Boy', with a strong sense of duty, never disobedient, focused on pleasing adults, initially my parents, later teachers and those in authority. That changed, briefly, during my final year as a trainee religious, when I became disobedient, even rebellious in response to an authoritarian regime, and in later life that new, assertive trait was prominent in a number of contexts. It seems clear now that in my early years I had learned to repress a great deal of what I felt, and of my personality, and had learned to be too much a conformist in my engagement with the world in general, and not just with authority figures. Part of my purpose here is to try to understand my early conditioning to be a 'Good Boy', to be emollient, even charming, in order to achieve my objectives and avoid confrontation, especially on an emotional level, and to reflect on what the considerable costs of that conditioning were. Crucial to this has been the likelihood that my mother's powerful personality, which so affected me, was shaped by her learning to cope with an alcoholic father.

'Good Boy syndrome' is sometimes used to describe the effects of an upbringing by parents who are overtly controlling or authoritarian, to encourage exceptional good behaviour or academic excellence, and which can also lead to hiding behaviour of which they disapproved. This was not my experience – my parents, for example, did not insist on success, or excellence in school-work, but were very tolerant of failure or struggle. But, looking back, I am aware of an expectation, particularly by my mother, of good behaviour and an absence of dissent – not that I have the least memory of wanting or trying to dissent. Indeed, I seem to have been a remarkably emollient, conformist child, but not the least, as I recall it, out of fear. Good behaviour was implied rather than insisted on, an emotional expectation rather than a rational one. It involved on my part, especially as the eldest of six children, a strong desire for approval, and a subtle encouragement to mirror adult behaviour. 'Good Boy behaviour' fits better than 'syndrome' for what I came to see as a damaging aspect of my personality, 'Good Boy' deriving from a colloquial expression often applied to me, or expected of me, rather than from child psychology.

In seeking to understand, and to try to repair, the costs to me and to others of that way of dealing with difficulties, I have also come to recognise that my 'Good Boy' persona remains a fundamental reflex in how I manage life, one that still needs to be challenged and overcome. In his essay 'On Repentance', one of his most sustained pieces of self-analysis, Montaigne wrote, 'There is no-one who, if he listens to himself, does not discover in himself a pattern all his own, a ruling pattern, which struggles against education, and against the tempest of the passions that oppose it.' Only in middle age did I begin to understand that my 'ruling pattern' involved essentially a level of dishonesty and dissembling, as part of my failure to engage properly, even with those closest to me, choosing to evade rather than to confront problems and deal with them. Only belatedly did I become aware of the damage that pattern was causing me and my relationships, and the need to be more honest, less threatened by disagreement or difference. Understanding what may have shaped that initial habit of being a 'Good Boy', the emotional cost involved, and the beginning of the process of freeing myself from it, has been at the heart of what impelled me to revisit memoir-writing.

In Part One the focus is on my childhood and early adulthood, while Part Two offers a series of reflections on what to me were key aspects of my later life, some of which illustrate both the residual difficulties caused by my 'Good Boy' persona and the efforts to modify it. Throughout, there are references to the essays of Michel de Montaigne (1533–92), which have been both stimulus and model; some of my later chapters are, in effect, in dialogue with key later essays of his. Part of my ambition for this book, indeed, is to share my enthusiasm for Montaigne's writings. As with all such from a distant past and different place, it takes a little time to attune to his voice, but it is so often an entertaining as well as wise voice, as to repay the effort. I give no reference details in my citations of Montaigne as their use is a matter of my personal response, not any kind of academic exercise. All of them come from the translation by Donald M. Frame (Stanford University Press, 1958).

I have found Montaigne to be less a guide on 'how to live', as a recent excellent study claimed, than a companion in retirement, speaking about shared concerns with insight, humour and empathy across the years. As will emerge, I share some of what he describes as his characteristics, for example the tendency later in life to give advice 'a little boldly', his preference for essays rather than 'extended narration', his instinctive, emotional rejection of cruelty and physical abuse, and his manipulation of the voice so as to achieve his ends.

His main – indeed he often claimed, his only – subject was himself, not in terms of what he had done or was doing, but of understanding how his thinking evolved over time in response to his experiences and his reading: 'it is not my deeds that I write down; it is myself; it is my essence'. A response to reading also marks this memoir; looking back over it I realise that it may appear in places to be as much about books that resonate with my experience as about memory directly. His constant reference to his reading was part of Montaigne's recognition of the novelty of attempting 'to follow a movement so wandering as that of our mind', and to describe it 'in the airy medium of words', an ambition that has created a powerful bond with his readers, helped by self-deprecatory humour and the frankness that more and more distinguished him.

Montaigne began his essays as a devotee of Stoic philosophy, while remaining on some levels a loyal Catholic. Stoicism, like Christianity later, was focused on learning how to master the body and its senses in order to deal well with life and to prepare for its end. Over time, his experience of fanatical religions and his efforts to describe his evolving thinking led him away from Stoicism to scepticism, questioning everything, suspicious of dogma, slow to judge, agreeing with Socrates that 'all I know is that I know nothing'. In his final series of essays his focus changed again from learning how to die to learning how to live, from intellectual questioning to wishing 'to know how to enjoy our being rightfully', from focusing mainly on the life of the mind to seeing the enjoyment of the body as equally important to happiness and understanding. In effect, he expanded and deepened the humanism in which he had been educated, and that had always underpinned his thought.

I have come to identify with that progression in Montaigne's approach to life, my early religious training also being in Catholic-inflected Stoicism, my professional training as a historian being in empirical scepticism, and the efforts at self-understanding in old age leading me to a more holistic appreciation of the interaction of mind and body, a deeper understanding of what it means to be human.

Montaigne has also offered me a way of writing that is different from the structured, evidence-based, academic approach. His essays are serendipitous, loosely assembled and full of digressions, following his thoughts as they arise and allowing room for reflection. Rejecting structure, or system, he called his writings a 'bundle of so many disparate pieces', 'a flow of babble', going along 'befuddled and staggering with a natural drunkenness'. This was not simply indifference to form but was dictated by his determination to describe and understand his fluctuating thoughts. 'I do not portray being:

I portray passing ... My history needs to be adapted to the moment ... It is a record of various and changeable occurrences, and of irresolute and, when it so befalls, contradictory ideas.' That is indeed how we live our lives, in contrast to the order normally imposed by the historian.

While I cannot at this late stage altogether abandon the habits of a lifetime, I have tried to follow Montaigne's loose, digressive approach in this attempt to write a 'memoir', one concerned both with recapturing childhood and with reflecting in old age on such scattered, rapidly receding memories of it as I have. This shapes the book's first section, a memoir of a postwar Irish Catholic childhood in a small town, and of my experience as a trainee religious from age fourteen to twenty-one. The second section, rather than bringing 'my story' up to date as narrative, deals with key aspects of my later life experience, not in the same sequential form, but in a series of reflections – on my personal life, on my move from Catholicism to humanism, on my working life as a teacher and writer, on my sense of identity, on retiring and on ageing. These are 'essays' as Montaigne envisaged his, as attempts, trials, or experiments in understanding, 'written in a general way and tentatively', rather than the polished formal writings we tend to associate with 'the essay' today. Together, they can also comprise a different, less structured form of memoir. My attempts, however, make no claims to be Montaigne-like. No writer since has succeeded in being quite that, and it is certainly beyond whatever writing skill I have. Yet, however inadequately, they aim to be in his spirit, contributions to a conversation with him and with other friends, some now dead, over a lifetime.

I have been a slow and late developer, like Montaigne aware of 'how much I still have to learn', and with comparatively little time to do so. These memories and reflections, while primarily an attempt to understand myself better, are also, as he wrote of his essays, intended for 'relatives and friends', in the hope that 'when they have lost me (as soon they must) they may recover here some features of my habits and temperament, and by this means keep the knowledge they have had of me more complete and alive'. If this attempt proves to be of wider interest, and finds space in what Montaigne called 'a nook in a library', that will be a bonus. However, they are also written cognisant of Montaigne's warning:

> Whoever puts his decrepitude into print plays the fool, if he hopes to squeeze out of it humours that do not smell of ungraciousness, dreaminess and drowsiness. Our mind grows constipated and sluggish as it grows old.

Yet, in another mood, he justified writing 'a record of various and changeable occurrences' such as mark

> a humble and inglorious life; that does not matter. You can tie up all moral philosophy with a common and private life as well as with a life of richer stuff. Each man bears the entire form of man's estate.

PART ONE

Growing up in Postwar Catholic Ireland

HOME

CHAPTER I

The Family

See, now they vanish
The faces and places, with the self, which, as it could, loved them
T.S. Eliot, *Little Gidding*

The main fascination of photographs of my parents together, taken before my own appearance on the scene, is that it brings them into focus as individuals rather than in relation to myself. I have only two such images, and they are of contrasting quality and mood. The difficulty of envisaging parents as young and full of hope, when in your first clear memories of them they are already middle aged, is compounded by the nature of old black-and-white photographs, which, as one art historian has remarked, 'seal people into a colourless world, as if they saw life that way too'. Furthermore, 'monochrome turns the present into the past; makes the past even more distant'. It also tends to make people look older than they then were, especially when the clothes of that era offered little to suggest youth. Yet, such photographs, looked at closely, can reveal a lot, and suggest new questions and speculations.

One of my photographs is professional, conventional and static, their formal wedding photograph in a Dublin studio in February 1942; the other, a few months later (judging by what they are wearing), is a relaxed, outdoor, informal photograph that also includes her sister Nancy (Figure 1). By then my mother was already pregnant with me, so I am in fact present, though unformed and invisible, and perhaps even unknown at that early stage to both of my parents. Neither of them was in the first flush of young adulthood; both had already had difficult life experiences. She, Johanna, outgoing, charming, full of energy and enthusiasm, was thirty-three; he, Art, self-effacing, gentle and humorous, was three years older.

In the informal photograph, probably taken by her older cousin and great friend May Gantley, they are on the quayside in New Ross, the small town in Wexford, in Ireland's south-east, where I was to grow up. He, wearing a formal suit and holding one of the cigarettes that were to kill him thirty-six years later, is sitting on a bollard, his raincoat spread over it, smiling faintly, probably joking; she is standing behind him, her hands possessively

FIGURE 1. Credit: Author

on his shoulders, smiling broadly, and beside her, equally delighted, is Nancy, who had been her bridesmaid – both wearing coats over identical light dresses in the cool early summer evening. The sisters remained close all their lives, sharing a deep sense of nostalgia, a simple piety, and uncannily similar handwriting. Looking at them here, in their vibrant early thirties, it is impossible for me not to remember their meeting in old age, when each had suffered strokes, which deprived them of speech. They were in different nursing homes, and when I brought Mother to visit her sister, they spent an hour smiling at each other and holding hands; it was unbearably poignant.

In Mother's old photograph album there are many pictures of her in earlier years, most with groups of friends, with sisters and cousins prominent; some on 'excursions' to the seaside, or to local sites, one to the megalithic dolmen at Newbawn, near the farm where I was to be born (Figure 2) – but none that I have found includes her shy fiancé, their engagement long a secret. She was a 'townie', growing up initially in Irishtown, where her family had lived and carried on various businesses since the mid-eighteenth century, and she remained so even after they moved to Ballymacar, a farm of eighty hilly and boggy acres three miles out of town. This was an effort by her mother, ultimately futile, to contain her

FIGURE 2. Credit: Author

husband's (my grandfather's) alcoholism, which was rapidly impoverishing them. But in her account, when we were children, he appeared as a romantic figure, full of stories of Australia where he had been born, his father having emigrated there in the mid-1850s and become a gold prospector, only to die within a few years. His redoubtable widow returned to New Ross, carrying (according to family lore) a number of gold nuggets, with which she bought land and houses, setting her spoiled son up for life – a fatal inheritance, as it turned out. He was a hale and hearty ninety-two when my parents married, dying three years later. Mother always maintained that he died then only because he went out on a frosty night against his wife's advice: for Mother he never really died.

Here she is, aged four, standing in front of her father in a family photograph, now in poor condition apart from this segment, an image of great significance for me (Figure 3). He is every inch the respectable *pater familias*, in his fine suit, with his submissive little girl, her hair beautifully done, carrying a basket (probably of the wildflowers she always loved), her eyes cast down, already learning how to manage him. Her closed eyes and the basket of flowers constitute for me what Roland Barthes (in *Camera Lucida*) called a 'punctum', that is the accidental detail of a photograph that 'pricks me' or 'which bruises me, is poignant to me'. In his search for the essence of his beloved mother in photographs after her death, Barthes finally 'found' her in a photograph of her as a five-year-old in a winter garden. 'I studied the little girl and at last rediscovered my mother', that is, her essence, especially her 'sovereign *innocence*', and 'the assertion of a gentleness'.

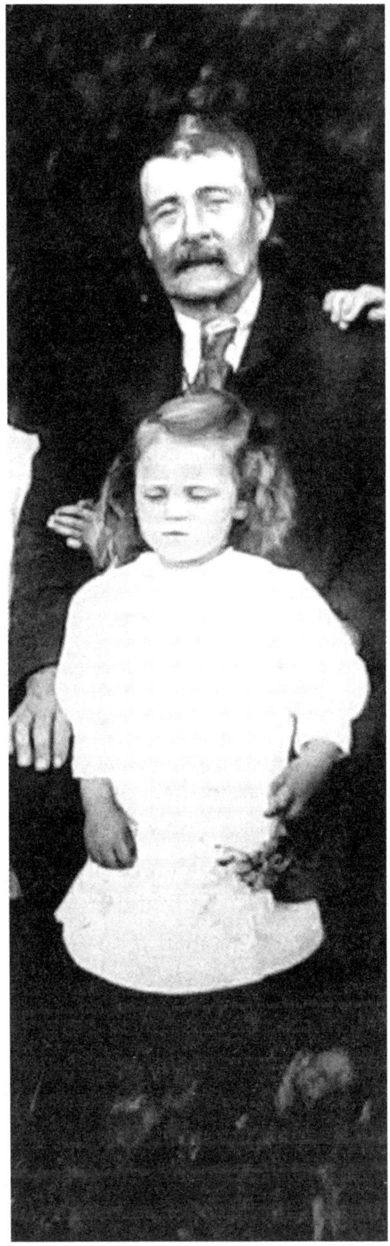

FIGURE 3. Credit: Author

In this photograph of my mother as a young girl I find a similar innocence and gentleness but also the guardedness and vulnerability of the wounded child, the child in danger. This is not speculation or hyperbole. In the damaged family photograph, of which this is a part, the face of the eldest girl was scratched out with some force, by herself, according to her daughter, my cousin Bride. In her short typescript of the family history, based largely on her deceased mother's account, Bride emphasises repeatedly the misery, including occasional violence, associated with our grandfather's drinking, something my mother could only hint at very late in her life, as we will see. But already, this small child at her father's knee must have been learning to cope with his sudden rages, in ways that were to shape her character – and mine.

He was a popular, elegant figure by all accounts, strolling late into town every day, leaving the farm to the mercies of a 'steward', twirling his silver-topped cane on his way to games of billiards or cards with friends. But his children had to leave school early and contribute to the shaky family income, my mother working in a shoe shop and going to night classes. In response to the insecurities of her upbringing she developed ambition and an iron will, and before she

FIGURE 4. Credit: Author

was thirty had opened her own shop around the corner from the quay where the post-wedding photograph was taken. She did so with the help of a bank loan, guaranteed by her mother's brother William, a successful businessman, and it was an unusually bold and ambitious venture for a young woman at that time. That is reflected in a photograph (Figure 4) in which she stands solemnly in front of her shop in her sensible shoes and shop coat, her name, 'J. Rice', in large letters over the door, a proclamation of her independence but also of her consciousness, throughout her life, of reviving a very old family tradition as business-people in the town. I have no doubt that she also saw her shop as restoring the family name after her father's slow decline. Up to the time she married she continued to live in the family home, which remained a romantic idyll throughout her life, just as her father continued to be idolised until her final years, when she revealed a little of the terror he could evoke. He must have visited her shop, if only to cadge some drinking money. Was he proud of her? She never said so. She never mentioned him calling in, or indeed anything that suggested a personal adult relationship with him. It seems likely that neither of my parents ever had a real conversation with their fathers.

FIGURE 5. Credit: Author

My father was a countryman, growing up in a family that had farmed the same land at Courtnacuddy, south of Enniscorthy, since at least the early seventeenth century. His mother died in the great flu epidemic of 1918–19, leaving himself and his siblings to cope with a withdrawn, authoritarian father, mourning her loss and coping badly with its consequences. Here, in their wedding photograph, they are the epitome of bourgeois respectability, reflecting less their economic circumstances (the farm was modest in size) than their strong clerical connections; that sense of social status can be seen later in his ambition and role as a Poor Law Guardian (Figure 5). My grandfather, Thomas, was an inefficient farmer, despite his meticulous records of crop rotation mixed in among the poems and curiosities of his commonplace books, one of which I have. His sons remembered him as more interested in reading, writing patriotic verse and involvement in nationalist politics. Widowed, he shut himself away from the family for long periods, his remoteness helping to create a remarkably close and lifelong bond among his children. All of them shared a gentleness, calmness and sweetness of temperament, a legacy from their mother, my father ventured when asked to explain something so striking and unexpected. His brothers,

FIGURE 6. Credit: Author

Jim, John and Nick, remained his closest friends, in that, if nothing else, emulating their father, whose only brother, John, a prominent priest, Gaelic Leaguer and promoter of local business, was not only his closest (perhaps only) friend but also his advisor, his word being law in the family, where he is still remembered as 'The Canon' – a stern, judge-like figure, indeed, as in this formal portrait (Figure 6). Thus, my uncle John was told, without reference to his own wishes, that he was going to Maynooth to train as a priest, and so to continue a generations-old family tradition, which he did, becoming in his turn the family's advisor and guide. At sixteen my father, likewise, was taken out of the Christian Brothers school in Enniscorthy, where he had been doing well, to begin work as an apprentice shop assistant in a large draper's in the town, its sanctimonious owner, doubtless, a friend of The Canon. The harsh conditions he endured there and his exposure to trade unionism made him a lifelong Labour supporter, and the ostentatious piety of his skinflint employer helped to turn him to a very private version of religion. Despite the active republicanism of his older brother Jim, prominent in the local IRA during the War of Independence, and a diehard anti-treatyite all his life, my father had also shown an antipathy to extreme nationalism, even as a schoolboy, something he shared with his Redmondite father, who fell out with Jim, his eldest son, over it.

After ten unhappy years as a shop assistant in Enniscorthy, the last few, as coincidence would have it, selling shoes, my father was liberated, suddenly and unexpectedly, by the man who had initially condemned him to town life. In 1931 Daddy's Aunt Biddy died, leaving the bulk of her estate to the Maynooth Mission to China, a prominent part of Catholic Ireland's growing spiritual 'empire'. A widow and childless, she had inherited a farm from her husband, and her brother The Canon, as executor (and, doubtless, architect) of her will, arranged its sale to my father (who, being penniless, was presumably given a loan) in order to keep it in the family. While a very good farm of ninety acres, eight miles from New Ross (five beyond mother's hard-scrabble Ballymacar), Courtdale came with problems, not least the fact that The Canon sold off all the stock and machinery to make some compensation to the original owners, the family my aunt had married into. So my father began with just the land and was refused a loan to stock it from the same bank that was to help my mother get started some years later. Land was seen as poor collateral in 1932, with agriculture plunged into crisis by an 'Economic War' with Britain after the new Fianna Fáil government refused to continue payment of the land annuities. These were a legacy of the British land acts under which Irish tenant farmers (including my paternal grandfather) had been enabled to buy out their land in the decades before the establishment of the Irish Free State. My father started farming, therefore, in a very difficult decade for farmers (a resolution not being achieved until 1938), and his only – and thoroughly justified – boast was that he had come through it with no debts and a productive farm, surviving during the worst times by selling his own butter (normally made by women) in the town.

So there he is on the quay in his wedding suit, his face a little less inscrutable than in most photographs, his whole demeanour calm, a successful man, a 'strong farmer', recently married to a young businesswoman, long loved. They were engaged secretly for a decade or more, she wearing his ring on a chain under her clothes, prudently waiting until they were financially secure. Their wedding had been equally secretive,

FIGURE 7. Credit: Author

in the University Church in Stephen's Green in Dublin, a city neither had visited before. The only witnesses were Nancy and my father's younger brother Nick, who had stayed at home and later inherited the family farm; the celebrant was his brother John who organised it all, and drove them to the farm at Courtdale after a wedding lunch in the Wicklow Hotel and a standard wedding photograph (Figure 7) in the studio of J.A. Stanley, more conventional and formal than the one on the quay, and lacking its sense of intimacy. Yet, each of the newlyweds, though unsmiling, projects (as I read it now) a quiet air of satisfaction at a dream finally fulfilled, a happiness long postponed. She sits stiffly on a rather shabby chair, dressed in the kind of dark, tailored suit she was to favour all of her life. Her stylish but comfortable shoes, and lack of jewellery, also remained a constant. He, more self-conscious in his three-piece suit (two pieces only thereafter), leans equally stiffly against a table, like his father (in this at least) a respectable bourgeois farmer. The next time Mother visited the Wicklow Hotel was to celebrate my BA graduation with lunch over twenty years later. 'Why all the secrecy then?' I asked her, and she waved the question away with 'You know how your father hates fuss'. A possible explanation for such hole-in-the-corner weddings would be a pre-marriage pregnancy, but my arrival ten months afterwards rules that out. It seems very likely that this deeply shy man could only go through the long-delayed marriage ceremony in the privacy organised by his brother – which puts his calm demeanour in both photographs in a different light. Or perhaps, it strikes me now, they wanted a quiet occasion, far from the flamboyant, volatile John Rice? I never heard Daddy speak of his father-in-law, so far as I remember.

The times were still difficult, the Economic War being succeeded by 'the Emergency' (as the Second World War was called in the Irish Free State). War news was everywhere, and while it might seem far away (though not to his brother Jim in Bradford), the war had recently come terrifyingly close. The village of Campile, fifteen miles from the farm, had been bombed (almost certainly in error) by the Luftwaffe two years earlier, and three women killed. Yet, how remote they were from the horrors then engulfing Europe came home to me recently, reading in W.G. Sebald's haunting novel *Austerlitz* how the mother of the eponymous hero was forced into the ghetto of Terezin in what is now the Czech Republic, around the time that I was born in the rural peace of Courtdale. The ghetto was one square kilometre in extent, and already had sixty thousand inhabitants. Wartime in Ireland was, for most people, a matter of coping with shortages rather than with danger. Rationing of all kinds, especially petrol, made business difficult, though farmers benefited to some degree from increased exports to Britain. Getting married and starting a family under the shadow of war must have added to the sense of its being a big adventure, a declaration of confidence, as well as a challenge.

Looking now at those smiling, optimistic faces on the town quayside, my father sitting on one of its largely redundant bollards, the scarcity of shipping making the quayside of this once major port effectively the town park, I am struck by my resemblance to my mother, often commented on as I grew up, making me, in her explanation, 'a real Gantley', that is, like her mother's family. The most striking proof of that came in my mid-forties when I met her first cousin Billy Gantley, son of her guarantor with the bank. Billy was a successful doctor in England, and the contrast between his comfortable bourgeois upbringing a few streets from my mother's shop (one brother became a dentist, another a Franciscan priest) and her genteelly

FIGURE 8. Credit: Author

impoverished one had long intrigued me. The combination of her spoiled father's idleness and his alcoholism doubtless explains the difference. I had no memory of meeting Billy before, and found the resemblance between us uncanny. Yet, despite my Gantley looks, as I sit into my car nowadays wearing glasses and a cap it is my father's face when in his seventies and similarly framed that looks back at me. Or so perhaps I like to imagine.

In contrast to their more sombre and formal wedding photograph, I treasure the intimacy of her hands on his shoulders in the photograph on the quay because my parents, like many of their generation, were not given to displays of affection, even in front of their children. Yet, we were instinctively aware of the great bond between them, as the core of the largely happy, stable environment in which we grew up, so different from both their experiences of childhood. While in general low-key and undemonstrative, my parents were also humorous, caring and encouraging.

After their wedding they set up house together beside the ruins of a small Norman tower house in the old farmhouse in Courtdale (see Figure 15 (next chapter)), where he had lived a bachelor life for a decade. There I was born, a week before Christmas 1942, a time of snow and ice so bad I could not be brought in their pony and trap to the church at Newbawn to be baptised for over a week, a source of worry for Catholic parents at a time of high infant mortality. Likewise, Mother didn't trust their frisky young mare for her daily journey to her shop in the town. Instead, she cycled the difficult eight miles there and back every day, right through her pregnancy and, once the weather cleared, after my birth. I was named, as was the custom, after my father's father, with the name of my mother's father second. Luckily I was an adult before I had any idea of the troubled legacy of each.

In the only photograph I have of my parents with me as a baby (Figure 8) it is summer and they are outside the farmhouse, he once again in his three-piece suit, with new frown lines on his forehead marking new challenges and responsibilities perhaps, and there may be a pipe nestled in his left hand. Mother, in a summer dress and again wearing stylish shoes, half hidden by the long grass, looks happy, holding their sturdy and inquisitive baby boy, also in a dress, as was still common in country places. Perhaps they had dressed up for the photograph or, more likely, it was a Sunday and these were their mass-going clothes. She was pregnant with her second child, Mary, and they had already decided, or were still debating, a move into New Ross to live over her little shop in Bridge Street. The shop was their main source of income, and her daily commute now only feasible long-term with a motor car, at the time a relative rarity and beyond their means.

As my parents pose in the sun, the life-changing implications of their move for their eldest may have been on their minds, perhaps even being discussed if the photographer was a trusted friend or relative. Perhaps there were ongoing arguments about it, and hence my father's frown. However, it never appeared to be his way to argue with her for long; she usually seemed to be the stronger, or at least the more assertive, personality. It seems likely that over time we all followed his lead in not opposing her. In her old age she told me that a major motivation in moving to the town was to offer better educational chances to their children. That it involved big sacrifices for him, leaving an occupation and place that he loved, was not mentioned. He would have realised also, perhaps sadly, because this mattered a great deal to any man from a farming family, that I would grow up as a 'townie' rather than the eldest son of a farmer, working with him and eventually taking over the farm. But perhaps there was no argument, as he may have had his own reasons to be glad to leave Courtdale, as will emerge. In any case, move they did, and so we grew up, six children born within eight years, living eventually in a large eighteenth-century house in the main street over

FIGURE 9. Credit: Author

a much bigger shop. It too proclaimed 'J. Rice' over the door, though my father now worked with her and she was in all other respects 'Mrs Dunne'. They still owned Courtdale, where her brother James managed the farm for some years and lived in the old house with his family.

A photograph taken about two years after the move into town gives a vivid insight into the transformation involved (Figure 9). In contrast to the informal family 'snap' taken outside the old farmhouse, this is a formal family portrait taken by the already renowned Annie Brophy in her studio in Waterford, with its romantic backdrop and props. It was a major – and expensive – statement of their new urban life, and growing prosperity.

In this picture celebrating middle-class success, my parents, sister and I are well-dressed 'townies'. My father's transformation from farmer to shopkeeper strikes me particularly – as does how uncharacteristically relaxed he seems in front of the camera. I am struck also of course by our shining top-of-the-range shoes, good advertisements for the shop which was clearly doing well. Looking at my well-nourished three-year-old self, it strikes me that I may never have been as well-dressed as an adult! My handsome, still young parents look happy and serene, my sister and I solemn but relaxed, fascinated, as I remember from later visits, by Annie's regular disappearances under the black cloth that hid most of her large camera on its wooden tripod and re-remerging every now and then to make a joke and adjust the composition: what might have been scary for children was, instead, intriguing theatre.

There is also a picture of me with my father, taken between these two contrasting family photographs (Figure 10). Now perhaps a year old, chubbier, blond-haired, wearing a dress still but also sturdy boots, I am being held by my father, his suit now somewhat shabby, but he is still wearing a tie. We are in the garden at Courtdale, or perhaps the laneway to the farm. I look a little apprehensive; he's not frowning this time but solemn as usual, for photographs were then a rare and serious business and he always hated having his taken. Away from the camera, he was a great smiler. Oddly, it is the only photograph of just the two of us that I have, me safe in his arms, a very potent image for me. It chimes with one of my earliest memories: my father, a powerful, calm figure, ploughing with a large grey horse onto whose impossibly broad back he lifted me, aged four or five, as he returned the horse to its stable across the nearby yard. My memories of the farmyard, and of the neighbours' older children teaching me to shout out a rude rhyme teasing my father, 'Art, Art, silly old fart', came from our regular later visits from town on Wednesdays when the shops closed at lunchtime, him carefully driving his grey Ford van, already ancient when purchased.

It is easy to see why the sensation of being lifted high in the air on to that scary perch and held by him as he walked the horse forward has stayed with me through the intervening years. He remained a calm and steady support

FIGURE 10. Credit: Author

to me until his death, younger than I am now, and has been mourned every day of the forty years since and remembered not least for his sayings and anecdotes, some of them now familiar to my children. His conversation had little originality, sprinkled liberally with common clichés such as Joyce strung together in *Ulysses*, which I first read in the seaside house my parents rented when their retirement home was being built. Reading the 'Cyclops' chapter, set in a pub, there was a shock of recognition in dialogue like:

> Will you have a pint?
> Would a duck swim?
> Will you have another?
> Sure a bird never flew on one wing.

Daddy certainly never read Joyce and at most might have vaguely heard of him, but he too was saturated in the demotic humour that so enlivens Joyce's writings. Like Montaigne, I feel lucky to have had 'a very good father' and, like him, 'I do not cease to embrace and cherish his memory, his friendship and his society, in a union that is perfect and very much alive'.

Many other memories of him are less dramatic or symbolic: as a child watching him leaning on the counter of our shop reading his paper, the *Irish Independent*, while waiting for the first customer of the day; as an altar boy seeing him, a distant, modest figure, at the back of a side aisle of our cavernous church while the other men who went to daily mass, mostly shopkeepers also, were close to the altar; as an adult sharing a slow pint with him in a dim bar or watching him transformed into a talkative, Joycean joker as he enjoyed his nightly two pints among his friends in the pub next door. In most of my memories of him he is calm and amused, but others are associated with great excitement, of excursions to Dublin on bustling steam trains to watch, as part of vast swaying crowds on the terraces of Croke Park, the county hurling team in its glory days. On these long, heady days out he was animated and talkative, but once home went back to being the quiet, almost invisible partner and support of his formidable wife, and the encourager of his children.

We were aware of his dislike of shopkeeping and the fact that he remained a countryman at heart, always regretting that they sold Courtdale, especially (Mother claimed with a certain asperity) after land came to be sold for more money per acre than they got for the whole ninety. In her account, after he died, the decision to sell was his and was due to sensitivity to what he felt was the resentment of some neighbours that he had come into a farm that had long been in the possession of another family, the Forristals.

A few years ago, I had an email from Peter Hansen, a professor in the Department of Animal Sciences in the University of Florida. He had read my *Rebellions* memoir and was fascinated by its account of my father's acquisition of Courtdale. 'My mother's family still lives at the Ferry Bridge [outside New Ross, on the road to Enniscorthy], and are Forristals of Courthoyle,' he wrote. That the family still described themselves in that way, eighty years after their 'home' farm had been sold, is a remarkable example of the attachments of Irish families to the land, but it also indicated something deeper – that they had farmed there for generations. So it proved, subsequent correspondence revealing that Peter could document family tenancy of the farm in the 1840s, and that he thought it likely they had been settled in the area since the 1660s. Further confirmation of this idea of a long connection with that farm can be seen in the fact that his family still call it 'Courthoyle', a direct translation from the Irish 'Cúirt Hoel', rather than the Anglicised 'Courtdale', as it had become by my father's time.

My father must have known some version of that story and been aware of how it might be regarded by the wider Forristal family, and by the local community. Even if no-one ever mentioned it, he may have felt any silent disapproval, and his enduring shyness would have made it hard for him to face it down. Yet, I have every reason to think that he was popular in the area, and his old neighbours were among his favourite customers in the shop in later years, the ones he came forward to meet with a grin and a joke. Most likely his feelings about leaving farming were mixed, and he wasn't all that unhappy in our market town.

My most vivid childhood memories of my mother are of us all traipsing behind her on long walks, often in the rain (a particular pleasure for her) and half listening to her naming the trees, flowers and birdsong or rehearsing again the magic days of her own childhood, as she remembered them, on the family farm at Ballymacar. We visited there regularly, a three-mile walk in each direction, often walking home in the dark as she was always reluctant to cut short her reminiscences with her brother Jack who had taken over that ever-more struggling and by now very old-fashioned farm. When at last the big ornate oil lamp was lit by Aunt Maggie (its soft glow slowly revealing the tenebrous kitchen with its large open fire featuring a 'crane' holding a large black kettle over it) our hopes of the longed-for departure would rise. I can still hear Mother's low, clear voice coming from the darkness with stories of her family as we stumbled forward on the dark road or hugged the ditch with the approach of a car, then a rare event. Today, the landscape of that walk and of the farm have been obliterated by an elaborate bypass of the town, which includes, prominently signposted, 'The Ballymacar Roundabout', giving that magical name of our childhood a new significance, albeit one that would have horrified her.

Another memory is of her baking her brown soda bread (she abominated the vogue for 'shop bread', especially the increasingly ubiquitous 'sliced pan') in the evenings in the large kitchen, with its coal-heated stove, or 'range', making it the only warm room of our uncomfortable house and hence in winter the centre of all family activities. She sang from her repertoire of hymns and romantic ballads as she kneaded the dough, all part of her favourite way to relax after long days in the shop. She sang mainly joyous Marian hymns like,

> Bring flowers of the fairest, bring blossoms the rarest from garden and hillside and woodland and glade … O Mary we crown thee with blossoms today, Queen of the Angels and Queen of the May.

As part of her deep-seated, probably unconscious denial of the often-fraught experiences of her childhood, shc also loved songs full of nostalgia for the old days, especially Moore's

> Oft in the stilly night, ere slumber's chain has bound me, fond memory brings the light of other days around me.

And she had a rich store of the sentimental ballads that still dominated the Irish radio wavelengths:

> When first I saw sweet Peggy 'twas on a market day. A low-backed car she drove and sat upon a truss of hay. But when that hay was blooming grass, and decked with flowers of spring, no flower was there who could compare to the darling girl I sing …

Gathered around her at the large kitchen table, her children did their homework (their father a helpful presence in the background), and when that was finished listened to the radio (known to us as the wireless), increasingly a great focus of entertainment for all the family. At some stage every evening the wireless was turned off and we knelt and said the Rosary, that repetitive, mesmerising (or giggle-inducing) mantra of prayers in honour of God and the Virgin Mary, and a feature of daily life in every house I knew then. We children often intoned, not without a little irony, the slogan of its great proponent, the evangelising and entrepreneurial American priest Fr Peyton: 'The family that prays together stays together.'

These memories of family life and my mother's central role in it also of course carry great symbolic weight. I never felt as close to her as I did to my father, perhaps because she was the authority figure in the family but also perhaps because she found emotional intimacy difficult after her own childhood experiences. This may explain why, though as a child I called her 'Mammy', as an adult I came more and more to call her by the more formal though still fond 'Mother', now used automatically in writing about her. I have decided to revert to 'Mammy' when it seems more appropriate, especially in these chapters on childhood. 'Daddy' never changed.

The stories our parents told gave us a powerful sense of family history and ethos. Mammy's, more often rehearsed and more glamorous, featured a close family relationship to Edmund Rice, founder of the Irish Christian Brothers, and the heroism of his cousin, her direct ancestor, killed by the military for harbouring women and children during the bloody 1798 battle for the town, according to family lore. Her mother's Royal Irish Constabulary father James Gantley was another heroic figure, dying of pneumonia, she told us, after searching in the snow for a woman fleeing an abusive husband. Most often rehearsed, however, were the glamorised early stories of her father John, featuring life in the Australian gold fields and the long sea journey back to Ireland. His heavy drinking would sometimes be mentioned in passing, but only as an explanation for the persona the family constructed for him after his death, as charming, lovable and extravagantly hospitable but also hopeless in business and too easily influenced by 'bad companions'. Only in her final years did she refer to the dark side of his addiction, the sudden mood swings, threatening behaviour and occasional violence, the untold story that in one way or another has probably helped to shape all of her children's lives as well as her own and those of her siblings. It proved difficult for her as an adult to deal with confrontation (indeed any disagreement) or with negative emotions, and she found the strength to face the uncertainties and challenges of life in a powerful will and an intensely traditional Catholicism. Yet, she was also generally cheerful, with a fund of humorous stories, particularly of the years before she married, such as a seaside excursion by train to Tramore which included the very overweight woman Aggie Browne in whose shop she had worked (and who features, far left, in Figure 2 earlier in the chapter). As Mammy told it, imitating Aggie's droll, drawled speech to our delight, the man who had donkey rides for hire on the beach paid her *not* to sit on one of his animals.

Daddy never showed much interest in his family's history, which we learned instead from Mammy, who was nearly as proud of its rootedness and clerical tradition as she was of her own similarly marked one. Instead, his stories revolved around his own experiences as a youth, honed by annual rehearsals of them with his brother Jim on the latter's visits back from exile (as he perceived it) in England. The hardships that he and his brothers suffered working on the family farm for a distant, severe father featured prominently, but also their attendance at dances and musical evenings in neighbours' houses, travelling long distances by bike. An anecdote Jim brought up every year concerned one such dance when he, still an eligible bachelor, was getting on great with a girl he fancied until my father interrupted them with, 'We better start home, Jim. Your wife will be wondering.' My father's only political story featured his mischievous schoolboy shout of 'Up the IRA' – the banned Irish Republican Army – when two Royal Irish Constabulary men came into the yard during a threshing looking for Jim, an active member of the IRA and then on the run. They arrested Daddy and marched him miles towards their barracks before sending him home with a kick in the pants. Part of the point of this story, as he told it, was his lack of sympathy with Jim's politics, and the humanity of the policemen.

Daddy's nostalgia for his years farming was evident in his humorous accounts of encounters with 'tinkers' (Travellers), of traditional remedies for animal diseases (such as digging out sods that contained the hoof-prints of a diseased animal and replacing them upside down), even in accounts of its hardships, such as walking cattle to the fair in the town starting at two in the morning and walking them home that night unsold. Perhaps the story most characteristic of him, and so my favourite, concerned the response of 'an old tinker' who had let his horses into a new meadow that Daddy had sown and was carefully bringing along.

'What do you think you are at?' Daddy roared at the old man, who leaned nonchalantly on a gate. 'Can't you see that it's all new grass? What have you to say for yourself?'

'Begob,' came the reply, 'I hope it won't do the horses any harm.'

'All I could do,' Daddy would conclude his story, 'was to laugh.'

His bachelor days were also remembered in anecdotes like waking up in his open trap in pouring rain outside his front door, his pony having brought him home unguided as he slept after a few too many drinks to celebrate selling all his butter on market day. His last port of call was often a little pub or 'sheebeen' at the edge of town presided over by a very old woman famous for her meanness. 'She would turn down the lamp so low that you could barely see the drink she gave you, turn it up to count your money as you paid, and turn it back to near darkness so that you couldn't see your change.' One thing I certainly inherited from my father is a fondness for telling (nowadays *re*-telling, as my family often points out) such stories.

As the eldest I probably developed a different relationship with our parents than my siblings did, especially the younger ones, who felt they struggled especially to get Mammy's attention. I never lost it. That was particularly evident in the ways I was encouraged from very early on to have a sense of seriousness and responsibility, not only helping in the shop but acting as host in the parlour to visitors if neither of my parents was free to go

Figure 11. Credit: Author

upstairs. This arose regularly during the annual visits of my Uncle Jim, at the time a gardener in a municipal park in Bradford (a sad comedown for the presumptive heir to the family farm), Aunt Betty, a teacher (who felt that loss keenly), and their pleasantly silent son John, a clerical student (soon to become the wider family's fourth generation of Fr John Dunnes, which more than compensated, his mother clearly thought, for his father's loss of status) (Figure 11). They stayed in my Aunt May's up the street and, after she moved to London, in the town's only hotel, the Royal, and called in every morning before setting out to visit various relatives. I would pour Betty a dry sherry, Jim a small whiskey and John a soft drink. Jim, much taller than my father (whom he often called 'the butty man'), was humorously and reassuringly familiar despite a strong Yorkshire accent whereas Betty was a rather scary figure for a small child (indeed, even for an adult) with her bright straw hats, white gloves and imperious manner, a bit like the Queen Mother. She had a tendency to lay down the law about various issues, to bewilder me with her vehement dislike of Pakistanis (it was a shock later to recognise her in Alf Garnett) and to interrogate me about school. The appearance finally of one of my parents would bring a welcome release.

I have no recollection of ever disobeying my parents as a child or even having a disagreement with them, much less confronting them. The extent to which that was true now seems to me not only remarkable but – having had four wonderful but often argumentative and sometimes combative (i.e. normal) children – even unnatural. One of the last things I remember my mother saying to me, before a second stroke robbed her of speech, was, 'You were always a wonderful son; you never gave us the least trouble or anxiety.' She meant it very kindly, mainly I think as reassurance after the breakup of my marriage. What she said moved me then and does so still, but it also resonates now with my sense of a powerful childhood drive to please, not to cause unhappiness. This was not due to any fear of the usual punishments meted out to children at that time (unknown in our house) but instead perhaps to a fear of emotional conflict, to a sense that this was something neither of my parents, and especially my mother, could handle comfortably. There was also, most likely, a feeling of responsibility common in eldest children and especially perhaps in sons. I was always a 'Good Boy', meeting unarticulated expectations of good behaviour, imbibed unconsciously, and with a sense of duty to make everything all right; this I have never lost. And this, I now realise, is how I most resembled my mother, not in looks.

Though she had been one of the youngest in her large family, she was the one who inherited her grandmother's strength and grew up determined to succeed and hold the family together, as well as to please her father and deflect his anger. However, this also involved emotional frailty and distancing. After her death especially this became a regular topic of conversation among her children, who all loved her while mostly feeling that sense of distance from her. We came to see the subtle, unstated form of emotional control she exerted over us as a consequence of her having to deal with an alcoholic father, and some of us have wondered how we may have absorbed, to a greater or lesser extent, and carried into our adult lives the strategies involved in dealing with alcoholism. Certainly, an inability to deal with emotionally charged conflict or even disagreement, learning instead to use charm and words to deflect confrontation, was for a long time a major problem for me and a factor, especially, in the failure of my first marriage. After it ended and I had a new partner, the extent to which my emotional disability was linked to my relationship with my mother came shockingly into focus. I found it impossible to tell her about my new life, desperately though I wanted and needed to, simply unable to face the emotional storm that I felt was bound to follow and the obliterating fear of her withdrawing her love from me. That crisis made me realise finally that I needed to confront and understand the nature and extent of the emotional problem that was the core of my 'Good Boy' persona, and I deal with that in the second part of this memoir.

During the year following her death, still trying to understand my relationship with her, in part by beginning to write about it, I had a very helpful discussion with the Palestinian scholar Edward Said. He had gone through a somewhat similar process in relation to his mother and was about to publish his memoir, *Out of Place*. He spoke of the intensity of their relationship throughout her life (she had died nine years earlier), despite for many years living on different continents. 'We wrote to each other all the time,' he said, 'and for years talked every day on the phone.' Feeling guilty at how little, comparatively, I had kept in touch with my mother, I responded, unthinkingly, 'That's wonderful.' He looked at me with a wan smile, a sardonic eyebrow lifted, and said softly, 'You think so?'

His devastating, bleakly honest memoir revealed what lay behind that quiet reply, a family life of deep emotional insecurity that had shaped – and still shaped – his life. His mother, whom he adored and with whom he shared so much, especially music and literature, would overwhelm him with affection only to withdraw it without explanation and become distant and undermining, a pattern endlessly repeated and always predictable. More consistent and equally undermining was the controlling, often bullying regime of his powerful father, the two combining to leave him without any 'sense of cumulative achievement'. Both parents also had complex insecurities of identity, which he inherited. Being a member of a Christian Palestinian family, living between languages, driven from Jerusalem when he was a child and ultimately from Cairo where he had grown up created his 'unsettled sense of many identities'. This devastatingly honest portrayal of his parents (and himself) also demonstrated his 'surprisingly strong residual love for them'.

Said told me that, in his view, the whole point of writing a memoir should be to understand yourself better. Despite his many books and his worldwide fame, he clearly felt that he had never interrogated or revealed himself properly. He was in the middle of lengthy, debilitating treatment for leukaemia when we met and it was not going well. In the four years left to him he was to publish much more, mainly on the Palestinian question and on music, but the memoir remains the key to all the rest.

Reflecting further, after reading it, on my relationship with my mother I realised that any threat of emotional withdrawal by her was unconscious and never deliberate, yet I nonetheless experienced it as real and was profoundly affected by it. I was always conscious too of being encouraged and supported by her and never undermined. Perhaps for those reasons, unlike Said with his mother, I retain no sense of hurt, much less anger, about my childhood, only a strong sense of empathy with her in my own struggles with life. Whatever her emotional limitations, she did her considerable best for us, which is perhaps the most important judgement that can be made of any parent. A key factor in understanding my relationship with her as an adult may be the effect of my leaving home when still a child (as it was for Said in relation to his mother when he moved to the United States at sixteen and remained there all of his life), so that after fourteen I didn't grow up with her and develop an adult relationship in the normal way, including through the tensions of adolescence. I remained to some degree not only a 'Good Boy' but also a child in relation to her.

As the disciplinarian in the family, however mild, our memory of her suffers perhaps in the contrast with that of our father, who was a very sweet, humorous man despite regular bouts of severe migraine; none of his children ever remember him as angry or even particularly insistent. From an early age the pleasure of doing things with him was enhanced by his humour. Methodical and calm in practical tasks, his response to my awkward, over-enthusiastic efforts to help was not impatience but the amused (again, commonplace) comment, still often wryly recalled by me, 'You are going at it like a bull at a gate.' Indeed, I am no handyman and whenever I attempt something a little challenging, having dealt with the frustration and remembered his comment, I still try to follow his methodical approach, seeing his hands going through the phases.

My childhood memories of my mother are also coloured by her care for me and her reassuring presence over a series of illnesses. Though indefatigably involved in sports, I was often ill, though not seriously so. Following a number of dramatic bouts of tonsillitis, I had the tonsils removed in the small local hospital when I was about six. I remember feeling lost and alone in the male ward after the operation and the woman doctor bringing in the offending organs in a little dish to show me. What she meant kindly as reassurance caused recurring nightmares. To aid my physical recovery our family doctor recommended that I drink a bottle of stout every day (at the time Guinness was advertised essentially as a health drink: 'Guinness is good for you'. It seems remarkable, however, that our doctor agreed). Mammy, a lifelong 'Pioneer' (an abstainer from alcohol on religious grounds, but also, no doubt in her case, a response to family experience), put her scruples aside, and when I gagged on the stout added milk and sugar. I drank that abominable concoction for several weeks.

Then for some years I regularly suffered from mysterious stomach pains, and no less mysterious after a week of tests in Waterford City Hospital, fifteen miles away. Being once again in a public ward in a strange place, especially with a crash victim swathed in bandages in the next bed, I was not too happy, and she visited every day, coming by train. The first time, heading for home she went to the wrong platform and ended up in Tipperary, and as a result we were all drilled in double-checking everything when travelling, which I still do. After the hospital she brought me to what we would now call a herbalist but was then known as someone with a 'cure' (in my case, I think, for the catch-all popular diagnosis of the time, 'worms'). I have a vivid memory of sitting on a red three-legged stool in the middle of a bleak cottage kitchen trying to drink a concoction, the foul, metallic taste of which still lingers in my imagination, brewed up by an old woman wearing a black shawl, seeming to be a witch from my story books. I also remember days lying in bed with a high fever, the flower patterns on the wallpaper expanding and threatening to engulf me. During one such illness, when I was thirteen, my spirits were lifted by the repeated playing on speakers outside a nearby record store of Bill Haley's 'Rock Around the Clock'. Having encountered traditional folk medicine some time earlier, I was now, in this illness, encountering modern popular culture at its most strident. The notorious film of the same name was coming to the cinema up our street and had already provoked teenage hysteria in Britain. I knew I would not be allowed to go, even if I had recovered in time, given my mother's horror of such music and all that it represented. She had been comfortable and approving, however, in the bare kitchen of the herbalist, a scene that could have been acted out anytime in the previous centuries. It is another reminder that I was growing up on the cusp of the divide between a slowly receding traditional culture and a burgeoning modern one.

As I look back, one of the most remarkable features of our family life was the good-humoured and affectionate camaraderie between us six siblings. We had no garden, and on winter evenings no recourse but to the warm kitchen, yet I recall none of the commonplace rivalries and conflicts. There was much joking, but also a strong sense of constraint. We were so well behaved that it seems somewhat unnatural in retrospect, all sharing a version of my 'Good Boy' persona yet in later life all developing strikingly

Figure 12. Credit: Author

independent views, some at odds with Mother's beliefs and, like me also, hiding this from her. In recent decades, on the rare occasions that my two Canada-based sisters are back on holiday at the same time and all six of us can meet (still with great camaraderie), we have talked about it, though always aware of how different from one another our experiences and memories of the family were and are. Being the oldest, and having left home at fourteen, I was in many ways outside the group and still get teased for it, for example for eating with our parents while the others ate separately – something I don't remember. My memories of those early days largely end when theirs are beginning (the youngest was only six when I left) and while we always got on well, it would be fair to say that I was close to none of them, especially the younger ones, in the way that they were to develop close relationships with one another. In our recollections my parents are not their parents; my family not quite theirs. My sense of solitariness in the family has, increasingly, been a minor sadness.

We were closest perhaps when on holiday for three weeks every summer in the nearby seaside village of Duncannon. Due no doubt to our lack of a garden, there are no photographs of our life at home, our box Brownie camera being no use indoors. However, there are a few out-of-focus ones of me with Mary as infants on a grassy section of the largely abandoned quayside near the house. Like my mother as a child in the picture with her father, I appear to have acquired already the habit I was to retain all my life, of picking bunches of wildflowers (Figure 12). After those early years Mammy seemed to lose interest in family photographs, possibly even a little in the day-to-day lives of the later children. Daddy hinted as much in old age to one of them. Six children (in eight years) and running a busy shop probably involved demands impossible to satisfy fully.

The box Brownie came into its own during our annual summer holidays in Duncannon. Many snaps show us shivering, wrapped in thin, damp towels against the usual cool showery weather, or in our 'togs', the boys wearing the permanently wet, chafing woollen versions of the time, the girls the more modern stretch nylon. There was intense competition for who would have the most swims in a day, and much tumbling about in the dunes above the beach, where Mammy sat in a sheltered spot, supervising our play. Daddy stayed in the town keeping the business going but came down, fourteen miles on his bike during the years when we had no car, on half days and Sundays.

A story oft-repeated by my mother in which I am being brought by him, still obviously very young, to Duncannon on the bar of his big heavy Rudge bike includes my first recorded speech. 'Time to get off here Art,' I was quoted as saying, as he started up Arthurstown Hill. Clearly, I was already prone to bossiness and advice-giving – 'a born teacher' – but I also treasure the anecdote because it is a very early example of the camaraderie that marked our adult relationship. It also causes me to think that quite early on my persona as eldest son sometimes involved staying in the town during those holidays, and helping in the shop as I certainly did later, going in and out on the bus. In my memory Daddy always avoided the beach, was never seen in swimming togs and ate in the little hotel nearby while we munched our sandy egg or banana sandwiches on the dunes. Indeed, he rarely played with us, as such, but the same was true for the most part of how their fathers related to my friends.

So, I was delighted to find a picture of him with us in the sand dunes in a recently discovered seaside snap (Figure 13). He is, of course, wearing his suit and tie, is now going grey at the temples and is putting on weight. Beside him, aged thirteen and ever the romantic (or 'a right gatch', i.e. fond of throwing shapes, as my friends sometime jeered), I am copying the pose of my hurling heroes, my stick showing one of the strengthening tin hoops he had riveted onto it; six weeks or so later we would be heading to Dublin together to see our second All-Ireland hurling final. Clearly it is another of those miserably cold seaside days and, like all of his children, he is looking

Figure 13. Credit: Author

rather grimly at Mammy taking forever, as usual, to operate the box Brownie camera.

That picture is also precious because it includes my mother's unmarried older sister and housekeeper Biddy (Bridget) and, unusually enough in family snaps, all six of us siblings acting up for the camera, no doubt to reflect the unseasonal weather. They were all to know Biddy better than I ever did; in my distant memory of her she was a benign, humorous presence when with us children but crippled by shyness and anxiety with most adults. She seemed much more old-fashioned and otherworldly than Mammy was and even closer in spirit to their childhood in Ballymacar. Years earlier when she and Mammy still swam with us in Duncannon, Biddy got into difficulties and was very frightened of the sea ever after. But she would sit quiet and still, safe on the dunes, looking out on it for hours. While I remember Mammy as usually emollient with us, she could be impatient, even sharp, with Biddy, as with our cousin Bride, who worked for a period in the shop and was a bright, happy presence in the house. As I grew older I became aware of Mammy's irritation with her siblings, especially those who, unlike her, had not managed the world very well and, she perhaps felt, had

Figure 14. Credit: Author

some of the hopelessness of their father. She was generous to them all, but sometimes impatient.

A year prior to that rather grim but also comical beach picture, we had all gone to Waterford city to celebrate my Confirmation and to have the final of three family photographs from our childhood taken by the wonderful Annie Brophy in her studio (Figure 14). While a traditional, rather stilted studio portrait, it captured something of the personality of each of us, once again in our best clothes and on our best behaviour, solemn rather than beach-cold grim, our handsome parents middle-aged and prosperous, proud of their decorously posed children. Of course the spotlight is again on me, recently Confirmed and more than ever the 'Good Boy'; perhaps my expression reflects that. This was the family I was to leave so abruptly two years later. I am fascinated by the serious faces of my siblings and the sense I have of them being at that indeterminate stage during which the adult face is starting to appear. I was to miss their growing-up, and my memory of them in the years before I left is hazy. This process of distancing from them has been one of the great costs of my youthful vocation. The Annie Brophy photograph is remarkable also because it includes Mammy, absent in all the family snaps I have because of course she controlled the camera – in which Daddy, in any case, had no interest. Photographs taken, we were doubtless released to savour some of the delights that Waterford offered compared to the limited resources of our small town, Woolworths and Bevan's bookshop being particular favourites.

Overall, my parents did succeed in their aim, perhaps never articulated as such, to provide for their children a more loving, encouraging and stable environment than either of them had experienced as children. 'Happy families are all alike; every unhappy family is unhappy in its own way.' So Tolstoy began the unhappy story of *Anna Karenina*. We were, in my memory, a happy family and for the most part unremarkable. We were a fortunate family too, lacking for nothing though without much money. At considerable financial sacrifice all six children went on to join the caring professions, the three boys becoming teachers initially, the three girls nurses. Three of us joined religious orders, though all left after some years to pursue different lives. The sense of responsibility and of service to others we were imbued with was shared by all and not just the burden of the eldest. Our parents educated us to go out into a world with which they had no familiarity. We moved away from them in more ways than that of distance, and there was sadness as well as pride for them in our far-away successes. They put us under no pressure to take over the successful business they had built up, selling it when our career paths were clear and when Daddy especially found the work too difficult. They built a house with a very large garden outside the town and we all visited regularly. They had a happy retirement, until he died, all too soon, from emphysema on my thirty-sixth birthday. In the first few years of their retirement he had been delighted to be back working 'on the land' developing an excellent fruit and vegetable garden at the back of the house. After he died it fell gradually into disuse, but she kept gardening indefatigably in the front.

Increasingly, however, she felt unable to live alone. She had talked of her nervousness at night as a child in Ballymacar when her father wasn't there; we had seen it for ourselves on holidays in Duncannon over the years whenever Daddy was in town. It was perhaps the only visible sign of how much this fiercely independent woman relied on her self-effacing husband's strength. Widowed, she kept up a brave exterior when her children visited but eventually had to reveal the extent of her fear of being alone at night, barricading herself into her bedroom after cheerfully waving us off. Characteristically, she not only made the decision herself to go into a nursing home and sell the house, but also picked the home she wanted. There, initially, she organised card games and played a leading part in its busy social life. A series of strokes made her final decade very difficult, but while she lost speech, she never lost her warm smile and indomitable spirit. I owe them both everything, and try to remember them not in the diminishment of their final illnesses but as they were in vibrant middle age (well captured in Annie Brophy's photographs): he in the pub next door joking with his friends, she in full flow in the shop inquiring after the families of her customers, looking after their needs, even those they didn't know they had – while we, their children, got ready to face the world in the safe haven they had provided.

CHAPTER 2

The Houses

The childhood home, we might say, is a machine for making memories
Brian Dillon, *In the Dark Room*

Thomas Hood's nostalgic poem 'I remember, I remember/The house where I was born', which I learned at my Christian Brothers school, has stayed with me, even though in fact I don't remember very much of my own birthplace, the old farmhouse, called Courtdale, with an ever-burning open fire at the heart of the sparsely furnished kitchen and a cool whitewashed dairy off it. I don't actually remember any of that detail, which comes from my uncle's very old-fashioned farmhouse, Ballymacar, that I do remember clearly and that my mother said was very like Courtdale. Yet, my father kept Courtdale for another ten years after we moved into the town, and his brother-in-law James Rice, with his wife Kathy, lived there and worked the farm. They had an only son, John, a little older than me, but I have no recollection of him being there. At twenty-one, an apprentice solicitor, he was to drown in the River Barrow when an old racing eight he coxed sank. He was a quiet, gentle soul like his father, and I think of him often and the life he never had. As my mother sometimes remarked, with added sadness, his death and later that of his father meant that the Rice family name in the male line had disappeared from the town after two hundred years.

In those years before he sold it my father spent every Wednesday afternoon, when the shop closed, helping on the farm. I often accompanied him, and my vague memories of the house come from those visits. As we turned into the avenue in our old Ford van, my father's sheepdog Sam, recognising the engine from away off, would be sitting expectantly on the wall beside the gate. I remember Kathy, whose humour was to twinkle into her nineties, tending to a cut on my forehead after a fall in one of the outbuildings; I remember the terror of a horse skittering across the yard from the stable; the fear of getting caught in the turnip-cutting machine in the haggard. My father's stories later gave the house an added sense of colour and excitement: his being exiled to sleep over the stable by his clerical uncle because the very elderly housekeeper he had inherited with the house lived in, and such co-habitation by an unmarried man was unseemly (his uncle's death a year later finally gave him decent accommodation); his sharing with James a purse of sovereigns found in the gap between the house and the remains of the early Norman tower house. I took this photograph (Figure 15) when I visited the house in the late 1990s and was greeted warmly by some of the family who had purchased the farm from my father nearly fifty years earlier. A substantial farmhouse when it was built, probably in the mid- to late nineteenth century, it was now a beautifully kept family home with none of the Spartan plainness I had associated with it. I was relieved to find that the ruin of the Norman tower house was a reality, though no longer looming over the house as it did when I was a child, its height having been lowered for safety reasons. But the fine yard and substantial outbuildings were as I remembered them, and the sharp outcrop of Carrigbyrne Hill behind.

My father was a good farmer, remembered particularly by his brothers as a first-class ploughman. He enjoyed the outdoor life, the sense of independence and the methodical nature of much farm work. Courtdale remained in the back of his mind as a lost Eden, and some of that romantic glow has endured for me. When my parents retired and built their house with a big garden on the edge of the town they named it Courtdale; their Jack Russell terrier, inevitably, was 'Sam'.

It was characteristic that my father's story about the remains of the old tower house was not about its history, in which he had little if any interest. Possibly the castle of 'Hoel of Karrathobren', mentioned in an early thirteenth-century charter of Earl Marshall's and in a sixteenth-century Bardic compilation of the O'Byrne's (the subject, in part, of my first publication), it gave its name (Cúirt Hoel), Courthoyle or Courtdale, to the immediate area and colloquially to our farm. The immediate neighbourhood was rich in historical remains and associations. Two major megalithic monuments were within a few miles, the remarkable 'four poster' stone circle of Robinstown, and the portal tomb at Newbawn. Carrigbyrne Hill, only seven hundred feet high but a dramatic feature of the flat landscape all around, was the site of the large rebel camp during the long, fatal delay before they attacked New Ross in 1798. Again, I don't remember my parents talking about the hill in that context but only as the location of the gathering on the last Sunday of July every year to harvest *fraughans* (as bilberries were known in Ireland) while picnicking and meeting friends. Around the side of the hill from our house was the field at Scullabogue where over a hundred men, women and children were burned

Figure 15. Credit: Author

to death in a barn by a group of local United Irishmen on 5 June 1798 while the battle raged in the town. Even as an adult I never heard that mentioned by anyone, a silence I came to understand when I researched the history of that day and of how it came to be remembered on its bicentenary. Across the road, a few hundred yards away on a low outcrop stands the remarkable Browne Clayton Monument, a ninety-four-foot-high Corinthian column modelled on Pompey's Pillar in Alexandria and constructed by a local landowner in 1839 to commemorate his friend General Ralph Abercromby who died in Egypt during the Napoleonic wars and had been commander-in-chief of the crown forces in Ireland just before the 1798 rebellion. Now restored after being struck by lightning in 1994, it is unique as the only such column with an interior staircase. Again reflecting his lack of interest in history, my father's only story about it concerned some of the local 'lads' who lit a fire at the entrance to scare their friends at the viewing area on top.

My father was to find my commitment to being a historian rather baffling. When I finished my MA thesis he weighed it carefully in his

Figure 16. Credit: Author

hand and asked me to explain what it was all about. After I had enthused a little about the fascinating complexities of the mind of W.E. Gladstone he replied, 'Aye, well, sure I suppose it will do no-one any harm.' Sardonic, amused, but obliquely encouraging, this characteristic remark has helped me to keep my research and writing in perspective. Being born in an area so rich in historical monuments spanning millennia might be regarded as an influence on my becoming a historian, but I only became aware of that richness as an adult. Likewise, I took a long time to learn the complex history of the early Norman town to which we moved, but enough of it was commemorated in song and story, and visible in its buildings, ruins and monuments, to affect me deeply as a child.

We first lived in New Ross over my mother's shop on Bridge Street, a small house of which I have only one memory, and that less of the house itself than of the butcher's shop opposite. Its shadowy outline can be seen above the steps which are reflected in the shop window, with its serried rows of shoes, before which Mammy proudly stands (see Figure 4 in previous chapter). The butcher, Tom Baily, himself a shadowy memory for me, featured in her stories as a great gossip who frequently strolled across the narrow hilly street to regale her with the latest. My 'memory' (more likely a projection of Mammy's account) is of watching him through the window of our shop with queasy fascination as he cut meat on the well-worn wooden block in his window. Our former shoe shop has long been a photographer's studio, the window now displaying more informal and colourful Communion and Confirmation family groups than those of Annie Brophy.

The house we moved to after some years (with the help, Mammy hinted, of the sovereigns found beside the walls of the old tower house) was very different and is lodged deeply in my mind. Remembering it in detail offers an important portal to some of the colours and sensations of my life then. A tall, late-eighteenth-century house in the middle of South Street, the main street of the town, it was probably one of a number built as a speculative venture for renting as business premises by the Tottenham estate. If so, it was finished just two years before the horrific battle for the town in June 1798, in the aftermath of which corpses were piled high all along the street. By the late nineteenth century it was described as a department store, owned by a P. O'Kelly whose name is still carved on a plaque near the roof. *The National Inventory of Architectural Heritage* described it in 2005 as

> an important element of the ... built legacy of New Ross, making a dramatic visual impression in South Street ... producing a robust Classical theme in the composition. Although compromised at street level by a replacement shop front (pre-1880) of minimal design interest, elsewhere the house has been well maintained to present an early aspect with most of the historic fabric surviving in place.

It may sound impressive to have grown up in a large late-eighteenth-century town house of some architectural and social significance, but we were not aware of that, knowing it instead as ramshackle, uncomfortable and lacking some basic amenities, poorly adapted to family living. I like this drawing of it by my sister Rosaleen, in part because to me it has a nostalgic, even romantic character (especially in her coloured version), perhaps because she was about to leave home when she drew it in her late teens (Figure 16).

We didn't just live 'over the shop', but partly *in* the shop. It had been unoccupied for many years when my parents bought its lease from Tottenhams, which helped no doubt to make it affordable. It seemed to us as children an immensely tall house, especially looking up the slope of Charles Street from the river, a view that one day caused me to freeze with fear, seeing my father on the roof, tied to the chimney by a rope, fixing slates. He was probably happier up there than in the shop. My fear of heights, in later years quite disabling at times, may go back to that experience.

My parents partitioned the ground-floor shop space with its long, curved counter, leaving a manageable and still large space in front for dealing with customers, with storage space at 'the back' which doubled as an indoor play area for us children on wet half days and Sundays and for many years contained the only toilet in the house. The first floor was converted into a kitchen/family room at the back and a very large 'parlour' at the front (formerly the hat department, an old lady told my mother), the full width of the house. Further upstairs were two floors of bedrooms, the top one occupied by a succession of live-in 'maids' before our Aunt Biddy, living up the town with her twin brother James (who had by this stage moved in from Courtdale), took over as housekeeper. In time I moved up to 'the top', as we called the attic, becoming the only one sleeping there, beside two large empty rooms used mainly for drying clothes in the absence of a garden. I was proud as well as pleased to have a room to myself finally after sharing with my brother, but also a little scared as I made my way up the dim, bare attic stairs each night to face its ghosts alone.

Indeed, the whole deep stairwell of the house could seem scary at night, especially going down for coal from the kitchen, when you had to turn left at the bottom and face a long, dark, largely unused corridor leading to the equally unused and gloomy back yard; at the start of the corridor and its threatening shadows the dark 'coalhole' was tucked under the stairs. The coal, not surprisingly, was shovelled into the bucket with nervous speed, its weight not noticed at first in the rush to get back upstairs. Also scary was the journey to the toilet at night, which meant crossing through the shop, dimly lit by the streetlamps, darting behind the counter to turn on a light then another halfway down to the toilet, with its smell of damp plaster and ancient drains, reversing the process on the return journey and making another dash for the welcome light of the stairs. Unsurprisingly, every bedroom had alternative, and more basic, sanitary arrangements.

Coming back to the house on winter nights – after being at the library or in later years at 'study' in school – also could involve a frisson of fear, waiting in 'the porch' (the deep recess between the shop windows) for someone to come downstairs to answer your ringing of the bell (there was, I think, only one key), the wait sometimes seeming even longer and more fraught by having to share the porch with the garda on duty sheltering from the rain, and even more so on the regular occasions when he had been joined by one of my teachers, out for a walk. Then when the big, heavy door was opened at last, another dash through the dark shop to the stairs. Little wonder that the same nervous boy became an obsessive checker of locks on doors and windows at night, especially in his isolated Cork house, still inhabiting in that way and no doubt in others his childhood home.

The walls of the house were half a metre thick and filled with rubble and horsehair, as my parents discovered when they were finally able to build a bathroom off the second remove, cantilevered out on sturdy steel beams. With such walls it was a lovely cool house in summer but freezing in winter, its ceilings very high, the only source of heat the coal-burning range in the kitchen. There was a fireplace in the parlour, lit only at Christmas, and effective only over a short radius. One Christmas when I had got a Meccano set from Santa and was anxious to keep it from my younger siblings I moved right across the room, where it was so cold my fingers got too numb to manipulate the little nuts and I was forced to move back to the marginally warmer area near the fire. On particularly cold nights I would get into bed fully dressed, wait for the bed to heat up a little, take off my clothes and put on pyjamas while still under the blankets, putting my clothes between them so that they would be heated by the morning, when I would reverse the process. Such Spartan conditions made it easier to adjust to boarding school, which in many respects was more comfortable, and certainly more modern. Little wonder that central heating and electric blankets are counted by me as among the greatest innovations of my lifetime.

The parlour had a large dining table I never remember being used as such, a couch and some armchairs and, at the end opposite the fire, a formidable antique sideboard on top of which were family photographs, including those of my clerical uncle and great uncle, and a great-aunt, a nun in a magnificently ornate wimple, or head dress, who had been a French Sister of Charity in Paris, remembered by Daddy and his siblings as the source of occasional exotic parcels. Among the ornaments on the sideboard was an old cut-glass decanter with an ornate, many-faceted stopper which gave endless entertainment when we were small. Looking through it, balanced precariously on the sill of one of the tall windows, the world outside appeared in multiple colourful images. There was a means of further colour-filled magic between the windows, a switch that turned on the Christmas lights for the whole street, and there was keen competition between us children for the privilege of operating it. A piano – another emblem of middle-class respectability – stood inside the door from the kitchen, and over it the only secular images that I remember being in the house, two romantic landscapes in cheap ornamental frames, a wedding present, which I now have, though in store, as their colours are faded, their frames fragile. I learned piano for a number of years with a stern elderly widow, Mrs Lee, and was sometimes persuaded to play simple duets with my sister Mary for visitors – 'Home to Our Mountains' being the only one that I remember. Neither of us enjoyed these performances and indeed the whole experience was joyless and soon abandoned, a source of regret as an adult, long devoted to classical piano music.

Despite the discomforts and small terrors of the house, in its heart, the kitchen, it was warm and welcoming, very much our family room. During the day when I was very young it was the domain of 'the maid' who looked after the housework and cooked the main meal ('dinner' was in the middle of the day for every family I knew) while Mammy worked her magic in the shop. All of this changed, as indeed did the whole spirit of the house, when Biddy took over the domestic duties. Painfully shy (I remember her fleeing to the attic on learning that our priest uncle was on his way up from the shop), she was at ease with us children, endlessly patient and indulgent but also with a quietly wicked sense of humour. More than a little in awe of her sister, she related much better to our self-effacing father. Like Mammy, she had her own fund of folklore and was knowledgeable about herbal remedies. I remember searching for herbs with her in the little roads near Irishtown where she lived, especially the 'Bosheen', along which 1798 rebels, mainly from my father's home area, had tried to advance late in the battle.

In the evenings the kitchen was our mother's domain, where we all found space to do homework or read or listen to the radio while she baked her brown bread and quietly sang her songs, religious and secular. Common to many of them was a romantic nostalgia which pervaded so much in her life and which I have inherited to a degree, less nowadays in lyrics than in the more plangent passages of romantic piano and violin pieces. She often harked back to 'the old days' when people didn't need to lock their doors, when many were 'poor but happy'. As a child I was encouraged by her and Biddy to sing for visiting relatives the maudlin ballad 'The Old House', made famous by her favourite singer, John McCormack.

Lonely I wandered through scenes of my childhood
They brought back to memory the happy days of yore.
Gone are the old folks, the house stands deserted
No light in the window, no welcome at the door.

McCormack finished each of his long series of farewell concerts, including one in New Ross attended by Mammy, with 'The Old House', for the effect its ending had on his devoted fans –

Why stand I now like a ghost and a shadow,
'Tis time I was I was moving, 'tis time I passed on

– this greeted with roars of 'No, John, no'.

Her 'old house' was Ballymacar, whose old folks were indeed gone and children scattered, though with her brother Jack and family living there it was not yet deserted, as it later became when Jack sold it, leading, sadly, to the estrangement between them. My mother's pervasive nostalgia also reflected her general dislike and suspicion of modernity and change. My father, however, had little nostalgia for 'the old days', instead remembering, in the banter that marked his relationship with his brothers, unremitting hard work under an authoritarian father.

The kitchen had a large bog oak table, a family heirloom, in the centre and a small table for the 'wireless' or radio against a wall. Over it were two religious pictures, 'The Sacred Heart' and 'The Blessed Virgin Mary', each with an electric bulb with a filament in the shape of a cross flickering before it; the former had all of our names inscribed in a space under the image, dedicating the family to God. A pagan deity between these two religious icons was the wireless, and there was consternation as well as panic when our old set burst into flames one night. To the rescue came Uncle John, who next day drove Daddy to Waterford where they bought a state-of-the-art replacement featuring a green light display with intersecting lines which narrowed to indicate the best reception as you turned the knob at each station. It was our first experience of 'high tech'; the religious red lights that flanked it had no such way of indicating whether you were any closer to God.

The family Rosary was our communal daily prayer, turning us briefly into an intimate religious community. Kneeling, we all took turns to lead a 'decade', or section of ten 'Hail Marys' following an 'Our Father' and ending with an invocation of the Trinity. At the end of the three 'mysteries' commemorating aspects of Christ's life ('Joyful', 'Sorrowful' or 'Glorious'), Mammy would add her own prayers for the family, known as 'the trimmings'. This nightly ritual was very much her initiative, and as with most things she was quietly insistent on good behaviour, without getting angry at our inevitable lapses. After it concluded, as we got to our feet, Daddy headed for his nightly two pints in the pub up the street owned by his sweet, nervous widowed sister for whom his presence until closing time was immensely reassuring. When she emigrated to London to live with her son, Daddy moved his custom next door to us, to the even smaller pub of legendary footballer Gus O'Kennedy, who needed no such reassurance.

After the Rosary we children could get back to the radio, which was increasingly tuned to Radio Luxemburg during the evenings, featuring 'Dan Dare, Pilot of the Future' but also 'Mario Lanza Sings', as well as the 'pop' music for which the station was famous. On the state broadcaster 'Radio Éireann' we listened during rushed dinners on school days to the serial drama 'The Kennedys of Castleross', and on more leisurely Saturdays to Leo Maguire's Waltons Programme, his memorable voice introducing the balladeer 'our own Charlie McGee' but also some of his own iconic compositions, 'The Whistling Gypsy', 'The Dublin Saunter', all recorded on the Waltons label. His son John, also a fine singer and composer of songs, was to become a great friend.

I had a collection of the cheap pamphlets of Irish songs and ballads that Waltons also published, and I was thus well equipped (as regards words, though not voice) to participate in the singing sessions in pubs which became a feature from the 1960s. But increasingly even Radio Éireann's lunchtime programmes featured modern popular songs from outside, with singers like Anne Shelton or Rosemary Clooney and, as I was leaving home, Bill Haley and Elvis Presley. On Sundays during and after dinner we listened to BBC comedies 'Life with the Lyons', and 'Round the Horne', followed by Radio Éireann's 'Din Joe' (with possibly the only tap-dancing troupe to feature on radio anywhere), and ultimately the more modern and daring satirical show 'Living with Lynch'. The radio programmes, listened to by young and old, and our ease in moving from Radio Éireann to the BBC and back illustrated better than anything else perhaps the hybrid culture that defined our post-colonial world.

This was further evident in our reading as children. We were allowed a number of comics weekly, *The Beano* and *The Dandy* inevitably and later *Bunty* for the girls and the story (rather than picture) paper *The Wizard* for me and occasionally *Tiger* featuring the footballing legend 'Roy of the

Rovers', later to have a comic of his own. Nearly all were published by DC Thomson in Dundee and were decidedly, and sometimes stridently, British, a fact we seemed not to notice. Likewise, when in need of a scrapbook for my newspaper cuttings on the Wexford hurling team I was happy to take the only one available, although it was issued for the coronation of Elizabeth II and featured the royal coat of arms on the cover. American comics like *Superman* had also begun to circulate but Mammy disapproved of these as somehow dangerous. When I came home one day with a number of them, loaned by a classmate who had American cousins, she was uncharacteristically angry and ordered that I hand back the comics and have nothing more to do with their owner. Only years later did I realise that her fear of contamination came more from the fact that he was a poor boy living in a notorious local council estate uptown. She could sometimes be a snob, my mother.

My own reading was shaped most by what was available in the local library (which opened in the Tholsel (the old Market House) a few evenings a week), where my friend Michael and I initially competed for the latest Hardy Boys mysteries and the stories of Greyfriars school (featuring Billy Bunter, 'The Owl of the Remove') before graduating to the adult section and books like *The Kon-Tiki Expedition* and *Seven Years in Tibet*. But buying books also became an early addiction, funded by serving as an altar boy at weddings and funerals or by generous visiting relatives. The town had no bookshop but Sheehan's newspaper shop sold schoolbooks and had a shelf of Nelson Classics, small hardbacks with thin translucent 'Indian' paper to accommodate massive volumes like *Dombey and Son* (which I finished with some relief during an illness). By then I had purchased all the available Dickens volumes and also many so-called children's books like *Robinson Crusoe*, *Kidnapped* and *The Swiss Family Robinson*. Before I left home at fourteen on my big adventure I had several shelves of books at the foot of my bed, all arranged and numbered. Today, I have only one volume from that little library, No. 25, *Tom Brown at Oxford* (1861). My name on the flyleaf, incongruously, is in Irish, and in the old script: Tomás Ó Duinn. While Irish was not well taught in my school, I became keen on it, following foundation courses on radio, even begging to be allowed downstairs when ill so as not to miss a lesson.

No doubt I had bought *Tom Brown at Oxford* because I had read and enjoyed *Tom Brown's School Days*, another of those 'children's' classics many of which are better described as exercises in tedious adult moralising. As critic Kathryn Hughes described *Tom Brown's School Days*, it was 'less a jolly romp of young toffs in white trousers, and more a junior *Pilgrim's Progress*'. Of course, young people are not averse to serious moralising if the story that carries it is sufficiently gripping, as Philip Pullman's novels have demonstrated in recent times. *Tom Brown's School Days* is at its best on the routines of boarding-school life, especially games, and indeed it laid down a template of enduring popularity: Greyfriars and Harry Potter's Hogwarts for example are in direct succession. *Tom Brown at Oxford* follows the same format, the moral education of a young man as he deals with various trials and temptations.

Reading it now, its most startling aspect, given the new life I was soon to experience, is its emphasis on 'muscular Christianity'. The author, Thomas Hughes, explained its meaning in the chapter given that title (Chapter 11) by contrasting 'muscular Christians' with 'musclemen' who glory in the body without understanding its moral purpose, whereas 'muscular Christians' follow the old chivalrous Christian belief that a man's body is given to him to be trained and brought into subjection and then used for 'the protection of the weak, the advancement of all righteous causes, and the subduing of the earth'. I was the kind of old-fashioned and serious-minded teenager who related to such messages, and I was to find uncanny echoes of them in the book of meditations by a seventeenth-century Spanish Jesuit that was the guiding text of my year as a novice only two years later.

I also have another book, saved from the dispersal over time of those gathered in the early part of my life, Charles J. Kickham's *Knocknagow or The Homes of Tipperary*, first published in 1879. It was not part of my original carefully numbered collection but was sent to me on my first Christmas away from home and inscribed (in my mother's distinctive handwriting) on the flyleaf, 'Christmas 1957. To dear Tom, with love and best wishes, from Daddy and Mammy'. It is a precious memento of them and of that time, the only thing of its kind that I have. It was the best-selling Irish novel ever to that date, with regular new editions. Indeed, the one I was sent had just been published by M.H. Gill & Son. Catholic, nationalist and rural, colourful and humorous, it had more than likely featured among the books in the childhood homes of both my parents, certainly my father's. Despite its poor organisation and lack of narrative drive, it touched deeply the folk memory, even as it echoed the *zeitgeist* of land and nationalist politics. But looking at it now, beside my copy of *Tom Brown at Oxford* published a decade earlier, I am struck by the similarities, not the contrasts. Just as Brown is described by its author as quintessentially English, so the hero of *Knocknagow*, Mat Donovan ('Mat the Thrasher'), is quintessentially

Irish, a popular sportsman and wit but also a man of great moral courage. Indeed, he could be described as a colourful Irish example of 'muscular Christianity'. 'Mat the Thrasher' was a regular reference point in my father's jokes and sayings, though I have found no direct quotes from the book that I remember in my father's repertoire. Probably the name was just a common invocation, like 'Paderewski', the iconic Polish pianist and prime minister who had died the year before I was born and was regularly cited by Daddy as shorthand for 'genius' or, more likely, 'show-off'. 'Mat the Thrasher' may have been shorthand for 'local hero' or, again, probably, 'show off' – a type of man Daddy would not have admired, nor would he have had much time for 'heroes'.

I don't remember my mother as a reader, apart from religious magazines like *Far East* (more heroic figures – missionaries in the Philippines going from one remote station to another on white horses) or *The Sacred Heart Messenger*, which included a serialised novel at the back, often by John D. Sheridan who also had a humorous column in their daily newspaper. My father always had a book on the go, all supplied by his brother John who would regularly appear unannounced, with big tins of sweets for us children and a box of books that he had finished with for Daddy. Zane Grey's cowboy books were great favourites of both and eagerly read by me, as were the Penguin Crime series in their green and white covers featuring authors like Margery Allingham, Ngaio Marsh, Raymond Chandler and Ronald Knox. My uncle also had a fondness for the slightly risqué series of crime novels by Leslie Charteris featuring 'The Saint'. These books ultimately collected in drifts throughout the house, in wardrobes and corners, and before I left home it was rare to find one I hadn't read, unless our clerical provider had visited recently.

My parents had one book that I remember, or rather a two-volume set – Piaras Béaslaí's *Michael Collins and the Making of a New Ireland*. It was a legacy from my Aunt May when she moved to London (she also left us her surprisingly sporty bike). The books had originally belonged to her deceased husband, Michael. They were put in the little-used drawer at the bottom of my parents' wardrobe and remained there. Both parents admired Collins and disliked de Valera; my mother probably voted Fine Gael (my father giving first preferences to Labour): our newspaper was the *Irish Independent*. Yet neither showed the slightest interest in Béaslaí's book. I found the large, green-covered volumes during one of my occasional furtive searches of their room, the most striking aspect of which was a small press on top of which were a number of statues on a lace-edged cloth. These included the incongruous but iconic 'Infant of Prague' (based on a sixteenth-century statue of the Christ child, with imperial robes and wearing a crown), the Blessed Virgin Mary (to whom Mammy was particularly devoted) and St Anthony with the Christ child. Opening the press doors underneath gave an illicit thrill, although the small, frail key was always left in the lock. Inside were various documents, prayer books and other small religious objects, including a purple stole (a small liturgical vestment used in hearing confession) which had been used by 'The Canon'. There was no kneeler in front of this Catholic altar but I have no doubt that my mother often prayed before it. Daddy may have done so too, for, while less ostentatiously and perhaps less conventionally so, he was just as pious.

Because our house could only be entered through it, the shop was also part of it, almost another family room. Our front door was an imposing one in a deep, plate-glass-lined recess between two large display windows, ideal for their original purpose of showing clothes but a perpetual challenge for Mammy in attempting to display the new season's shoes, women's on the left as you walked in, men's and children's on the right. Once inside the door the 'long counter' fronted ceiling-high shelves of women's shoes first, with men's beyond a half partition. On the right behind the 'short counter' were children's shoes and, under the counter, sheets of leather with its distinctive smell, sold by weight to customers who wanted to repair their own shoes and gradually replaced by various stick-on rubber products. My father would occasionally sole shoes, mainly for old customers, cutting the leather with a curved knife, stripping off the damaged sole and tacking on the new. Highly finished or waterproof they were not! We also collected shoes from customers to bring to the local cobbler.

At busy times Mammy dealt with women and children, Daddy with men, while those of us children on duty helped wherever needed, with Mammy doing the fitting and final approving. Working with her was an education in how to interact with customers, watching her greeting everyone and asking after family members, showing endless patience, pulling box after box from the shelves in the attempt to meet the customer's needs – and almost invariably making a sale. Daddy would admit defeat sooner and often said, only half admiringly, 'Your mother could sell sand to an Arab.' She loved the social aspects of selling and had an extraordinary memory for the details of customers and their families, her face lighting up with pleasure and interest as she greeted each one. She had turned the childhood charm, developed to manage her father, into a business as well as a personal asset. No doubt I did the same.

She was less engaged by the book-keeping aspects of the business, and retirement was eased by her dislike of the role, gradually given to shopkeepers by Revenue, of collecting a new tax (value-added tax). I can still hear her triumphantly announcing, after consulting with a sympathetic priest, that VAT was immoral and so she had no obligation to collect it for the state. Compared to the meticulous accounting system used by the father of my friend Michael in his shop, my mother's was very ad hoc, lacking even a proper till, for example. Cash taken in was put in a drawer under the counter, counted once a week and lodged in the bank, with no reckoning of the money taken from it as needed for shopping or for our pocket money, which operated on an honour system. Little wonder that my own noting of money in and out has always been slapdash, and my tax returns (even today with its simple online procedures) always in arrears. Mammy kept the accounts, such as they were, and also did the ordering of stock, in days spent with commercial travellers who hauled their heavy sample cases onto the 'long' counter. She enjoyed the excitement of seeing the new 'lines' and had a good eye for what would sell. Of course, she also remembered the names of the children of these travelling salesmen, making friends of them as part of the strategy to get the most favourable terms. (When late in life she failed her driving test for the final time, the biggest blow to her pride seems to have been her inability to persuade the examiner to pass her!) Daddy kept out of the travellers' way, glad to deal instead with any customers who might have called in during the long ordering process. He tolerated rather than enjoyed shopkeeping, his treat being the regular long discussion about farming with old neighbours, which always involved him being teased for his easy life in the town. He would trigger this by his answer to initial greetings of 'How are you, Art?' with 'Not too bad for a poor man with six children, trying to make a living on the side of the street.' He, in turn, would tease them for having little to do nowadays, with their tractors and other machinery, and he would sing the praises of the farm horse.

On Saturday nights when we finally closed, the last shop in the street to do so, the counters and much of the floor space would be littered with the boxes there had been no time to put away. We all pitched in, and order would only be restored at eleven o'clock, or later. Working there, or merely going in and out, was a very important part of our socialisation. Many of the customers were country people, sometimes whole families coming in twice a year to get shoes for parents and children, sometimes rough-talking men buying working boots or wellingtons. I vividly remember one farmer bargaining me down for a pair of 'wellingtons', and when this was agreed after a nod from Daddy, he turned sideways and opened a large safety pin inside his coat which secured a thick wad of money, from which he peeled a pound note.

Most of our customers, however, were from the town, many of them availing of our approval system, i.e. being allowed to bring home up to five or six pairs of shoes to try them on – or, more often than not, having them delivered by one of us children, a chore that could involve toiling up one of the town's many steep hills, and a lengthy postponement to joining in games with friends after school. Their generous approval and credit system was to cost my parents dear when they came to sell the business and unrecovered monies owed (even after several requests) amounted to a significant proportion of the sum they got for the shop – with the defaulters, mother often remarked, mainly from better-off rather than poor customers, many of whom paid dutifully in instalments. My parents were very far from the stereotype of the money-grubbing, tight-fisted shopkeepers 'who fumble in a greasy till'; indeed, as she later sometimes claimed, they were not in business primarily to maximise their income but 'to have enough' and a good conscience; such was my observation too.

One thing we all learned from the shop was that we did not want to be shopkeepers, and we have cause to be grateful that our parents made no attempt to persuade any of us to take over the business beyond a reminder that the option would be there. It has struck me that if she had put any pressure on me after I left the Christian Brothers at twenty-one, I would almost certainly not have been able to resist her. Nowadays, on my rare visits to the town, when I buy the newspaper and the occasional book in our old, now much-changed shop I look to see if they have any equivalent of Nelson Classics. Sadly, I have yet to find one. But I have been pleased to see, on occasion, some books of mine for sale, making me feel that I haven't quite left the old place yet.

Clearly, I retain a romantic, even nostalgic memory of my childhood home, akin to my mother's memory of her beloved Ballymacar but without similar shadows. Did I dream about it in the years after I left it so definitively, and for a strikingly different environment, at fourteen? Not that I remember, but I must have done so at times as an adult. It is a pleasure to recall it in detail now.

What was I like as a child during those years? My siblings, across the divide of my disappearance, remember me as rather distant, if (largely) benevolently so. Clearly, I was already well rehearsed in the 'little adult' role I was soon to inhabit more fully. At home I was a serious, sometimes solemn child, studious, well behaved, no doubt a bit of a prig. Despite it being rather crowded and without the added dimension of a garden, the house allowed some space in which to be solitary – the large, little-used parlour, the pleasantly chaotic 'back' of the shop, and above all the attic rooms on warm summer evenings where, even before my bedroom was moved up there, I could sit on a windowsill high over the river and read. But I read everywhere, and a lot, creating private space even in a crowded, noisy room. Like my father I was a very different person outside the house with my friends, with long carefree days exploring town and countryside, joining enthusiastically in games of all sorts, arguing vociferously, sometimes angrily, having a volatile but usually short-lived temper – in general with a personality largely suppressed within the family. But in school too, partly out of fear, and in church, increasingly from religious fervour, I was serious, conformist, a further manifestation of the 'Good Boy'.

CHAPTER 3

The World Outside the Home

Our shop, in the middle of the main street, was also our portal into the wider world of our ancient, economically depressed but still vibrant small town, New Ross, population around five thousand, as it had been for centuries. Another nostalgic poem remembered from school is Henry Wadsworth Longfellow's 'My Lost Youth', which begins:

> Often I think of the beautiful town
> That is seated by the sea;
> Often in thoughts go up and down
> The pleasant streets of that dear old town
> And my youth comes back to me.

New Ross remains for me also a 'dear old town', and traversing in memory its 'pleasant streets' does indeed provoke glimpses of my long-lost childhood. Walking those very changed streets nowadays, by contrast, has more the effect of emphasising how far away that childhood is. Virtually all of the forty or so shops that lined our street then have nowadays a different owner and business, most with new, modern shop fronts (Figure 17). Apart from the topography, I could be in a very different place, and indeed my very familiarity with the pattern of streets and the network of lanes off them serves to emphasise the distance from my memories, as great as that of my image in the mirror today is from my childhood photographs. Yet, those memories of the small world outside our home offer ways into recapturing and understanding aspects of that childhood available nowhere else, as Marcel Proust had discovered in his detailed remembering of 'Combray'.

While the sea was some miles away from my hometown, it was a daily presence, as our mighty river, the Barrow, ebbed and flowed with the tides and brought ships to the quayside, including some sail-powered coasters still in my childhood, bringing timber and coal from Dublin and sending back grain and malted barley in return. Our house faced Charles Street, opening up a view of the river, and every morning from my attic room I checked the

Figure 17. Credit: Author

tide, as I was to do for many years from my house in Cork, looking down on a similar ancient, tidal waterway.

As children we were dimly aware that our town had a noble history, founded by the Normans and once enclosed by walls (elements of which survived). Regular deaths by drowning in our dangerous river brought reminders in the local newspaper of the curse put on the town by the Crutched Friars when driven out in the thirteenth century, threatening three such deaths each year. But we had little awareness otherwise of the town's remarkable early history, which the dominant nationalist ethos of the time regarded as foreign.

This view was reinforced by the fact that 'New English' Protestant families, principally the Tottenhams, dominated the town from the Williamite colonial settlement of the late seventeenth century, replacing the 'Old English' Catholic merchant families whose tombstones can still

Figure 18. Credit: Author

be seen in the ruins of St Mary's the medieval parish church, emblematic of a lost history, a broken tradition that survived in nearby Waterford. The Tottenhams developed the town in various ways, such as building the commercial premises in which I grew up. By the end of the eighteenth century they owned many of the town's buildings, as they do to the present day despite being absentee landlords since the early nineteenth century.

They owned the small, bleak house leased by the Rice family in Irishtown since the late eighteenth century, and they sold it a few years ago after the death of my Aunt Kathy, the last Rice to live there (Figure 18). When researching the family story of my ancestor's role in 1798 (which centred on that house) I visited the old-fashioned town office of the Tottenham estate to ask if they could help me to document my family's tenancy. The woman in charge was very helpful, but it quickly became obvious that its older records were unsearchable, their chaotic nature evident in the shelves of heaped documents covered in dust that lined the walls. I subsequently learned that they had been unable even to document the estate's long-acknowledged legal title to one of the town's largest properties, the Royal Hotel. I doubt if they were legally entitled to sell the Rice family home, in which they hadn't invested anything for many decades, but the family understandably didn't want to challenge the sale. It was time to let the old place, and its stories, go. Together with its largely derelict out-buildings it seemed a modest premises to have been, as family lore had it, the home and business quarters of a successful merchant, my ancestor John Rice, the family story of whose death at the hands of the military in the aftermath of the battle of 5 June 1798 sparked the research for my book *Rebellions: Memoir, memory and 1798*. Its status for us as the ancestral family home of the Rices put their long connection with New Ross, as Catholic business people operating outside the town's power structures, in historical perspective and was a matter of enormous pride and consequence for my mother.

The Tottenhams headed the group of 'Protestant Ascendency' families that built the splendid Tholsel, or town hall, in 1749 and dominated its politics for over a century as town 'sovereigns' and as MPs, first in the Dublin parliament and then at Westminster. The town's lack of interest or pride in much of its history may owe something to the fact that it was seen as 'their' history, which is a pity as the story of the town is a significant and complex one.

I came to realise this fully only in 2006–7 when, at the request of Wexford County Library, I edited an anthology of texts and images to celebrate the eight hundredth anniversary of the town's first royal charter. I called the anthology *New Ross – Rosponte – Ros Mhic Treoin*, the names that chart its modern, medieval and Gaelic names. Founded by William Marshal, earl of Pembroke, it had become New Ross around 1200 to distinguish it from the earlier manorial settlement of Old Ross, near my birthplace (our move into the town thus had distinguished historical precedent). The Normans also called it Rosponte (the town of the bridge), while the original Gaelic settlement was called Ros Mhic Treoin (the wood of the son of Treon). By the end of the thirteenth century it had become the most important port in the country, but then its slow decline began having been bested by Waterford, its larger neighbour downstream, in an intense competition for royal favour. A more enduring conflict with the surrounding Gaelic lordships led to the erection of fortified walls in 1265, celebrated in a colourful long poem in Norman French, for centuries the official language of the town. The population was decimated by the Black Death in the mid-fourteenth century, half-destroyed by fire on several occasions, and its famous walls battered and breached by a succession of Gaelic, Royalist and Cromwellian forces. Like the country as a whole, the town had a period of peace and growing prosperity after the Williamite

Figure 19. Credit: Author

victory at the end of the seventeenth century, only to have that peace shattered – and its walls again breached – by the horrifically violent battle for the town in the 1798 Rebellion. In its aftermath New Ross settled back into the slow, sleepy stagnation that still characterised it in my early years.

Downtown, the flat ground beside the river where we lived retained the medieval street pattern. The principal streets had been broadened and developed in the eighteenth and nineteenth centuries but there was still a warren of medieval lanes off them and off the steep hills to the upper ('Irish') town, with evocative medieval names like Sugar House Lane, Folly House Lane, Windmill Lane and Brogue Lane. A hundred yards to the left of our shop door was the large townhouse built by the Tottenham family around the time that they built what became our house; within two decades they had left the town for good, and their town house had long housed the Convent of Mercy nuns when I attended infant school there (Figure 19). Across from it was the handsome 1806 Catholic church, built with the help of the Tottenhams, one of a number of healing interdenominational ventures in the aftermath of the rebellion, and now a theatre. A hundred yards to the right of our front door was the Tholsel (Market House) (Figure 20), then, as now, the centre of the town's civic life but also the focus of the fiercest fighting in the 1798 battle, as commemorated by the statue of a heroic rebel pikeman in the medieval market square in front of it

Figure 20. Credit: Author

brandishing a fist at this symbol of Protestant power (Figure 21). The chief importance of the Tholsel for me as a child, however, was the little public library which then occupied its large ground-floor room and opened only a few evenings a week. More than any other institution, perhaps, it shaped the course of my life by making me a reader, right down to the present day as I sit writing among my books.

While ignorant of much of the town's chequered past, as children we were very aware of its role in 1798, reminded daily not only by the statue of the pikeman but also by the series of well-designed plaques detailing aspects of the battle that were scattered throughout the town and which I copied into a notebook, perhaps for a history project. We knew it was the decisive battle of the rebellion, which effectively ended with the heavy defeat of the rebels. Yet, we got a perverse thrill from the mention of the town and its battle in a famous patriotic ballad we learned at school lamenting how 'The bright sun of freedom grew darkened at Ross'. This ballad and others reflected the town's sense of the rebels' bloody defeat as, essentially, glorious.

For my family the battle had an extra romance because of the story, often recounted by my mother, of the killing by soldiers of her great-grandfather in its aftermath, for attempting to save the lives of women and

Figure 21. Credit. Author

children by hiding them in his business premises in Irishtown. A small project to research his story, meant as a gift to my seriously ill mother as the bicentenary approached, led me ultimately to a more complex account of the battle and its horrific death toll of approximately 1,500 in a conflict lasting little more than twelve hours. Bodies were piled up in all the places of heaviest fighting, including my street, and there is a contemporary account of women walking past a wall of corpses for several days after the battle on their way to the shops, including perhaps the new premises that was, in time, to be ours.

It seems safe to conclude that the sense of the past that I got from my environment and my family when growing up influenced my ultimate ambition to become a historian. It may even have shaped what was to be the focus of my research and writing throughout my career, on Ireland's history being profoundly a colonial one. Perhaps the *longue durée* of my ancient town, with its multiple languages and rulers, however dimly understood, helped me to see that colonial experience not as a history simply of repression but as a complex, shared history producing a mixed culture. I had grown up with a mid-twentieth-century version of that complexity, between languages, at home in an Irish Catholic and nationalist environment but also in a Norman town and with aspects of elite and popular English culture. Like all colonised people, including the mixed inhabitants of my town over many centuries, I was a cultural hybrid.

As well as carrying the imprint of its history, daily life in the town of my childhood followed traditional patterns, even as it began to reflect the slow transition to modernity. Not only did the last of the sailing ships still operate, but wooden crates of shoes were brought from the railway station to our shop on a large dray, drawn by a massive shire horse; most country people still came to town by pony and trap, the less well-off by donkey and cart, tying their animals up in the back yards that were long a feature of many businesses. Farming was largely unchanged from my father's youth, powered by horses, not tractors, and many farms, like those of my father and uncles, still had no electricity – though most looked forward to the government's electrification scheme finally reaching them.

If sent to get 'messages' from a nearby grocery shop, I came back with an armful of brown paper bags of carefully weighed food, much of it locally sourced and none pre-packaged. We persisted with raw milk, delivered twice a day to the house, long after pasteurised bottled milk became the norm (when crates of it were stacked every morning outside the shop opposite) – part of Mammy's resistance to what she believed to be the blandness of the modern. In various small as well as large ways we were raised to be traditionalists. While I was fascinated by the little available to me of the new, cosmopolitan popular culture, most of the fundamentals of my childhood were little changed from when my mother was a child in the town or indeed even from her father's childhood over ninety years before my birth. Yet, change was coming.

New Ross was still primarily a market town, as it had been for many centuries, dependent on its rich agricultural hinterland, but its economy began to be transformed during my schooldays with the establishment of a small cable-wire factory and then a major investment by a Dutch firm in a modern plant producing chemical fertiliser. This revitalised the port, stemmed the flow of emigration a little and gave a new sense of hope – and identity – to the town.

The dominance of the Catholic Church in many areas of life was the most visible proof of enduring cultural traditionalism, but it was facing a number of challenges, though initially some were only dimly perceived as such. The stylish *art deco* cinema up the street from us, with its uniformed staff, garish posters and seductive foreign glamour, may have seemed less of a threat because of strict censorship laws. Its regulars included many from the respectable *petit bourgeoisie*, among them my parents in the days of their secret engagement, though not after they had children. Ultimately developing a fear of the cultural challenges it posed to us, Mammy didn't allow me to go to any films other than religious ones throughout my primary school years but she had to give in when it came to my younger siblings (though always insisting that they sat in the dearer seats upstairs and not with the rowdies on the wooden benches close to the screen). Other harbingers of modernity, like the slow growth in car ownership and the beginning of the dancehall craze which it facilitated (as did the radio, with its promotion of local 'showbands'), contributed to the suddenly rapid transformation of the town and its culture in the 1960s.

The town I returned to from the Christian Brothers in 1964, after seven years absence, was a different, more 'modern' place. This was evident even in the ethos at home, especially the greater freedom of choice allowed my siblings, who were, astonishingly to me, sent by Mammy, after closing the shop on Saturday nights, to the chip shop, only recently seen by her as a den of iniquity. It had been off-limits to me not only because it attracted a 'rough' crowd but because it had a jukebox, on which for a few coins you could play the popular music of the 1950s.

My old friends now had access to cars and drove every weekend to the new dancehalls to meet girls. However, I had lived through those years of change in an environment even more traditional than the town of my childhood, and had been left behind. While I adjusted reasonably well to the shock of the new, that doubly deeply ingrained traditionalism meant that I never fully embraced the modernity rushing towards us. I became a dutiful rather than dedicated follower of fashion, in frequenting dancehalls for example or listening to the exciting new music of the 1960s and '70s. It is tempting to imagine that one of the attractions for me in becoming an academic and historian was the licence to live culturally in earlier times, where I was more at home.

My parents seemed happy to have few outlets outside the home, my father's moderate pub-going being the main exception. Mammy loved card games (not something I inherited, despite her occasional encouragement) and sometimes played in the whist drives organised for local charities. She also went to meetings of the Apostolic Work Society in the Legion of Mary hall, at which devout women made some of the smaller ancillary elements of Catholic liturgical vestments (such as soft white cinctures and colourful stoles) for Irish priests on the 'foreign missions' in Africa and the Far East. She was a devout member of the Children of Mary (a nineteenth-century devotional organisation for women) and attended its weekly prayer meeting or 'sodality'. She treasured its blue cape and the blue ribbon with its 'miraculous medal' – reflecting devotion to the Blessed Virgin as miracle worker in interceding with her Son – and both were put on her in her coffin as she had asked. Neither of my parents had close friends outside their families. Daddy's pub friends (all known by their first names) and Mammy's friends from church-related activities (all known by their married surnames) were met in their social settings, or casually on the street, or as customers in our shop; none visited the house. This also seemed to be the pattern in the homes of my friends. When her children moved away to study and work, Mammy was suspicious of the friendships they made and would occasionally remind them that they could only rely on one another and on the extended family throughout their lives. Certainly she – and indeed Daddy – lived by that.

My mother clearly saw the great annual escape from work to the seaside as an opportunity to spend more time with her children. It seems likely that she always had some guilt about working full-time, even if it was downstairs. Every July, starting on her birthday, the tenth, we spent three weeks in Duncannon, a small, pretty seaside village, its cliff-top fort commanding the mouth of Waterford harbour, its front lit on clear nights by the raking light of the Hook lighthouse a few miles away. Its long sandy beach was a great attraction, flat and firm enough for annual car races and safe for swimming. Its ancient small harbour beside the fort, from which James II left Ireland after the defeat of his armies and where you could buy fresh fish from one of its small trawlers, added to its character. The fort contained the putative cell of 'The Croppy Boy' of 1798 fame. 'It was in Duncannon that young man died', according to the popular ballad, regularly featured on radio and in concerts.

These holidays were also seen by Mammy in traditional terms, replicating as far as possible those she loved to recall in her romantic memories of childhood when her family decamped every summer, before money got tight, to Fethard-on-Sea. Duncannon was fourteen miles from home and, as for many years we didn't have a car, we were brought there in a series of trips by the unflappable 'hackney man' Johnny Doran in his splendidly large and ancient American saloon, possibly a Dodge, beautifully burnished and rarely driven at more than twenty miles an hour. He had to go even more slowly on the first trip each year bringing Aunt Biddy, a very nervous passenger, cocooned on the back seat in a nest of blankets, sheets and pillowcases and tasked with readying the rented house we would occupy. For some years we stayed at apple-cheeked Mrs Maher's on the street near the church. Her hallway had a framed certificate and medal, awarded posthumously to her husband, killed in action in the British Merchant Navy, one of many fishermen who had enlisted in the Second World War from small Irish ports. Then for many years we stayed in Mrs Annie White's near the harbour with its collection of outhouses refurbished by her fisherman husband Bob, whose delight it was to row the many miles upriver to every circus that visited New Ross. Their cavernous kitchen was a location for impromptu concerts; recently I discovered that I still knew all the verses of 'The Red River Valley', often sung there. Finally, we stayed near the beach with Mrs Gilbert White, a nervous woman who had spent years in London and had 'notions'. With all our landladies Mammy conversed endlessly, when not shepherding us all down to the beach. There, she supervised our non-stop activity from the sand dunes where she sometimes sat, needles flying and talking to her Apostolic Work friend Mrs Cullen, aunt by marriage of Louis Cullen, later to be one of Ireland's most important historians, and a good friend. At that time he was a postgraduate student, of whom she was prone to boast.

Daddy's escapes from the house were nightly, but only next door to the unusual pub owned by the sprightly, twinkling Gus O'Kennedy, a sporting hero, winner of four successive All-Ireland Gaelic football medals in his youth. His small licensed premises were entered through an even smaller shop, which sold radios – and later televisions. Its bar clientele rarely varied – a few shopkeepers, the town engineer, a teacher, the town's printer and (very usefully at times) the garda (police) superintendent. Each had his own stool, each his own (largely modest) drinking habits, and each his own method of paying for his drinks (several outside pub hours by cheque, some at the end of each session, some as each drink was served). The conversation was largely the same each evening, much good-humoured teasing and joking, rehearsal of familiar stories and comments on the events of the day (but no political arguments were allowed). Its only other rule was that nobody could buy a drink for anyone else. It was like an exclusive club, which I was privileged to join in my early twenties, my father being allowed to buy his impecunious student son a pint after a solemn vote of all present.

Its exclusivity was deliberate policy by an owner not interested in expanding the business. When you entered the little shop a bell would tinkle, and Gus would see through an angled mirror who it was that had come in. If it was a stranger or someone disapproved of, he would skip out to the shop counter (he had also been a champion dancer) to tell the unwelcome caller that the bar was full. I once heard him announce this when only three of the regular dozen had so far assembled; nobody commented. There was one exception to its exclusively male assembly, a woman who sometimes appeared with a male friend, sitting with him at a small table rather than at the bar with everyone else. When I asked my father about them he told me that they were great friends, each unhappily married to someone else. None of the regulars paid them any heed; small-town life could show a charitable reticence, at least in this singular club.

Some years ago my brother-in-law John Quigley, long a resident of Canada and an early internet forager like many exiles, sent me a film clip discovered by him on YouTube. It featured the BBC's Alan Whicker doing a TV feature in 1963 on the Irish background of J.F. Kennedy prior to the American president's visit to New Ross, the town of his ancestors. In his usual patronising, fake-sounding version of upper English-class tones Whicker interviewed a number of the president's Irish relatives (quaint Irish peasants), and the programme ended in Gus's bar, uniquely crowded for the occasion, the regulars swamped by blow-ins. At the far end of the bar, however, in his usual spot, beside his usual neighbour Pat Cullen the sardonic printer, is my father, who raises his glass and laughs when urged to by a ballad singer at the end of a song written for the occasion. This grainy image is an unexpected and precious reminder of him in his mid-fifties, amused but not quite approving of the carry-on (a bit Paderewski), his laugh mocking (Figure 22). These shadowy brief minutes capture much of what I remember of his nightly transformation from quiet supportive husband and father to talkative joker, among company where he felt at ease and could forget his migraine.

Figure 22. Credit: 'Gus O'Kennedy's pub, 13 South Street, New Ross', Youtube, posted by Phil O'Kennedy, 21 March 2013.

As a child, the thing I most shared with my father was love of hurling, and especially enthusiasm for the great Wexford team of that era. The greatest thrills of those years were going with him and one or two of his friends to the big games in Dublin's Croke Park, travelling by steam train, sitting quietly among these quiet-spoken men on the shabby bench seats of the train's dusty compartments, adorned with faded framed photographs of Killarney and other tourist spots. I brought a good supply of comics, and on one occasion a paperback of the life of the great Hungarian footballer Ferenc Puskás which I had been thrilled to find the day before in our newsagent's. Teased by one of Daddy's friends that I would not be allowed into Croke Park with a book about a soccer player, albeit one who had humiliated England in Wembley a few years earlier (soccer being then 'banned' for GAA members), I feigned lack of concern but made sure the book was well concealed as my father lifted me over the turnstile, free of charge as always, with the encouragement of the man operating it. We never had stand tickets but stood on the Cusack stand corner of the terraces at the Canal end, a steel barrier in front of us to lean on and a good view of the whole pitch. My first All-Ireland final was 1954 against Cork, their great hero Christy Ring going for a record eighth All-Ireland medal, Wexford going for their first title since 1910. Indeed, the history I was most engaged with then was that of Wexford teams, and their mixed fortunes over the decades.

On this first All-Ireland occasion we went to Dublin the day before the match and Daddy and I stayed for two nights in a guesthouse at the top of Harcourt Street, opposite the train station, beside which Ireland's first all-night garage, newly opened, was brightly lit. It was my first time staying overnight in Dublin and the only time, as far as I can recall, that I shared a room with my father. It all seemed very glamorous and exciting.

My small flashes of memory of the actual game mainly feature Ring and the Wexford heroes the Rackard brothers (from Killanne, close to my father's Courtnacuddy), especially my hero Bobby who had the job of 'marking' Ring. Cork won at the last minute with a Johnny Clifford goal, which I can still see, at least as it was featured in the *Evening Press*, launched the next day and stylishly delivered to street sellers and shops in purple bins mounted on trendy Lambretta scooters as we walked down O'Connell Street. I would by then have already read in my father's *Irish Independent* the match report by their great sports journalist John D. Hickey, a colourful writer who influenced my prose as much as anyone in those years.

> ... in that hour of mighty combat ... vanquished gained almost as much distinction as victors ... The game made Ring the most fabulous hurler of all time [but] there is no disputing that Wexford's Bobby Rackard was the man of the hour. Utterly disdainful of flailing hurleys, he time and again came through a forest of them, ball in hand ...

Two years later, Wexford, now finally champions having beaten Galway the previous year, had their revenge on Cork, and John D. reached for his most purple prose to describe the two abiding memories of that game:

> It was all stupendous, and then as if to give us something completely new, an incident that we will relate to generations yet unborn, we had the inspiring and never to be forgotten spectacle of Nick O'Donnell and Bobby Rackard rushing to carry shoulder high from the field their 'arch-enemy', Christy Ring ... But the spirit of admirable good fellowship was not confined to one side. When, as the result was still in the melting pot, Ring shot a pile-driver at Art Foley, the Wexford goalie brought off one of his several miracle saves, but he had hardly more than done so when the Cork maestro went in and congratulated the net guardian on his spectacular work.

The next day the *Independent* included a posed photograph of the winning team, with autographs of the players. More smudged grey and white than black and white, it may have seemed a dull souvenir of a vibrantly colourful day but to me it radiated glamour and excitement. Instead of putting it in my sports album, I was given money for a frame and hung it in the kitchen among the religious images. Well, it had seemed a quasi-religious experience.

After this game, as on all other such occasions (Leinster finals, League finals) bar the 1954 All-Ireland, we travelled back to New Ross on the train, now moving even more slowly than on the way up (on one trip I saw with mounting anxiety one of my father's friends walk alongside the train for a while, with others, picking blackberries), arriving home well after midnight (ensuring excellent overtime for the crew, as the passengers noted, almost approvingly). Before going to our own house, however late, we always called in to see my Aunt May, who had a couple of bottles of stout for Daddy and a warm lemonade for me, the train being 'dry', the carriage system (and no doubt the licensing laws) ruling out a bar.

My memories of my father during those magical 'excursions' (as we called them) was of imperturbable good humour and unobtrusive care of me, joining in the excited discussion of the match, delighted at every aspect of the day out – mass heard standing at the back of Westland Row Church beside the station when we finally arrived, dinner up the road in the scarily formal Mont Clare Hotel, the walk in the midst of colourful crowds across town to the match, including a quick pint en route, time permitting, in the Shakespeare Bar (with me joining other boys outside on the footpath, nursing our soft drinks, all sporting our team's colours and wary of one another), the walk up the canal, past the three-card-trick men with their collapsible tables for a quick getaway, the noisy, swaying excitement of the game, followed by a mixed grill in the huge restaurant of the Metropole Cinema, the unnecessary rush for the train which never left on time.

A recent newspaper feature included a 1953 photograph of Dublin Airport's Collar of Gold restaurant run by Johnny Oppermann, one of the most fashionable (and expensive) in the city. It brought back another vivid memory of the Monday after the 1954 All-Ireland final when my clerical uncle John drove up from Gorey to meet us and bring us to the airport restaurant for lunch. Its enormous windows looked out on the (infrequent) arrivals and departures of the new Vickers Viscount planes. What I best remember about that lunch, however, was trying to work out the hierarchy among the waiters by the amount of gold braid on their uniforms. On our way out of the airport, passing probably the only shop, my uncle noticed me

Figure 23. Credit: Author

looking at the array of comics on display, brought me over to the counter and uttered the magic words, 'Give this young man one of every comic you have.' It compensated for the newspaper accounts of our traumatic loss the previous day. Years later, when I got to know my uncle better, I found that he was well known in Gorey, where he was then a mere curate, for giving away whatever money he had and that his equally generous impulses towards his family were mainly courtesy of his bank, in an era when priests had generous credit facilities. When the family had stopped going to Duncannon, Daddy took holidays for a number of years with Uncle John, touring widely, staying in small hotels in quiet seaside places like Ballycotton, times of great happiness for them both (Figure 23) before John's bad health made it too difficult.

I hardly noticed our house's lack of a garden, having the freedom of the town and surrounding countryside to a degree unimaginable in today's more fearful world. My close friends were also 'downtown' boys, sons of other shopkeepers, while many of our classmates and sometime rivals were from 'the top of the town', up its series of steep hills, some living in the recently built council estates. I was aware of the largely unarticulated difference in social status and privilege, but this was fudged by the fact that teachers, guards and insurance men – all low-paid but prestigious occupations – were among those who lived in these 'council houses'.

Once out of school and if not needed at home, our freedom was limited only by the requirement to be back for meals. We played hopscotch on the quieter streets, marbles in the lanes, had bicycle races (fast and slow) on the quay and, despite its dangerous currents, learned to swim in the river, initially from the boathouse landing with a canvas belt around our waists tied to a long pole. Later, using our efficient, if awkward, breaststrokes we swam in the quieter waters of the 'pill' (inlet) at the Ferry Bridge a few miles above the town. From our early teens we took out heavy rowing boats (life jackets were unknown), going upriver with the tide and back on its turn from where the Barrow meets the Nore.

In contrast to such quiet days on the river, the annual regatta day had an air of frantic excitement, the river on an ebbing tide full of rowing eights and fours from all over Ireland – Athlunkard from Limerick, Commercial and Garda from Dublin, the Lee from Cork, Enniskillen and Portora prominent among crews from Northern Ireland. As some races were for All-Ireland titles, the regatta attracted every major crew on the island. Bookies roared the odds on the quay, and the surge of boats toward the finish line was a thrilling sight. One year at least our window, usually full of ladies' fashion shoes, displayed the regatta's ornate silver trophies.

Escaping the easily reached limits of the town, we roamed the fields, exploring, going on impromptu cross-country runs or picking blackberries to sell to Mr Grace, who exported them to England in large barrels. Across the river in the sloping fields where the fertiliser factory was soon to be built we found a spring, bubbling into an old broken black cauldron; in a very faint memory, a man nearby exposed himself briefly. Another day in that area we watched a colourfully dressed woman, sitting on the steps of a horse-drawn caravan, tossing grain or seeds into the wind from a wide shallow basin.

The 1940s and '50s are often depicted as a grim, bleak period in Irish life (and so they were in many respects, especially for the many unemployed men and their families), but while this impression may be reinforced by the often blurred black-and-white photographs of the time, much of the life I lived as a boy was in vivid colour. Exotic strangers were a common sight in the town: strongmen and fire- and sword-swallowers occasionally performed their feats outside the Tholsel; ballad singers sang on street corners on Fair days, when fast-talking 'cheap Johnnies' sold their incredible

Figure 24. Credit: Author

bargains from stalls on the quay; Fossett's and Duffy's circuses paraded down our street to announce their arrival.

Though seldom allowed to go to the cinema, we were brought to every circus by Mammy, who had loved to go when she was a child. Small though these circuses were, I am now struck by the fact that they all featured the classic acts, like Pierrot and Joey clowns, trapeze and tightrope walkers, ponies and lions – all accompanied by a live band, its composition changing as the musicians came and went to do their acts in the ring. Fossett's Circus was the great favourite because some of the family wintered and went to school in the town. Some years ago I went to a performance of Fossett's Circus in Cork and talked to the current owner and ringmaster, daughter of Teddy Fossett who I remembered from childhood. Few of the traditional elements remained but the sense of magic that circus has always meant for me still lingered.

Homegrown colour and excitement on the streets were provided regularly by the town's two bands. The Confraternity Band (from the Men's Confraternity in the parish church), a jaunty brass ensemble, wore bright blue blazers and white trousers. The martial New Ross Pipe Band (recruited from the local FCÁ (Fórsa Cosanta Áitiúil, or local defence force, i.e. part-time soldiers) wore stylish slashed green jackets and orange kilts and were led by a tall drum major twirling a large ornamental staff. As small boys my friends and I would march beside them in turn, chests out, arms swinging, on their regular parading through downtown.

The two bands came together each Corpus Christi, the ancient Catholic feast day in summer, one leading, the other bringing up the rear of the long, colourful procession of school children and religious groups, my mother participating with the Children of Mary in their colourful blue capes and white veils (Figure 24). At the head of the procession walked a priest carrying the Blessed Sacrament (Corpus Christi, Body of Christ) in its resplendent gold monstrance, under an ornate processional awning carried by Confraternity stalwarts. One of the most coveted roles of the liturgical year as a senior altar boy was to walk behind the priest while swinging the exotic silver thurible in which incense was burning, its distinctive, well-remembered smell wafting over the priest, honouring the host, as you swung.

All the shop windows, including ours, had an altar, decked with flowers; yellow and white papal flags fluttered from windows, and there was colourful bunting across the streets. The procession wound its long way from the Good Shepherd Convent (with its hidden Magdalene laundry, its inmates not in the procession) in Irishtown to the parish church, in the grounds of which an altar had been erected. A similar display of Catholic devotion happened then in every town and village in Ireland, the footpaths crowded with reverent onlookers.

Years ago when our sons were small I brought them into Cork city centre on some urgent shopping expedition, despite it being Sunday. The city centre was crowded with shoppers (followers of the new religion) and as we emerged from the toy store I was suddenly reminded of what day it was. Down the street, closed to traffic, came a small, rather sad Corpus Christi procession led by a brass band. The procession's most remarkable features were a colourful group of recent arrivals from Africa, dancing and singing, and just in front of the priest carrying the host, two or three old men, Papal Knights in court dress, including ceremonial swords. The procession passed through the crowds of shoppers, some curious, most (like my boys) indifferent. It was a snapshot of the profound change in Irish society since my childhood – modern Ireland looking on, uncomprehending, at a remnant of a traditional Ireland and its recently dominant but now marginalised Catholic Church.

The main focus of my fun and games was 'Murphy's Yard', a large enclosed space with only an old wall – perhaps part of the medieval town wall – separating it from the river. Old stables and magical caves burrowed into the cliff on which the houses of John Street were built overhead. There, among the Murphys' multifarious business activities (principally poultry and salmon) a large gang of boys and girls, friends of the Murphy children, were allowed to play, under the calm, amused gaze of their father. We had hide and seek and other non-gendered games, but for us boys the main activity was hurling, hotly contested games, hours long. The yard also featured a crude toilet built over the river's edge, into which offal would be thrown at times, attracting teeming swirls and coils of eels, which were caught and killed before our squeamish eyes.

Three of us also had our own gang for a time (John Murphy and Michael Hanrahan being the other two), and scratched on the shield of a long-abandoned sports prize the initials T.T.T. (The Terrible Three). I have no recollection of further activities, terrible or not, but I vividly recall the intensity of our friendship, and one aspect of it that was at odds with my 'Good Boy' persona at home. The family of my best friend Michael had a fond, but teasing, argumentative relationship, very different from the calm of mine. Playing our games, I would on occasion suddenly erupt in anger at being teased and flounce off home, declaring I would never speak to Michael again. Of course we would meet after dinner or next day and resume our activities as if nothing had happened. No doubt such short outbursts were an important safety valve, given my usual carefully controlled behaviour.

The account of my childhood thus far may seem rather idyllic – 'Huckleberry Dunne on the Barrow'. The idyllic elements, even discounting the element of nostalgia, were as I remembered them, and I felt safe and happy in my traditional home and surroundings – except for my experience in the Christian Brothers school, which I first attended aged six. For three years before that I was one of a small number of privileged, mainly 'downtown', boys at the infant school of the Mercy Convent, later attended by my sisters. During those years of 'Babies', 'Infants' and 'Senior Infants' we were treated with great kindness and gentleness, 'babied' indeed. Only Sister Immaculata, who taught us religion from a small red catechism, seemed a large, scary presence. Sixteen years later, summoned by the nuns to their convent on my first visit home as a professed religious, I was astonished and amused to find that the monstrous nun of childhood was a tiny, smiling figure; no doubt it was the catechism with its theological abstractions, incomprehensible to small children, that was scary. In preparing for First

Figure 25. Credit: Author

Holy Communion, however, such rigour was softened and each of us was assigned a senior girl to help us (mainly, as I recall, to colour in the holy pictures of our Communion book), and though I cannot remember who it was that looked after me, I know I was delighted with all the fuss. I find this photograph (Figure 25), taken (possibly by one of the nuns, although it has the look of an 'Annie Brophy') in the convent garden, very moving, not only the intense seriousness of my face and the conventional devotional pose but also the care and common sense of my mother's choice of a good tweed suit, the coat a little too large, to allow for growth (repeated in her present for my fifteenth birthday as described in Chapter 4), and the sturdy 'Start Rite' sandals from the shop. This is another 'punctum', as Barthes called the incidental details in a photograph that are poignant and revealing of inner realities, in this case of my devout, dutiful childhood and my mother's anxious love.

While the Communion went well (despite a stressful breakfast in the convent parlour, with a nun hovering behind each of us), all of this was poor preparation for what I encountered a few months later when my mother brought me up the High Hill to the Brothers (the only time I remember either parent coming to the school). I retain a vivid memory of peering out fearfully from behind a mobile blackboard at the crammed rows of strange boys – over seventy of them, as I recall. While there had been no corporal punishment in the convent (or in my home), now virtually every class for the next six years was punctuated by beatings with the infamous 'leather', not for bad behaviour but for missing questions or getting homework wrong. I have no memory of having been beaten myself (though I must have been), but I was traumatised by the daily and often extreme violence inflicted on other boys by teachers both lay and religious. I was, and long remained, a timid person, and I worked very hard to escape punishment. But I was also a shopkeeper's son and therefore treated more favourably. Even at the time I was aware of the additional savagery involved in the singling out, day after day, of the poorest boys, whose circumstances must have made homework significantly more difficult, and often impossible, and with no money for books or materials. The brutalisation of the boys generally often transferred to their behaviour at playtime in the yard, where only the protection of my more tough-minded and hard-fisted friend Michael saved me from bullying.

School sports did offer some compensation, especially hurling. I was a goalie, a role in keeping with my romantic personality – heroic, saving the team from disaster, just as I planned to save the world. I could carry off the odd spectacular save but was never good enough to make the school team – too excitable, too nervous. Also on the positive side of school, there were choirs and an annual musical, and I learned, perforce, a lot of poetry, for which I remain grateful. Sports day, 29 June, was elaborately organised, with every boy in the school dressed all in white (Figure 26). Here I am on my final sports day, six weeks before I left home to join the Christian Brothers, looking, to my eyes now but probably not reflecting my thoughts then, vulnerable, apprehensive and distressingly young. The whole school was involved in exercises of 'Swedish Drill' (a European-wide craze, part of a

Figure 26. Credit: Author

cult of the body from the early nineteenth century), in complex formations covering the entire marked-out sports ground, the smallest boys using staves, the oldest twirling fiendishly difficult clubs that had ropes instead of wooden handles. After the drill came a remarkable array of athletics events, from egg and spoon races for the youngest to pole-vaulting with bamboo poles for the seniors. In my last years before leaving the school I fancied myself as a middle-distance runner, another romantic role, also allowing individual self-expression without the threat of physical hurt. With my friends I would do many circuits of the town's streets on long summer evenings, each circuit reckoned by us, with some exaggeration, as a mile.

Again, I had a certain style and could run forever, but when I tried to take up running as an undergraduate in University College Dublin years later I quickly learned my limitations and so my dream of running an Olympic marathon for Ireland, like that of playing hurling in goal for Wexford, soon faded, though never completely.

But, overall, my memories of school up to age fourteen are of fear in the face of relentless cruelty. This may make it hard to understand why I then insisted, against my parents' better judgement, on joining the Christian Brothers before my fifteenth birthday. One thing that made it possible was that I could not articulate, even to myself, my abhorrence of what I had experienced, not at that age and in that society which largely approved of hitting children. I had learned to cope with it on a personal level and it was less severe during the two years I spent in the secondary school. It was only some years later when I first taught as a young Brother that I realised the extent to which I had been traumatised by my earlier experience, quickly refusing to use the 'leather' I had been issued on the first day.

The main reason I joined the order (more accurately called a congregation) was that I was very religious, unsurprising given my background but with an intensity that is difficult to relate to now. That again owed much to temperament. I was, and remained, a romantic, not in the sense of attachment to any cultural or political doctrine (which I have never felt strongly) but in the role I envisaged for myself in the world, dedicating my life to doing good, especially through education. My religious fervour was highly emotional, again unsurprising for my age, and possibly an outlet for the emotions suppressed at home. I can still see my young self on many private visits to the church staring avidly at a statue or the tabernacle, praying for a sign, for confirmation that God was calling me – a kind of self-mesmerism, guided and intensified by the pamphlets of the Catholic Truth Society on vocations, available on a rack in the church porch. There were also pamphlets, heavily coded, on the need to repress sexual urges, and perhaps in retrospect the sensuality of my religious fervour represented in part a meeting of that need. At the time, however, my sense of self was heroic, a spiritual version of my literary and sporting heroes.

The Catholic Church had offered the most vivid and intense cultural experiences of my life until then. The imposing parish church was like a huge theatrical set, with its soaring spaces, its colourful glass, its prominent pulpit and the elaborate high altar carved by the father of Patrick Pearse, no less. Being an altar boy heightened the hugely seductive effect of the liturgy on me, much of it sensory – the music, the vestments, the incense, the bell-ringing – all of it coming together on great liturgical occasions, solemn funeral masses and high masses, some ceremonies involving the presence of the bishop, seated on his throne, wearing his mitre. The Easter ceremonies had a powerful emotional force, especially the dramas of Good Friday, and of Easter Saturday at midnight when the Resurrection was represented by the processing of a candle through a darkened church, its flame used to light those of the congregation while a single tenor voice soared from the choir loft with the exuberant '*Exultet*'. Its refrain, '*Haec nox est*' (This is the night), still echoes in my memory.

Taking an ever more prominent part in those very theatrical performances as I progressed up the altar boy hierarchy was wonderful, and even sleepily serving early-morning mass before a half dozen people was to feel privileged and chosen, at ease on the altar and in the sacristy, spaces reserved otherwise for the priests. We were dressed in a version of clerical garb, the long black soutane and lace-fringed white surplice, and trained, after a fashion, to make the responses in Latin. I was indeed seduced and enthralled by the wonder and mystery of it all.

Even now, despite having lost the religious beliefs associated with them, the sounds of traditional Gregorian chant, so admired by Haydn, Mozart and Beethoven, can send shivers up my spine. Some time ago, after the funeral mass of an old friend – the historian Brendan Bradshaw – listening to his fellow Marist priests sing unaccompanied the 'Salve Regina' I was reminded why this simple twelfth-century hymn is regarded as one of the most haunting and perfect of musical compositions. I was also reminded of another colourful event in the town of my childhood, the annual Festival of Plain Chant, part of a European-wide revival at that time and thus another example of influences from outside taking root in small Irish communities. Every school in the district gave public recitals in venues throughout the town, competing for prizes, singing from the common Gregorian (ninth-century) repertoire, especially from the *Missa de Angelis* or Mass of the Angels (*Kyrie*, *Gloria* and *Agnus Dei)* – and from Benediction (*Tantum Ergo*, *Adoro Te)*. As a grand finale a massed choir of all the schools sang the full *Missa de Angelis* in the parish church, conducted from the pulpit by Fr Gall, the tall, charismatic priest from St Peter's seminary who organised it all. The swelling sound reverberating through the vast spaces of the church was thrilling, as was the sense of belonging and community. Dressed up in our sports-day whites, we Christian Brothers' boys enjoyed it as a day off from school but also as fun and excitement rather than duty. How very far away it seems.

We are now painfully aware that underneath the colour and the ritual, behind the rhetoric and unchallenged authority, was a cesspit of sexual abuse of children in their care by priests and religious, perpetrated by relatively few but covered up and essentially condoned by church authorities, religious and diocesan, the exposure of which has done more than anything else to destroy the moral authority of the Catholic Church in Ireland, to a degree utterly unimaginable in my childhood. Of course, the abuse was not only sexual and physical but also an abuse of power, seen also in the treatment of unmarried pregnant women and their children in Magdalene laundries and in mother-and-baby homes; and in the treatment of the few teachers, writers and doctors who challenged that power. As a child I questioned very little, and never the church, which would have been unthinkable. I lived unaware, cocooned in the general culture of public piety and of silence, particularly in sexual matters, of which I was in any case profoundly ignorant. At the top of the town, near my Uncle James' house, the imposing Good Shepherd Convent had a laundry, which my mother occasionally used. I assumed that the nuns did the washing and starching and was unaware of the women incarcerated in the convent, even though my altar boy duties sometimes brought me into its chapel, in the choir of which my uncle later sang. The women were largely unseen, even by those living next door. My Aunt Kathy told me when the scandals broke, 'You got glimpses of them working in the fields.' But of course every adult was aware of them.

If I had learned of those invisible women and had asked my mother about them, I'm sure she would have told me that the nuns were very good to the poor girls. Yet she most likely knew of families incarcerating their wayward daughters in such places, and of the law aiding and abetting them in this. Of course, she would not have seen it in those terms, and if confronted with the reality would have refused to believe it of the nuns (and even more the abuse by priests) – perhaps she would have been incapable of doing so. Claire Keegan's brilliant novella *Small Things Like These* (2021), set in New Ross thirty years later, captures the continued conspiracy of silence about the Good Shepherds and the almost unimaginable heroism it would take, even for a respected businessman, to challenge the church once terrible abuse was uncovered. Two years later, the publication of Maureen Sullivan's memoir of her horrific experience as a very young inmate there, *Girl in the Tunnel*, dispelled any thought that Keegan's portrayal of the life suffered by the women was exaggerated.

That conspiracy of silence about the whole gamut of abuse was all-encompassing, not least among better-off Catholics with clerical connections, like my parents, who could have exerted pressure or at least raised concerns. Perhaps my parents did. A fellow altar boy told me in his late sixties of being abused by a priest who was in charge of us and had a great reputation for holiness in the town. Remarkably, my friend told his shopkeeper-father, who went immediately to see the parish priest, and the abuser was moved to a rural parish next day – free to abuse again. The potential of such pressure as that exerted by my friend's father is clear, even if the steps taken by the church authorities, in this and many other instances, only compounded the original crime.

My own religiosity was much influenced by the consciousness of the great clerical tradition in my father's family, four generations, including my own, of Fr John Dunnes. There was some puzzlement that I had chosen to go for the lowlier life of a Christian Brother, still highly respected of course but without the power and mystery of the priest. This choice was no doubt influenced by my mother's family, which had fewer priests but the greater distinction of having produced the founder of the Irish Christian Brothers, Edmund Ignatius Rice. Our heroic ancestor, killed in the aftermath of the bloody battle for the town in 1798, was his cousin and probably had an outlying branch of Rice's successful provisioning business, centred downstream in Waterford. In school we prayed daily to 'the founder', as we did at home as part of the family Rosary. My mother was devoted to him and to the cause of his canonisation, that is, official recognition by the church that he was a saint, which was why he was prayed *to* rather than *for*, part of a process designed to encourage the necessary miracles. His inspirational story – the successful Catholic merchant devoting his life and wealth to the education of poor boys after the death of his wife – proved irresistible to me and no doubt weakened the resistance of my mother, who would have preferred, very sensibly, that I waited until I was eighteen before undertaking such a life-changing step. I could defy her because she opposed only the timing while greatly approving the ambition. I was, more than ever a 'good boy'.

She was also reassured by the 'Postulator', the Brother who visited schools recruiting 'postulants', young boys aspiring to join the order, that I would simply be a schoolboy in a boarding school for the next two years, during which I would not be asked to make any further commitments. She knew from my avid perusal of the missionary magazines she subscribed to – such as *Far East* – that my romanticism tended in that direction, and she was given direct assurances by the wonderfully urbane visiting Brother, as we all sat ill at ease in our seldom used 'parlour', that there would be no question of that for many years – a promise not honoured.

And so my childish commitment to a religious vocation was accepted, and my mother put aside her concerns and focused on assembling the clothes I was to take with me, according to the meticulous list that arrived by post sometime later, sewing a name tag on each item and packing them all neatly into a new trunk (finally consigned to the dump over fifty years later after decades of storing my children's toys). While for me it was, no doubt, a time of mounting excitement and growing self-importance, it must have been heart-breaking for her and my father, but I was given no hint of that, even as I was brought to the town's little train station, my trunk stowed in the guard's van and myself placed carefully by her in a compartment containing two nuns with the request that they would look after me and make sure I got out at Bray, where I would be met. The true state of my parents' feelings and the extent of their sacrifice were only brought home to me many years later by my siblings, who remembered them sitting silently on the settee in the parlour that evening as the light faded, holding hands, the only time any of their children ever saw them doing so. Perhaps they sensed they were mourning, as well as my loss, the end of my childhood. While I did indeed live the life of a boarding schoolboy over the coming years, I also became, in terms of how I was treated and the expectations of me, a small adult, a young religious, with my black suit for Sundays and feast days and with my commitment to my vocation underlined by the knowledge that I would not be coming home for Christmas or Easter vacations, and only for a brief holiday in the summer. It was indeed a dramatic and radical break, reinforced, as now seems clear to me, by a deliberate process of estrangement from family and home.

Recently, when discussing the policy of recruiting boys at fourteen with an old friend, still a Christian Brother, I was taken aback at the vehemence with which he called it a form of child abuse. But I had to agree that the term was not too harsh. The congregation's disregard for the ultimate wellbeing of the children in their care (most notoriously in the 'industrial schools' they ran) extended even to the cynical cutting short of the education of the boys who sought to join them, robbing us of crucial years of development and stultifying and distorting our emotional lives. We were all – those who left and those who stayed – profoundly damaged by it. This is, in part, the subject of the following chapters, but they also record the nurturing sense of community, the kindness and mentoring received from many of the older men and the encouragement of my growing love of teaching, that marked the seven years I spent with 'the monks', as the Brothers called themselves informally, rather than with 'the congregation', the official regime which blighted so many lives.

LIFE WITH THE CHRISTIAN BROTHERS

CHAPTER 4

Training

THE SCHOOLBOY POSTULANT

I don't remember the slow journey by steam train to Bray in August 1957 where, no doubt, I was handed onto the platform by my solicitous guardian nuns and taken over at once by the Brothers deputed to meet me, together with boys from all over the south of Ireland – eighty-two in all, arriving over several days. Our trunks were stowed on a lorry and we walked as a group the mile or two to Old Conna where, twenty years earlier, the Brothers had taken over an eighteenth-century mansion belonging to the Plunkett family and renamed it Coláiste Chiaráin.

Right from the beginning I felt happy in my romantic boarding school, for so it seemed. Entering the grand entrance hall of the old house, with its fine staircase, I had, for the only time in my life, a strong sense of *déjà vu*; I had, I felt, lived here before. But if in my memory I felt instantly at home in Coláiste Chiaráin, that is unlikely to have been true of the fourteen-year-old, cosseted, timid boy I was then. Was the initial experience of leaving my family and finding myself in the midst of a large group of strangers not traumatic instead, the trauma then and later suppressed? My lack of any memory of homesickness during those early days was to be repeated in relation to returning to the Brothers after the few visits home over the coming years, a fact I found upsetting, as well as puzzling to record as I wrote and revised this memoir. Feeling a vague sense of guilt, wondering if I had been singularly unfeeling, I looked for possible explanations. My very romantic sense of vocation and of being on a great adventure may have helped me to overcome the upset involved. More prosaically, the intense drive to conformity and identification with the group that boarding schools or armies or religious orders develop would have been a powerful influence. An important aspect of this, as Colm Tóibín noted about his own experiences of boarding school, was the attraction of 'the orderliness of life in that school' and 'the thought that I can decide almost nothing for myself'. There was also my subtle conditioning at home to suppress negative emotions and to win approval by being a 'Good Boy'. Now I had a wider and more challenging arena in which to act out that role. Then again, my lifelong tendency has been to look forward with optimism rather than backward with regret, a tendency that may also of course be a way of avoiding emotional upset.

Whatever the explanation, this suppression of emotion on the radical break with my family clearly left scars, as my unease at recording it showed. It was some consolation to learn recently that such suppression was not unique to me. In a commissioned internal report on the culture of the Christian Brothers, in 1998, G.T. Faulkner, an Australian Brother, having interviewed many members and former members, wrote that 'personal grief at loss of family was severe, even when not consciously recognised'. It led to retrospective 'intense anger' for many Brothers and former Brothers, anger at themselves for their 'seemingly cavalier' response to the separation, and at the congregation for not recognising the enormity of the break and helping its very young postulants to deal with it. I don't feel anger, only sadness, and upset for the soft young boy that I was and for my companions in unacknowledged grief.

Instead, the Brothers attempted, successfully in my case, to help us to suppress or sublimate the trauma involved by total cultural immersion, and by ceaseless physical activity. No doubt this was meant kindly, as being in our best interests: also it seems clear now that they did not have the training required to understand and meet our emotional needs. Instead, we were expected to emulate the military discipline of the young Spartan boy in the well-known story, not showing his pain as the wolf cub concealed under his coat gnawed at his breast. And indeed there was a strong Spartan feel to our new school. The lawn in front of the old house had a range of formidable gym equipment, including rings and parallel bars, reflecting the vogue for Germanic-style gymnastics as a form of manly character-building; this was reinforced during the year by weekly gymnastics classes with a tough army instructor who put us through the rigours – and terrors – of the pommel horse. In a field nearby was a large swimming pool, using cold water from a stream filtered through gravel beds – another aid to the muscular, manly Christianity that was our version of the Spartan code.

Crucial for me in this apparently painless transition was the emphasis from the start on games, and especially the daily opportunities before term began to play intense, competitive hurling; some of my new classmates were very talented. This I did despite a lack of boots (forgotten in the packing) for several weeks, playing in goal in my slowly disintegrating purple and gold Wexford socks. Allied to all of this enthusiastically embraced, character-forming exercise was an equally intense experience of prayer and meditation, mainly in the bright chapel, a former ballroom, with views down to the sea through a row of high windows.

Attached to the elegant old house was a large hall – more prefab than extension – which was our study/classroom/recreation area/concert hall and heated, as I remember it, by an enormous Russian-style stove. Attached to the hall was a similar building, divided into sleeping cubicles and bathrooms but with no stove; breaking ice on the water in our washbasins was a regular occurrence. We ate in the basement area of the old house. The regime was indeed Spartan, disciplined but kindly, and with real camaraderie among the boys. It had many of the basic characteristics with which I was familiar from English boarding-school stories, from *Tom Brown* on. We were muscular Christians, with a Gaelic Catholic twist. The gregarious side of my nature, evident previously in my life outside the home, doubtless helped me to adjust to boarding-school life, as did my 'Good Boy' drive to conform and win approval. The more solitary element found expression in prayer, rather than private reading for which there was no time and certainly no encouragement.

The other boys came from all over the southern province (south of a line from Dublin to Galway), and we all quickly learned the home place of each (the memory of which I retained, as I discovered recently when sent a list of our group). It was one way we kept our identities – I don't remember much talk about families; perhaps it was discouraged. It was easy to make friends, and I recall little bullying or bad behaviour. There were regular warnings against 'special friendships', which we found puzzling. They were forbidden, we were told, on grounds of charity and community, of not favouring any comrade over another. We were given no sense of the old fear in religious orders of homosexual activity, of which most, if not all of us, were entirely ignorant. That is the nearest we got to sex education that year, in my recollection.

The biggest challenge for most of us was that all the academic subjects (including science and Latin) were taught through the Irish language, in which I was far from proficient. It said a lot for the teaching we received that I could play a lead role in an Irish play, *An Fear Siúil* (The Tramp) at the Christmas concert. It also said a lot about how well I had adjusted to my new life, however difficult it may have been at first. The rhythm of our days quickly became second nature: early rising, mass, breakfast, household chores, classes, dinner, back to class, games, supper, study, recreation, evening prayers – all strictly supervised. Eating in the refectory was a challenge initially. You quickly learned that if you didn't get and guard your share as the dishes circulated you might have little to eat.

The cooking was done by non-teaching 'lay' Brothers; others ran the attached farm. I was never clear about their status in the order, but it was evident that they lacked the usual formal education. They were a feature of each of the Orwellian-styled 'houses of formation' in which I lived and were often more approachable than the teaching Brothers. In retrospect there seemed to be a hint of a caste system, such as existed also in some orders of nuns.

There were many talks about good behaviour, even about etiquette, which we studied from a small book, none of which I remember except such advice as became useful in later life when setting a table or replying to a formal invitation. However, one sermon from a visiting priest giving a 'retreat' (days of intense prayers and meditation) stayed in my mind because of the great relief it gave me. This priest, whose name I wish I could recall, set out to prove – contrary to the dire warnings we had heard all of our lives – that it was almost impossible to commit a mortal sin, that is, a sin so grave that you would suffer eternal agonies in Hell if you died unforgiven. In contrast to the graphic, quasi-pornographic descriptions of hellfire and damnation delivered by an emotional Jesuit priest to terrify schoolboys in James Joyce's *A Portrait of an Artist as a Young Man*, we heard a calm argument that the conditions required by Canon Law for such a grave sin – of 'serious matter', 'full knowledge' and 'full consent' – could rarely be met in full. Ever the optimist, I was happy to embrace the idea, which no doubt saved me from nightmares and helped me to avoid scruples, a common affliction of pious young men and from which some friends were to suffer.

Long walks in a 'crocodile', three abreast, were a regular feature and much enjoyed, with their opportunities for conversation and jokes and brief glimpses of the outside world. Some that I remember were formidable, especially a long trek to the Sugar Loaf mountain, the stiff climb to the top, the pell-mell back to the road and, I think, the welcome sight of a bus to take us back to the college seven miles away (perhaps the bus also brought us – making it a less heroic test). In the evenings we listened sometimes to the radio, especially on Sundays to the BBC's 'Grand Hotel', an important introduction to a range of light classical music. At Christmas and major feast days the hall became a makeshift cinema, showing wholesome fare like sedate old musicals starring Nelson Eddy and Jeanette MacDonald. Sometimes there were newsreels, months out of date, and in one of them I finally saw the poor-quality black-and-white film of Ronnie Delany, with his awkward upright style, winning the 1,500 metres at the Melbourne Olympics a year earlier – an improbable triumph I had first been thrilled by while listening to a radio commentary at home after returning from serving early mass.

As part of the large farm attached to the college there was a beautiful walled 'kitchen' garden which had the Plunkett family motto *Festina Lente* (hasten slowly) over the entrance. Periods of 'manual labour' introduced us to an old monastic tradition – *laborare est orare* (to work is to pray) – but, more practically, they also provided another physical activity to tire out adolescent boys. In my earlier memoir I described the sudden appearance one winter day of my clerical Uncle John, with the superior of the college and the provincial of the congregation, on the steps looking down on the walled garden where I was harvesting Brussels sprouts. With remarkable deference, the Brothers apologised to me and to my uncle for allowing recruitment to the Indian mission by a visiting Brother contrary to a promise made to my parents. I, of course, had volunteered enthusiastically for that romantic life of hardship and sacrifice and wrote in delight to tell my parents, who, appalled, turned to my uncle, as they did in all emergencies. *Festina Lente* was apt indeed!

The day I most vividly remember of that year, however, was my fifteenth birthday, on 18 December. As usual, we assembled before classes began, and letters from our parents were handed out by the superior, who had the exotic name of Zeno. Parcels involved a different procedure. They were opened, and any edibles consigned to the common pool. This happened to the tin of biscuits my mother had sent, but her parcel had also contained the book *Knocknagow* (a Christmas present, as mentioned earlier) and a fine Donegal tweed jacket in her favourite brown colour ('hides the dirt'). The superior handed the jacket to me; I put it on as instructed and immediately took it off again, explaining that the sleeves were too long and I would wear it later in the year. 'You will wear it now,' he told me, 'your mother spent good money on that coat.' And so I did, embarrassed for many weeks by the way the sleeves virtually covered my fingers.

Many years later I was to discover not only that I shared a birthday with my future wife, Clare, but that she was born about ten miles away on the day that I was embarrassed by my fine new sports coat. It is the only birthday (including my latest) that I remember clearly. Our family had never made a fuss of birthdays, and I had no interest in celebrating even significant ones like my sixtieth or seventieth or eightieth. Why not? I wonder now – a fear that such celebration would tempt fate, or perhaps show a lack of modesty? A touch of the Paderewskis?

Figure 27. Credit: Author

At the end of our 'juniorate' year in Bray we were allowed a visit home for two weeks, during which we were expected to wear our clerical black suit and tie, worn on Sundays in the college. Since leaving home the previous August I had seen my parents just once, when they came to the Christmas concert. My distance from them already was highlighted as they proudly watched me perform in the Irish-language play, without being able to understand a word of what I said. (My father's joking pretence to speak Irish featured common nonsense phrases like 'tá sé mahogany gas-pipes'.) During the seven years I spent with the Brothers I continued to live in a bilingual world, which was to become important to my sense of identity and to my academic work, as described later.

On my summer visit home such distances shrank temporarily and I was able to resume my familiar life in the family and with friends – but only to a point. I had moved away, was changed, was marked for special things. In this photograph, out for a walk with my best friend Michael (Figure 27), who had loyally continued to write to me despite knowing that I was not allowed to write back, all that distinguishes me is the darker (clerical) colour of my jacket, but that represented for us both the radically different path I was now on and to which I would shortly return. I don't recall any memory of feeling special or privileged, but I was embarrassed by praise from relatives and neighbours and in a visit to the nuns who had taught me, and I must have been made to feel such; it may not have been healthy for a fifteen-year-old.

Overall, I don't remember this interlude or the return to my new life as unsettling, much less upsetting; there seems to have been no reassessment, no second thoughts, and no suggestion from my parents or anyone else that it might be good to reflect on my decision. The return to my religious family was made easier by the anticipation of renewing friendships and going on to a new, modern college, as it had been described to us. Carriglea Park, near Dún Laoghaire, renamed Coláiste Iognáid Rís (Edmund Rice College), was indeed impressive. With its large refectory, its gleaming modern kitchen (I remember the wonder of its industrial-sized dishwashers), its terrazzo-floored corridors, well-appointed classrooms and airy dormitories, it was a far cry from the old-fashioned make-do of Bray. We were encouraged to be proud of our new college and its proof of the remarkable growth in vocations to the congregation.

What was not explained to us (and what I missed in my account of my life in the Brothers in *Rebellions*) was that only four years earlier Carriglea had closed as an 'industrial school', one of a number of the notoriously grim institutions run by the Brothers and set up originally to care for 'neglected, orphaned and abandoned' children. Its expensive refurbishment had obliterated all traces of its recent past. If we had known that history when we arrived in 1958 it would probably have made little impression on us, as such institutions, though considered grim, had not then the notoriety they have now for cruelty and sexual abuse. However, I found it shocking to read the Ryan Report's findings on Carriglea industrial school, published since I wrote my earlier memoir. It cited inspectors' reports to the Department of Education over many years, documenting the poor repair of the buildings, the lack of trained staff, the poor diet, the lack of recreational activities or training for the boys – all justified by the Brothers in terms of the inadequacy of state support. Yet, it emerged that when the boys were transferred abruptly to other industrial schools, some far from their families, to make way for us, there was a large financial surplus – and that this money, which should have been used to improve the lives of the poor boys in their care, was used by the Brothers instead to refurbish the old buildings for the benefit of those relatively privileged boys who had sought to join the order. I am haunted by that thought and find the callous attitude behind it difficult to forgive. Today, the old industrial school building, our

'Coláiste Iognáid Rís', is part of the Dún Laoghaire Institute of Art, Design and Technology (IADT), and what had been our chapel was, when I visited some years ago, a recreation area, with a pool table and jukebox. IADT has a fine academic reputation but also one as a happy place for students, so the old building may finally have laid its ghosts to rest.

Unaware of the Coláiste's grim recent past, we resumed the familiar routine of prayer, games and study. Those of us in the senior school (doing the state Leaving Certificate) were kept separate from the juniors for much of the time. Friendships across the divide, we understood, were particularly discouraged, an extension of the earlier ban on 'special friendships'. We seniors were encouraged by the more liberal, adult tone of our head, Brother Purcell, known to all as Johnny, and by the excellence of many of our teachers. They needed to be excellent, because they had been set a very difficult task. Instead of taking the normal two years to do the Leaving Certificate, we were to do it in a year. Because the Brothers had their own teacher-training college, in Marino, Dublin, they could ignore the normal highly competitive standards for entry to primary teaching, only meeting the absolute requirement of a pass Leaving Certificate, with honours in Irish. The teaching we got was good, mainly in terms of the rote learning that was all that the Leaving Certificate examined then (and largely since). Our staff was selected, I imagine, on the basis of proven skill at teaching to the exam, reducing everything to lists and formulae that could easily be mastered. When I left the Brothers I was deeply uneducated, except in how to do state exams. Of course, the same might be said of those who went through a more conventional education, even in elite private schools. But we were being trained ultimately to be educators – indeed, education leaders – and the Brothers had a particular duty of care in relation to us which they interpreted very narrowly, even cynically, in terms of our emotional as well as educational development.

The magician who got us all through honours Irish was the exuberant, often engagingly incoherent Brother Horgan, commonly known as 'Jeff'. In my memory he also taught us geography and botany, that is, nearly half the Leaving Certificate programme. I have quoted one of his regular staccato sayings to generations of my history undergraduates in the hope that they might learn the humility proper to research and teaching: 'The more you know – you know you know – the less.' We were not aware that it was a version of an aphorism attributed by Aristotle to Socrates and a favourite saying of Montaigne's, but I think Jeff probably was. We treasured his eccentricities and got through our texts. In Irish these included some serious challenges, especially the Middle Irish prose text *Tóraíocht an Ghiolla Dheacair*, with its alliterations, its accumulations of adjectives and adverbs, its convoluted plot and magic. More accessible, but also technical and taxing, were the medieval *Fiannaíocht* poems, some of which regularly rise to the surface of my memory to this day. Recently, listening to a blackbird in the garden, this came to mind unbidden.

> Binn sin, a loin Doire an chairn/Ní chuala mé in ard san bhith/
> Ceol ba bhine ná do cheol/Is tú fá bhun do nid.
> (Beautiful your voice, blackbird of Derrycairn. I had not heard
> anywhere a song finer than yours, as you tend your nest)

An additional pressure came from the radical change, forced on students countrywide at the start of that year, from the traditional Gaelic script, grammar and spelling we had used up to then to the new 'caighdeán' or standard Irish, with its simplified grammar and spelling, and the use of English (or, more properly Roman) characters. This was now mandatory in all the subjects we did – while still using traditional textbooks. It appeared to us a fiendish form of torture.

In retrospect, making us do the Leaving Certificate in one year was an appallingly inhumane and anti-educational policy. It subjected us to extreme pressure and severely limited our education (we did what was perceived as the easier botany course instead of chemistry and physics, for example); it accelerated our development, pushing us into third-level training at sixteen, and thus compounded the basic problems associated with treating adolescents as adults and failing to address their emotional and developmental needs.

I was shocked – not least at my enduring naïveté – when Mr Justice Ryan speculated, in part answer to my evidence to the tribunal he chaired, that there was an economic calculation behind the one-year Leaving Certificate; it was considerably cheaper. Such a calculation was also involved, as was widely believed in the congregation, in the policy of sending their trainee teaching Brothers to teach full-time for several years in their schools after only one year of the two-year teacher-training course (done consecutively in all other teacher-training colleges). Only then did they return to do the second year. The main motivation here, Mr Justice Ryan suggested to me, was to ensure that Brothers qualified as teachers close to final vows, when they were less likely to leave and waste the investment made in them. Of course, the Brothers were not alone in foregrounding this economic perspective. The key government report ushering in the new modern planning of state education a few years after my Leaving Certificate was titled *Investment in Education* (1962), a very inadequate basis on which to develop national educational policy, and its foregrounding by the Brothers an appalling betrayal of their mission.

One consequence of our hectic schedule of study and games was that it allowed no time for the kind of wide reading for which I had developed a taste in my final years at home. I can recollect no fiction or poetry I read in Bray or Carriglea and realise now that this was not simply a matter of time constraints. Private reading and the broadening of horizons that go with it would have been a threat to the narrow religious conformity that dominated our education. If there was a school library in either place, I have no recollection of it. This failure to encourage individual development and the habit of critical inquiry was to make it all the more difficult for traditional religious orders such as the Christian Brothers to cope with the huge cultural challenges that were to face them.

Despite the academic pressure, I enjoyed my year in Carriglea, buoyed up once again by intense games of hurling, during one of which my nose was broken, though of course in our Spartan regime not treated. Many years later a specialist examining my throat was fascinated instead by my nose. 'Can you breathe through it?' he asked. When I replied in the affirmative, he shook his head, muttering, 'You shouldn't be able to.' After another high-testosterone game I lashed out and punched in the face a boy I felt had been bullying me – the only time in my life I lost my temper to that degree. Of course such incidents were ubiquitous in the boarding school stories I had read years earlier. I was living the life of an Irish Catholic Tom Brown.

But the academic pressure was intense, and we were also living on our nerves in terms of our overall development despite the camaraderie and normal good humour. What we were not doing was growing up emotionally, dealing with adolescence, other than by sublimating our little-understood feelings in ceaseless activity. It was an intensely masculine, indeed masculinist world, its values those of the soldier, even its religious training emphasising strength, discipline and endurance. Frowned on were softness, emotion or sensitivity. More than ever, but now in this military mode, I was a 'Good Boy', a happy conformist, and feeling no strain in that so far as I can recall. Aware now, after many years of teaching and parenting, of the complex nature of male adolescence, and reflecting on my own passionate nature, it seems to me likely that I felt in fact a deeply buried unhappiness or anger, now beyond recall, during those years of quite draconian 'formation'. But I had no language for it then and no means of expressing it.

Instead, I remember life in Carriglea mainly in positive terms, a time of friendship, intense physical exercise and academic challenge. A major contributor to that positivity was the superior, who, in his own eccentric way, treated us as the young adults we had, perforce, become. His weekly talks, with their anecdotes and often strange advice, were much enjoyed. Standing, or rather rocking, in the middle of the room, a small portly man with jet-black hair the fringe of which he constantly smoothed with a moistened finger, he chatted rather than lay down the law. His way to cure the flu, he told us, was to walk to Howth and back, and his solution to a lack of clean socks was to rotate the ones you had on different feet. Every week there were further gems of homespun advice, including, I dimly remember, some oblique comments on sexuality. I was a victim of his humour at the end-of-year prize-giving. When I was called forward for my only award – winning the billiards competition – he announced that the prize would go instead to the runner-up as I had been seen by him several times practising with the handle of the brush with which I was supposed to be cleaning the hall (the cues being locked away). It was, I had to admit, a fair cop.

After the Leaving Certificate exams we were allowed home for another short summer holiday, which, once again, I remember only as a pleasant interlude with family and friends, marked again by no reassessment and left with no remembered regret. But I was now sixteen, facing into a year of even greater seclusion and intense spiritual training, while more aware of girls and sexuality from listening to the talk of my friends. Yet I appear to have proceeded smoothly down my chosen path, untroubled by doubt. It's as if, having made the commitment at fourteen, I was incapable of questioning it. In all of this there was a passivity that now appears uncharacteristic and troubling, the result of the two years of conditioning that I had experienced, much of it subtle.

THE NOVICE

There was now a new excitement as well as a daunting prospect to look forward to – leaving the secular world (even further) behind and spending a year as a 'novice', a religious undergoing a year of spiritual training after first 'taking the habit', that is, the induction ceremony during which you put on the garb of the Brothers – long black soutane, with a broad cincture around the waist, and a clerical half-collar. While it is possible to see my two years as a postulant (a candidate proposing to enter religious life) in terms of boarding-school stories, it is extremely difficult to explain to a modern reader the radical nature of the shift to trainee religious, living in what was in many ways a medieval world. So I realised some years ago when visiting St Helen's in Booterstown in south County Dublin with my teenage sons. Previously my novitiate, it is now a luxury hotel.

Built in the mid-eighteenth century and remodelled in its present form at the end of the nineteenth, the house had been home to a succession of Anglo-Irish families, most notably Viscount Gough, commander-in-chief of the British Army in India. What had been a romantic chapel in my time, and was originally a ballroom, was now the hotel's glitzy, opulent lounge bar, but the original marble pillars remained and helped me to locate the place I sought.

'There,' I told my eldest son, pointing to the floor beside one of the pillars, 'was where I prostrated myself, arms out wide, face down, having put on the long black robe, or "habit". I was now a "novice", being inducted into the Congregation of Irish Christian Brothers, my new family, even taking a new name, Brother Bosco. I was your age, sixteen.'

'What do you mean,' he replied, 'you prostrated yourself? How medieval is that! How did you come to do such a thing? And did you not realise that your new "family" included paedophiles and perverts?'

I was struck afresh by the immense cultural gap that separated my childhood from that of my sons, who have no religion or sense of nationalism, are more fluent in German than in Irish, citizens of the world wide web and thinking of Berlin as a preferred future home. At sixteen I had been an intensely devout Catholic, a fervent traditional nationalist, immersed in the Irish language and a Gaelic games fanatic. How could my sons even begin to understand my teenage self, in his new religious 'habit', face down before a Catholic altar and his religious superiors, when I myself struggle to identify with Brother Bosco, searching for fleeting fragments of memory across a chasm of sixty years and now immersed in an utterly transformed culture. Indeed, I am in many respects much closer now to the worldview of my sons than to that of my earlier self, much as they might demur, amused at any notion of our common modernity.

'So, what did you do during your year here?' asked my younger son, now near the age I had been when I first left home on my big adventure.

'Well, it will indeed seem medieval to you two, a year of prayer, religious studies, long silences and absolute obedience, cut off not only from family but from the world outside. We were teenagers but not treated as such. The emotional and hormonal stresses of teenage years were not acknowledged, and we dealt with them by ignoring them and by directing our energies into relentless physical activity – long walks, sea swims, Gaelic games and what was referred to as "manual labour".'

'Sounds a bit like the army; you must have been miserable,' my younger son said. 'Can we have a Coke?'

As the pair wandered off, it struck me forcibly, almost jarringly, that in fact I had been largely happy in my medieval year, buoyed up by religion and by friends, often more amused than affronted by the traditionalism of our eccentric novice master, who unfortunately made much of me because of my relationship to 'the founder', to whom he was devoted.

As I looked out the hotel window at the unchanged terraces at the back (their flower beds even planted as they had been then, with scarlet salvias fringed by white alyssum), random memories flooded in: early-morning meditation in the study hall, at which I was regularly the chosen reader, standing at the top of the hall, sleepily coping with passages from the writings of Alonso Rodriguez, a sixteenth-century Jesuit mystic and trainer of novices; singing magnificent six-part Palestrina hymns as part of the choir at the Christmas crib, imaginatively placed in the atmospheric underground passageway that led to the chapel, housing originally (and probably now again) the wine cellars. Across the passageway was the dark room where the habits and coats of deceased members of the order were stored after cleaning and then distributed (by me for a time) to us novices as work-a-day outfits to spare our own tailored versions. I remembered the back-breaking work of moving a pile of large stones from one part of the garden to another, as ordered by the novice master, who then ordered them all moved back, without explanation; there were, again, the intensely combative hurling games played in all weathers; the recreation periods during which occasionally a trunk full of 'secular' books (all by Catholic or Cold War authors), kept under the billiard table, was opened.

In the same room, once a week we had elocution and voice lessons from a flamboyantly dressed young actor, Barry Cassin, one of only two outsiders we saw regularly, the other being the equally flamboyant chaplain (Jesuit, of course), who roared up every morning on an ancient motorbike. I remembered pleasurable hours in the gardens and glasshouses selecting blooms for the altar, another regular job. Above all I remembered friends, some of whom slipped away silently as the year went on (their absence never adverted to) to resume a more normal life. However, most managed to find

Figure 28. Credit: Author

coping strategies to survive the experience, and one of them, Leo Wright, still in the congregation, has stayed a lifelong friend.

'But didn't your parents mind you leaving home so young and seeing you so cut off from your family?' asked one of my boys.

'I'm sure they minded a lot', I said, 'though they didn't let me see that. They were very religious, and accepted the sacrifice involved for them in my joining the order. They would have preferred that I was older, but they made no effort to persuade me, much less forbid me. It must be hard for you to understand that. You can imagine how your mother and I would have reacted if either of you had proposed leaving home to join a religious outfit at fourteen!'

My sons exchanged amused glances at such a far-fetched idea. 'Yeah, right,' said the youngest. 'Is that why we were brought up without religion, in case we would use it to escape the family early?'

How bizarre it all seemed now viewed through their eyes, but aspects of that year, good and bad, were to have a major impact on my future life, and some remain with me.

Leo recently sent me this photograph of our novitiate group, forty-six in all, taken after we received the habit (Figure 28), together with a list of our names in alphabetical order. I find it poignant now to look at the eager, well-remembered young faces, each emerging in sharp relief against the black background of our new soutanes. This photograph could be read as an image of Catholic Ireland at the height of its power and influence when large numbers joined religious orders, the Irish Christian Brothers being among the most successful recruiters. But for me it is a picture, above all, of youthful idealism and a reminder of shared experience, its intensity borne out by the fact that I could match the name to a face in most cases despite a gap of sixty-four years. We were about to live together through a very challenging year, a spiritual boot-camp for sixteen-year-olds, and I remember no unpleasantness, only comradeship. The vast majority would leave, most within a decade, having been recruited far too young to make adult commitments or to benefit properly from the experience. But our idealism was real, and our youthful attempts to live up to it seem serious and impressive to me in retrospect. As discussed above, the Brothers clearly had a concern that boys might join the congregation simply in order to get a teaching qualification, but I remember no hint of that in the speech or behaviour of my fellow novices. Our idealism had a strong religious basis, of course, but it had also an element of the romantic youth culture soon to sweep through western democracies, determined to change the world with protest and music. Four years later when a student in University College Dublin embracing many of the values of that culture, I don't think I was embracing something radically different, and I retained a sense of continuity in relation to many of the causes I espoused then in my later working life. I remained a romantic throughout.

My noble-seeming pose, as I stand at the far left of the back row, doubtless reflects my response to the solemnity of the occasion but also perhaps that romantic sense of vocation. In a 'snap' taken the same day with Danny Brennan, a fellow novice from my hometown, I look more relaxed, my childish face at odds with my adult religious garb and carrying no mark yet of the radical changes in my life experience since I left home. Such an individual photograph was possible because it was taken by Danny's brother, already a member of the order (Figure 29). There are, of course, no photographs of me on that day with my parents – no parents were invited. With my new name, and wearing its uniform, I now belonged, more emphatically than ever, to my new religious family. How did they look after me?

Figure 29. Credit: Author

Looking at those images of my sixteen-year-old self, full of idealism and certainty, I wonder if I would like the new Brother Bosco if I could meet him now, or would he seem rather narrow, unthinking, naïve, even pompous – however charming? He would certainly be appalled and uncomprehending at my secularism and pervasive scepticism. But of course I do also recognise me in him and him in me, both romantic idealists and 'Good Boys' in spite of my later scepticism and my efforts to be less anxious to please. Wordsworth's famous paradox comes to mind: 'The Child is father of the Man'. The simple experience he uses to illustrate this, and to demonstrate how such a sense of wonder enriches our lives, resonates all the more now as I too 'grow old'.

My heart leaps up when I behold
A rainbow in the sky;
So was it when my life began;
So is it now I am a man;
So be it when I shall grow old,
Or let me die!

What most made my heart leap up on the day I became a novice was my sense of vocation. Unlike the sight of a rainbow, it did not continue to retain its sense of magic. A crucial question to ask in remembering my year as a novice has to be: Why was that so?

Many of my recollections of the novitiate are indeed romantic; some are amusing. But, as was emphasised endlessly to us, a major objective of the year was to *test* our vocations. Surely there must have been a darker side to how I experienced this intense spiritual trial while also coping with growing up, still only sixteen/seventeen years old? Did I have no doubts, no 'dark night of the soul', that thrillingly romantic image from the poetry of St John of the Cross which featured sometimes in talks and meditations? Did I not rebel against the very strict discipline? Were there no sexual awakenings? Unsurprisingly perhaps, given my already well-established pattern, I have no recollection of any of that. The relentless routine that was designed to keep us busy and exhaust us physically, burying adolescent urges and confusions, seems even here to have been enough to fill my days, largely pleasantly; any sense of rebellion, even irritation, at some of the more extreme demands made were absorbed, it seems, in communal ways of coping.

The nearest thing to rebellion I can remember was my private refusal (though, I learned later, shared by many others) to use the 'discipline', or small whip of knotted leather thongs, distributed by our novice master at the start of Lent with the injunction to use it on our bare backs in our sleeping cubicles as a form of chastisement of the sinful body, as had been done by early saints and martyrs. But while many of us noisily beat our

Figure 30. Credit: Author

pillows instead, this was less in rebellion against the thinking behind the medieval practice than an extension of the general belief that our novice master was somewhat mad, as well as eccentric. With his shock of white hair, vague manner and tendency to mix things up, he seemed a combination of saint and one of the Marx brothers. One morning, for example, he told us solemnly to have our football boots ready in our laundry bags and our clothes for washing ready for inspection. It is not surprising therefore that we were, as I remember it, more amused or embarrassed than aghast at his insistence that we wear our swimming trunks when having a bath! It was only in retrospect that the pervasive fear of the body and the emphasis on its subjugation in that culture appeared to me to be so damaging. I feel sure that I was not alone in sometimes coping badly with sexual and emotional relationships in the years after I left the Brothers. A more quantifiable problem with my novitiate, however, was that my vocation was not challenged spiritually or intellectually – only superficially, and eccentrically – and that emotional needs, crucial to personal development, were either ignored or repressed.

Figure 31. Credit: Author

My family were allowed to visit me some weeks after I became a novice. I was helping with the harvest on the farm attached to the monastery, delighted, as I remember, to have a turn standing up top of the noisy, vibrating steam threshing machine, feeding the loosened sheaves of corn into the hopper, filthy from the straw and chaff, deafened by the noise. I was suddenly summoned to the visitors' parlour where, after a quick wash and change, I found my parents and siblings, last seen a few months earlier and a world away. My brothers and sisters were in high spirits after a visit to the zoo and full of a scary encounter with an elephant. No photograph of that survives, only one with a calm giraffe, but there are several pictures of their visit to see me. They must have looked with curiosity on a creature almost equally exotic, their older brother, in his new long black cassock and clerical collar, looming over them in one picture rather like the giraffe (Figure 30). I, in turn, must have felt that my distance from them had now been formalised and completed. Was I sad about that? Or did I even have such thoughts? Only recently my sister Mary sent me another, un-remembered photograph from that visit, of me standing rather bashfully between my parents, who look solemn, as befitted the occasion (Figure 31). It is the only photograph I have of just me and the two of them since I was an infant – the two pictures, it now strikes me, marking birth and a form of rebirth. No doubt they were proud of me, but they may also have felt a little bewildered, even sad, to meet me suddenly transformed into an adult, of a solemn, semi-sacerdotal kind. I find that I cannot imagine what my own feelings may have been, my new name and garb accentuating further my distance from them. By now well-schooled in downplaying feelings about family, I doubtless focused on acting out my new role, with my modest smile and shiny shoes.

The novitiate operated, in part, as a school, and once again we had some excellent teachers, particularly in music and scriptural studies. We did a detailed reading of the Gospel of St Matthew, using a modern, annotated text, with footnotes that used research from history, archaeology and Biblical scholarships to interrogate the Gospel and its traditional interpretations. It was an exhilarating, somewhat shocking challenge to orthodox opinion, the only one that I remember in those years. It was also my first exposure to a 'revisionist' approach to evidence that was to feature so strongly in my later academic work.

I don't recall who taught us that untypically radical scriptural studies class, but our education in church music, for which I will be forever grateful, was with Plunkett Nolan and ranged from the complex Renaissance polyphony of Palestrina to the traditional simplicity of Gregorian plainchant, already familiar from childhood. Sometimes nowadays I listen to a CD of Benedictine monks singing Gregorian chant and am deeply moved by it, though conscious of the male power and tradition, as well as the beauty and spirituality, it represents. My early training in church music has, doubtless, contributed to the marked change in my musical tastes as I get older, from the large-scale architecture and booming soundscapes of symphonies and operas, through chamber music, to single instruments, especially the cello suites, violin sonatas and piano works of J.S. Bach. Like early church music, in their simplicity and spaciousness – the room for silence between notes – they too are deeply spiritual and thought-provoking, as of course are Bach's choral works. It is also no accident that the music I listen to most is from the eighteenth century, where much of my research and teaching has also been centred.

I next met Plunkett Nolan nearly fifty years later when this gentle, sophisticated man, remarkably unchanged in appearance, was an observer on behalf of the Brothers when I gave evidence at the Ryan Commission hearings. (Indeed, he had that role throughout the many sessions on the Christian Brothers, a difficult, upsetting task.) I had coffee with him and the other Brothers present after the session. They were pleased, I think, at the largely positive view I had given of my time in the order (less critical than the view I was to develop later), a relief after the many gruelling days listening to details of abuse of the boys in their care and how badly the order handled it. He was very friendly, and tried, without much success, to remember me when I was a novice.

'I can only picture you,' he said finally, 'soloing up the wing during a hurling match against the Northern Province.'

'What a nice way to be remembered,' I said, after admitting that I had forgotten the event. 'I wasn't very good at it, but I so loved playing.'

It was a cheering reminder that even as a devout novice, Brother Bosco was still also a sports-loving teenager. Recently, I had a powerful confirmation of that when trying to remember better the retreat walk described below. I had a sudden, vivid memory of my old-fashioned football boots stepping off that rough path and up the short incline to the sports field. I am in my sports outfit and clutching a piece of paper. It is, I realise, the team selection for the game Plunkett remembered and I am delighted because I have been picked – far from a foregone conclusion. The strong, unbidden sense of myself as a happy sixteen-year-old in this strange and stressful environment, an example of what Proust called 'involuntary memory', was greatly consoling. And so, having been first given the gift of Plunkett's memory, I had its picture of me endorsed, and made more real years later.

A remarkable feature of the religious culture of the Christian Brothers, as I experienced it, was the commitment to combining the 'active' life – teaching in the wider community – with aspects of the 'contemplative' life, as laid down in the Rule of St Benedict. The daily office recited by priests, though by us in the shorter form known as the 'Little Office of the Virgin Mary', was a key aspect of the latter. As novices we chanted it daily in the chapel; out in teaching communities it was more usually simply recited. Later I was to learn that there was a tension between the 'active' and 'contemplative' aspects of the vocation of the Brothers. The latter tended to be regarded as a simple, satisfying commitment to personal devotion, and from that limited perspective it had been dealt with reasonably well in the novitiate. The 'active' life, however, involved engagement with the world outside which, paradoxically, we were taught to view as sinful and dangerous and in general the Brothers were obliged to have as little as possible to do with it. They lived in their monasteries as if members of an enclosed order in a hostile environment rather than of an active order involved also in the wider community, which they served. This extended even to keeping the lay teachers in their schools, beside whom they taught, at arm's length. They were seen as contaminated by the world, their vocation to teach compromised by marriage and children. This sense of alienation from ordinary life, this fear of contamination by it, was strongly emphasised in the novitiate as a core value of our vocation as religious.

At the end of the novitiate year we had a thirty-day 'retreat' of seclusion, silence, prayer and meditation to prepare for the taking of our first temporary vows (i.e. renewed each year until final vows) of poverty, chastity and obedience. I can see us still, bedraggled soldiers of Christ, in our patched workaday soutanes and heavy work boots pounding day after long day in silence the lovely path through the little wood in our extensive grounds, today covered by expensive houses. As well as working off our animal spirits, the idea was that we would meditate on the last talk as we walked, avoiding eye contact to minimise the temptation to speak – which, remarkably, in my memory no-one did.

This intense religious marathon was led by a very traditional Jesuit and famous retreat-giver, Fr Tom Counihan, following his understanding of the detailed plan laid down by the founder of his order, St Ignatius Loyola, in his *Spiritual Exercises*. These evolved over the decades from the 1520s when they were first devised as a guide for his small groups of early followers on how to best lead a Christian life. Only in recent decades has the order come to terms with the powerful current of mysticism in Loyola's writings, obscured from the outset in order to survive the probing of the Inquisition. I learned this recently in conversation with my friend Terry O'Reilly, an expert on Ignatius and on Spanish mysticism. He told me that *The Spiritual Exercises* are interpreted very differently nowadays from my experience of sixty years ago. Then, the dominant motif of the thirty-day retreat, as I remember it, was military. Though his training was, in fact, as a courtier, Ignatius was presented as a former soldier who had brought military discipline to the defence of the Catholic Church against Protestant heresies. That Jesuit tradition was reinforced in the aftermath of the French Revolution when the order was restored to papal favour and given the lead in the modern spiritual wars against secularism, atheism and socialism. Counihan, it seems, represented the end of that tradition. A small, intense, uncomfortable figure, he radiated a spiritual fanaticism. A priest of the Society of African Missions left this record of his disturbing experience of Counihan during a thirty-day Ignatian retreat many years earlier, urging the use of scourging with a 'discipline':

> Fr Counihan would take you to his room and teach you how to use it. He'd leave it under the pillow and tell you that you could come at any time and use it there. He would flog himself to show you how to do it. I flogged myself once, and I said, 'never again'!

Our novice master, for all his otherworldliness, would never have countenanced such inappropriate behaviour – even by a famous Jesuit.

In the 1970s a new generation of Jesuit retreat-givers and writers on Ignatius, notably Fr Joe Veale (previously well known as a charismatic teacher of English in Gonzaga College), developed a very different approach, based on a return to the original vision and spirituality of *The Spiritual Exercises*. Although I became aware of it only recently, Joe Veale's role in Ignatian studies has particular meaning for me, because of comments he made on my essay 'Seven Years in the Christian Brothers', published in *The Dublin Review* some months before he died, as work in progress from my then forthcoming memoir *Rebellions*. These were passed on to me through a mutual friend and stayed with me. They were a major influence on my decision to revisit my experience of religious life, as will appear below.

The new Jesuit view of the Ignatian legacy also implies a different model of the vow of obedience, one closer to the Benedictine ideal of a shared listening to God and obedience to the community, not simply to the abbot. That would certainly have been more attractive for me than the old-style military model, which was what was proposed on our thirty-day retreat and implemented in practice in community life, particularly when differences of opinion arose. We were to be soldiers of Christ, and that meant absolute, unquestioning obedience to superiors. This was the core meaning of the vow of obedience that we took from the retreat.

Reading through *The Spiritual Exercises* now I get a very different impression than that articulated by Counihan. Ignatius wrote a structured, quasi-mystical guide to spiritual growth through developing a relationship with God and an understanding of oneself. The tone is measured and encouraging, not hectoring. The gradual intensification of focus on Christ as exemplar, however, does point to the aspect of my experience of those absorbing thirty days that has stayed most vividly with me. The focus on the Passion of Christ in the third week of *The Spiritual Exercises* had a heightened emotional tone; it was a time, as Ignatius wrote, 'to draw upon all my powers to grieve, to feel sorrow and to weep'. Our retreat-giver was at his most animated and theatrical in several graphic sessions of exhortation to imagine the sufferings of Christ, described in lovingly rehearsed detail, '*as if it were happening to yourself – now*' – the scourging, the crowning with thorns, the nailing to the cross. This I recall as deeply upsetting, not in the reflective sense intended by Ignatius but rather in seeming a quasi-pornographic exercise, like many of the lurid depictions of suffering and death in medieval religious art – or indeed the report of Counihan's private tutorials in using the 'discipline'. While the primary focus was on the body of Christ as Redeemer, it could be read, on a different level, as another negative view of the male body, whose torture here, however, was portrayed as the key to our salvation.

Our spiritual training included regular 'examinations of conscience' to discover the inescapable 'sins' we had committed. In the novitiate this sometimes took the form of prostration on the floor, one at a time, in front of the novice master high on his dais and our fellow novices in their desks behind us as we openly confessed such 'faults' as we could think up as acceptable for the occasion – a listing as banal and meaningless as those I had used since first Confession, aged seven: disobedience, sinful thoughts, neglect of duty. It seemed even then a ritual more comic than meaningful. On the other hand, there was discouragement of what might have been valuable in learning to deal with the complexity of emotions involved in being teenage males – self-understanding and self-validation rather than self-accusation and self-abasement.

While the fact was never addressed, that I remember, our training and worldview were certainly intensely male. Reinforcing this was the fact that we didn't see a single female all year, except on walks, during which, the instruction was, we were to emulate the anchorites in the desert and 'avert your eyes'. Indeed, the culture would be considered 'macho' today on many levels while also, paradoxically, including a traditional negative view of the male body as a source of sin and an enemy to be overcome, a traditional feature of European monasticism and especially of the Celtic variety with its extreme versions of mortifying the flesh.

As part of my early-morning reading duties as a novice I may well have read the following characteristic passage out loud to my sleepy, teenage companions at the start of a daily meditation. It comes from our guiding text for that year, *Practice of Perfection and Christian Virtues* by Alphonsus Rodriguez, SJ, first published in 1609 and, remarkably given its glaring inadequacies, used as a training manual for novices in many religious orders until relatively recently.

> To animate us more to this exercise [of mortification] it will be of great help always to act on the principle that we laid down at the beginning, that this outward man, our flesh and sensuality, is the greatest adversary and enemy that we have, and as such is always at work making mischief for us, lusting against the spirit, against reason and against God ... St Bernard affords us good consideration, saying that we must deal with ourselves and with our body as with a sick man entrusted to our care, who asks for and desires much that would do us harm, and must be refused accordingly.

This was not simply a counsel of perfection; it informed the novice master's instruction that we literally scourge our bodies and his decree that we counter the danger of masturbation by wearing swimming trunks in the bath (not that this explanation was provided). It even informed the huge emphasis on physical exercise, which was as much about the exhaustion of the body to discourage its 'lusting' as it was about health and fitness. Continued unexplained warnings against 'special friendships', combined with regular citation – also unexplained – of the order that the risen Christ gave to Mary Magdalene, '*noli me tangere*' (touch me not), added to the pervasive sense of the body and indeed of human relationships as dangerous and problematic. The Australian author of the 1998 internal report on the culture of the order, referred to earlier, commented that such injunctions contained 'the basic ingredients of homophobic isolationism'. The fact that such negative views of sexuality were hinted at rather than explained had to be confusing as well as troubling for the ignorant adolescents that we were, already carrying the burden of similar evasiveness and negativity from our home and school formation.

Not surprisingly then, the vow least commented on, in my memory of the intense instruction leading up to the taking of our first vows at the end of the novitiate, was chastity. Also unsurprising is the fact that everything I remember suggests that it was presented in negative rather than positive terms, as mortification of the flesh rather than as a sacrifice designed to remove a major obstacle to our service to God. I remember no acknowledgement of the now obvious fact that such a vow would present major challenges and need strategies of understanding and coping. We were to rely instead on the male toughness and ability to endure hardship, valorised often as core strengths of the Christian Brother.

I am not qualified to make meaningful connections between that male culture – with its negative view of the body, its discouragement of emotion and of tenderness, its unexamined vow of chastity – and the sexual abuse by a small minority of Brothers of vulnerable children under their care, but I have no doubt that there were such connections and that they were important. One, again oblique, application of this perverted sexuality can be found in a circular letter on the vow of chastity by the superior general of the congregation in the 1920s. It connected 'softness', or 'heedlessness or effeminacy' in (male) teachers with the encouragement of 'the child's ... natural charms', which could be to the ruin of both. One inference was that the (feminised) child was as much instigator as victim of sexual abuse, a common clerical view that long survived in the Catholic Church and doubtless still does in some quarters. Another was that Brothers who were 'soft' or 'effeminate' were most likely to be tempted. Thus, the vow of chastity was primarily about offering an endorsement of male strength; little wonder if maimed male self-esteem and male aggression followed. Thus, as well as the potential danger it posed to children, there was also a big emotional price to be paid by all male religious for this approach to sexuality, made worse by denial and evasion and its lack of compassion and understanding.

In the recent debates surrounding the scourge of clerical abuse of children in Ireland this negative spirituality has been often ascribed to an Irish form of Jansenism, the seventeenth-century, largely French, heresy marked by a pessimistic view of human nature and a moral rigour, based in part on a negative view of the body. Certainly, Jansenism had some impact on Irish Catholicism well into the twentieth century, most apparent in its view of the unworthiness of all, even the sinless, to receive Communion. My father, for example, deeply believed this, only taking Communion once a year and then because the church insisted on it, whereas my mother went to mass far less frequently but took Communion every time. However, Jansenism, although it certainly regarded the body as potentially evil and a source of shame and guilt, is an inadequate explanation for the sexual repression that so marked Irish Catholicism. Indeed, it is debatable whether Jansenism was ever a major influence in Ireland, and it may be more convincing historically to see sexual repression as a product of the mid-Victorian moralism that Cardinal Cullen harnessed in his reformation of the post-Famine Catholic Church. Its sexual mores suited many Famine survivors, enforcing celibacy on younger siblings, for example, to help consolidate landholdings and succession to the family farm, as the historian Joe Lee pointed out many years ago.

The Congregation of Irish Christian Brothers, as I experienced it, thus echoed a complex European tradition in its religious life, but it also often echoed the mores of rural Ireland, which supplied the great majority of its members. Despite its many fine qualities, Irish rural culture, much lauded by my mother, could also feature a harshness, narrowness and philistinism that ill equipped many of the priests and religious it produced to deal with the modern world or to develop a more generous understanding of their vocation. The survival dynamic in Irish rural life may also help to explain the strongly 'macho' culture of many Brothers – the emphasis on hardiness and suspicion of softness, the obsession with sports involving intense physical contact and, most tellingly, the justification of the brutal regime of physical punishment in the schools. This was defended by parents as well as Brothers as a crucial means in achieving their ambition of educating boys out of poverty or, more generally, improving their life chances. Even the gentlest, most thoughtful Brothers that I met tended to support and indeed practise routine corporal punishment.

Joe Veale's hope in writing to our mutual friend, that in any future version of my memoir I would try to place 'the macho culture of the Brothers in the wider context of an Irish masculine culture', cannot be met fully here, though it has been a major influence on this attempt to reflect more on my experiences in religious life. Recent research across a range of disciplines, but especially literary studies, has begun to explore 'Irish masculinities', and all I can do is make a small contribution by reflecting on my own experience. Nor can I deliver much better on his hope that I 'disclose the personal experience of celibacy'. I left religious life before it became a big problem for me, but I have little doubt that had I stayed I would have experienced what he described with searing anger in his old age (he died in 2002) as the results of 'spiritual assumptions that dehumanised'. These created 'a desert in the heart ... the longing for human contact ... the ache for a little tenderness and gentleness'. And while I remember no overt expressions of misogyny during my time with the Brothers, I feel Veale was right in his conclusion that 'the clerical world ... was aggressively masculine, philistine and assured of its superiority to women'. It simply didn't arise for a young Christian Brother then, because women were entirely absent from his world.

I remember even less emphasis on the vow of poverty in preparing for first vows, perhaps because it was the easiest of the vows to enforce. When it was invoked to justify confiscating my few books, records and photographs as I was leaving the order it seemed as bizarrely legalistic as it was hurtful; there was always some latitude allowed in relation to such personal items, partly in recognition, I imagine, of the fact that the Brothers did indeed live lives of poverty.

The only vow that needed clear, unambiguous exposition, it appeared, was obedience. It was taught as a simple and absolute imperative, the total surrender of the self to the will of God, manifest through the superior. It was presented in military terms as the core value of the religious life, with the religious as soldier of Christ. There was no room for collegiality, no tolerance of different points of view, no encouragement of personal exploration of the meaning of one's vocation. It was a view of obedience utterly out of tune with the emphasis on individual agency and independent thinking in the world outside the walls of the monastery, but out of tune also with important elements of the monastic tradition as practised in many orders. It was to prove decisive in my decision to leave four years later.

In general, looking back, our novitiate year seems to me, as his long experience of religious life seemed to Joe Veale, 'deeply shaped by a debased rhetoric of obedience and a skewed spirituality'. Certainly, our spirituality – the key focus of the novitiate – was skewed rather than deepened. While scriptural studies and religious music were well taught, the same could not be said of religion and the spiritual life. Rodriguez's text was so archaic in its ideas and language as to be useless in that regard, and I don't remember anything else that we studied in this area apart possibly from some passing references to modern Catholic thinkers like Teilhard de Chardin, Thomas Merton and Dom Eugene Boylan. Instead we got a parody of elements of classical monastic training – the meaningless tasks to test obedience, the fetish for manual work, the use of the discipline, the theatre of public confession. Personally, I don't think my spiritual life benefited very much from that regime and worldview, that I had a better, deeper sense of vocation at the end of the year. When I came to question my vocation, I had learned no way of doing so meaningfully.

While I also gained little insight into myself or my feelings, I did learn to share an unfortunate and flawed communal sense of confidence during those 'years of formation'. Unthinking obedience, the certainty of being right, and being members of a male elite with immense power in Irish education were crucial to the remarkable success of the Brothers up to this, its high point in Ireland – and to its catastrophic failures. For the individuals imbued with it, this unreflecting confidence, bordering on arrogance, proved not to be a good legacy in later life, whether inside or outside the order. Yet, initially, that confidence and my adherence to the vow of obedience were to help me to face an early and severe test within months of leaving St Helen's.

CHAPTER 5

Teaching

The move to Marino teacher training college was much anticipated – a pattern of those years, each offering something new and exciting. Liberated from the intense, enclosed religious life of the novitiate, we would commence preparing for the active aspect of our vocation – teaching. We had taken our vows, wore clerical dress all the time now and were members of the congregation rather than mere 'postulants'. Marino had the additional glamour of being the world headquarters of the congregation, and the fact that the superior general and his council were soon to move to a new headquarters in Rome only added to our sense of pride at being part of a large international organisation. Just as British schoolboys were conscious of the reach of their empire through maps featuring their possessions in red, we were familiar with the map of the Brothers' spiritual 'empire' across all five continents.

Unlike the modified aristocratic houses in which we had spent two of the previous three years, the imposing stone mass of St Mary's, Marino, with its fine chapel, had been built by the Brothers fifty years earlier, though on the site of such a house, owned by the sophisticated, patriotic Lord Charlemont in the late eighteenth century. With the purchase of the remains of his small estate the Brothers also acquired fine gardens with ornamental buildings, one of which, the jewel-like Casino, now regarded as one of the most important small eighteenth-century buildings in Europe, was in a dilapidated state, little appreciated in the narrow Catholic nationalist ethos of the time.

The change of pace and tone in our lives was striking. Though the phrase wasn't used then, we were now third-level students, attending lectures and soon to be involved in practical teacher training. The teaching staff that I remember were very good, especially Claude Hamill, whose intelligence and love of English literature made a big impression on me. After a month or so of lectures we went out to local schools for three weeks of supervised teaching practice. I was lucky in being assigned to the class taught by Jackie Brosnahan in nearby Donnycarney National School. Well known nationally as the ebullient head of the Irish National Teachers' Organisation, his classroom was an oasis of calm, with no resort to corporal punishment during my hours there, and he was immensely encouraging. But the most important lesson I learned from those weeks was that I loved teaching; which was just as well.

On the Friday evening, as I recall it, at the end of our teaching practice I was summoned (as was Leo Wright) to the office of the president of the college, an urbane Cork man, Finbarr Casey. No doubt we were perturbed and wondering what we had done wrong. But instead of censure we were given what was presented as a compliment: we were to leave our course next day and teach for a year in one of the Brothers' schools, while preparing for a university degree in science by doing Matriculation exams in physics and chemistry. The reason for this unusual move, it was explained to us, was that the state's Department of Education had told the order that it had too few qualified science teachers in its schools, being reliant instead on Brothers doing summer courses. The basis for selecting us was that we had come first and second of our group in Leaving Certificate (pass!) maths. Of course, neither of us questioned the decision: our brand-new vow of obedience passed its first serious test. There was no discussion, no query as to whether either of us had any interest in doing a science degree (we hadn't). We left in a state of shock to pack our trunks and to say goodbye to our friends, another abrupt loss in my life. Three days later we were facing our new classes, for which we were immediately to have full responsibility, Leo in Sexton Street in Limerick, I in Francis Street in Dublin.

In retrospect, of course, this was another poor decision by the congregation that took scant heed of our welfare or development and was in that sense a continuation of earlier decisions of the same kind – recruitment at fourteen and the one-year Leaving Certificate. A more obvious and collegial response to the Department of Education's strictures would have been to send some of its experienced but unqualified science teachers to university, but that might have created staff problems in the schools and be more expensive – or so I assume the thinking was. Instead, two raw, inexperienced recruits, neither yet eighteen years old, were sent into a very challenging environment, to sink or swim. And we were to feel privileged!

Our sense of shock was compounded three days later – Armistice Day, 11 November 1960 – when each of us was assigned a 6B, Primary Certificate class in our respective schools. At the time, with comparatively few going on to secondary education, the Primary Certificate (a state exam, colloquially known as 'the Primo' in Dublin) was then a key qualification, essential at the lower end of the job market where most of our new students were destined to start. Thus, the responsibility placed so unexpectedly on us was

Figure 32. Credit: Author

even greater and emphasised further our lack of qualifications. In recent years Leo and I have commemorated that abrupt Armistice Day start to our teaching careers, marking the fiftieth anniversary with lunch in a Cork hotel (Figure 32). This also celebrated a friendship, so important to me not least as a bridge back to my time in the Brothers, across the divide created by being cast into outer darkness when I left, causing me more distress than I understood for many years.

As well as being launched abruptly as teachers, we were being sent 'on the mission', as the Brothers called – significantly – being out teaching in the schools. The world outside 'the monastery' (as each community house was called) was thus re-imagined as a foreign, pagan place, though we had all come from it. As missionaries, our engagement with the threatening world around us was to be strictly limited. Like our bodies, our environment was seen in negative terms, not the best conditioning for those dedicated to teaching adolescent boys from that world.

It was a great help that my new home, the Synge Street monastery, was a large, supportive, relatively easy-going community and included several retired brothers as well as those teaching in the attached prestigious primary and secondary schools, or in the much less prestigious Francis Street primary school, a mile away in the Coombe, Dublin's oldest working-class district. The walk there was a daily treat, through the magical St Patrick's Close, past Marsh's Library, of which we knew nothing, then the great medieval cathedral, of which we knew that we were forbidden to enter as a centre of Protestant heresy. The folkloric reputation of its great eighteenth-century dean, Jonathan Swift, would have been more sympathetically viewed in our world, and his ghost might have smiled on our mission to teach the poor boys of the inner city.

The school had a new building, incongruously squeezed into the warren of streets off Patrick Street and abutting the high wall of St Nicholas of Myra church which loomed over its playground. Its catchment area was going through a period of transition, with families moving out to the new housing estates like Crumlin and Ballyfermot. Recently, watching a short film online of President Michael D. Higgins visiting the school in January 2018 to open its new library, I was delighted to learn that it is now a very successful and innovative 'DEIS' school (Delivering Equality of Opportunity in Schools), one of a number of such schools in deprived areas given extra resources. The main event of the president's visit was held in the two upstairs classrooms in which I had taught, the folding partition opened to make one big space.

While the school I joined sixty years ago was certainly grimmer and more one-dimensional than its current incarnation, I also remember it fondly for the humour of the boys, their enjoyment of games and their honest efforts at learning. On one of my first days a boy came up to the front of the class and asked if he could leave early as he had to go to 'dianere'. He enlightened me that this meant the Eye and Ear Hospital nearby, and he gave his name as Ricky Nelson (a well-known pop singer, though unknown, of course, to me), to the delight of the class – and to my amusement when I had it explained. They were full of chat in the yard during breaks, and in the playing field in Dolphin's Barn where I organised hurling leagues (a sport new to the school, I think). Some were desperately poor and disadvantaged; the better off had fathers who worked in Guinness and lived in apartments supplied by that paternalistic firm. The humour of the boys echoed that of their mothers, encountered often in passing their hall doors as I walked to school: 'Come here to me, Brother Dunne, you are much too soft on that young fellow of mine, a right waster'; 'Like his da,' her neighbour might chime in. All around there was a real sense of community, slowly disappearing and becoming lost in gentrification, some boys bussing in

Figure 33. Credit: Author

from the new council estates and getting their dinner from their grannies. The middle-class incomers, of course, were far more likely to send their sons to Synge Street school.

I was lucky in that my new colleagues were welcoming and helpful, apart from the principal, who I thought initially to be rather authoritarian and brusque. This judgement doubtless owed something to the fact that the decision to give me the most challenging class in the school appeared to be his, and I can only see it now as a cynical avoidance of the task of getting one of the experienced teachers to replace whoever it was that had left the staff after a few months of the school year. (I now wonder if the odd coincidence of Leo and myself being both assigned Primary Cert classes points to another bizarre decision from on high.) I knew almost nothing of the curriculum, or of responsibilities like keeping the class roll or producing weekly, monthly and yearly teaching schemes (these I must have inherited from one of the community, as I was not equipped to produce them). When I first went through the roll I found that one of the boys would be fifteen on my eighteenth birthday, five weeks later. I was reassured to discover that the boys were unaware of my extreme youth, when the one who shared my birthday told me confidently, walking back from a games session, that I was forty-five!

Someone not fooled, however, was the archbishop, John Charles McQuaid, when officiating at the opening of the new building. The staff lined up to be introduced, and when he got to me he stopped, his sharp eyes amused. 'Rather young, are we not?' he said, a remark that did little for my confidence. His judgement is borne out by a staff photograph (Figure 33), taken probably the same day, in which I look exactly as I did at the start of my novitiate, truly a young 'gearc' (Irish *gearrcach*, a fledgling) as the Brothers called a raw recruit. The three other teaching Brothers were experienced educators in their mid-twenties, and they gave me a lot of support, both practical and psychological.

As well as help from colleagues on the staff, I was closely monitored – for obvious reasons – by the well-known schools' inspector Tomás Ó Dónalláin, whose daughter Áine Hyland was to become a colleague in UCC. He appeared regularly without warning, and without preliminaries would request, '*An Rolla, led' thoil; cóipleabhair Ghaeilge, cóipleabhair Béarla, cóipleabhair Matamatica; scéim laethiúil, scéim míosúil, scéim bliantúil*' (The Roll, please; Irish, English and maths copies; the daily, monthly and yearly teaching plans). He would then sit at the back of the class with a '*lean ar aghaidh*' (proceed), and start looking over the material, while listening. Sometimes he stayed all day. He was not unpleasant, just remote, and if he ever gave me advice, I don't remember it. But in general he seemed to approve, and I survived.

Despite the disadvantages I suffered from being immature, untrained and inexperienced, I did manage to carry off the daunting task given me; all the boys, or so I recall, passed the 'Primo'. Clearly the confidence that I had acquired over the years was a big help, beginning with being the eldest son in a family both of whose parents had succeeded in difficult circumstances in their early working lives, later in my sense of privilege as a member of a great religious teaching order. Facing a class not much younger than me, as a Brother in religious garb, I was immediately in a position of power, even when I declined to join in the school's general ethos of corporal punishment.

Entering the school building initially, I was brought to the principal's office and handed a standard-issue 'leather', familiar from the school beatings in my primary school which had so traumatised me. I had also developed ideological grounds against its use, having, rather controversially, chosen in novitiate the religious name Bosco, after the founder of the Salesians, who had condemned corporal punishment in teaching children – substituting instead 'reason, religion, kindness'. The leather's weight and rigidity when held in the hand was a surprise and added to my sense of revulsion. With it came the injunction: 'It's either you or them and they understand nothing else.' Insecure initially as I was and daunted by the task given me, I did try using it briefly only to find that I was also temperamentally unsuited to hitting the boys, finding it personally upsetting and humiliating as well as cruel. In this, as I was to learn many years later, I shared that squeamishness of Montaigne's, who attributed his hatred of cruelty to both 'judgement and nature' and above all to his 'softness' which caused him distress at even the routine killing of chickens for the table and 'the scream of the hare in the teeth of my dogs'. I also realised that its use was so much the norm throughout the boys' lives as to be ineffectual. I learned that there were alternative ways of imposing discipline, principally by keeping the class busy and also by use of the voice, changing its pitch and tone and volume as taught by the colourful actor Barry Cassin in novitiate and which remained a great resource. Teaching, of course, is a branch of acting – or is it the other way around?

I know that other Brothers also refused to use 'the leather', and for similar reasons, and it would be wrong to see its use as uniquely a mark of the order. Indeed, as the Ryan Report detailed with its usual forensic rigour, the Christian Brothers issued a series of regulations in its general Chapters from 1900 to the 1960s strongly condemning the use of corporal punishment except in exceptional circumstances and urging protocols 'of moderation and decorum' that would minimise its harm. Indeed, there were exhortations for the congregation to take the lead in the growing campaign worldwide to abolish it altogether in schools. All of which, as Mr Justice Ryan comments, makes it difficult to understand why the Brothers consistently protected those members who were shown to be guilty of extreme physical abuse. And clearly there was no sustained attempt to ensure that the Brothers' regulations were obeyed, despite admissions that abuse was widespread. Remarkably, I have no recollection of the subject ever being mentioned in my years in the 'houses of formation'. In Ireland, at least, it appears that it was seen as an ineradicable feature of the society generally. In Francis Street, as in other schools, it was probably used as much by lay teachers as by religious, and it was strongly supported by most parents. In all three of the schools in which I taught as a Brother some parents berated me for not beating their sons, believing it was necessary if they were going to succeed.

My trouble in getting on with the principal had nothing to do with corporal punishment, so far as I can recall, but it was brought into focus by his tendency to barge into my classroom unannounced and speak to me about some issue in front of the boys. Perhaps this was his response to my extreme youth and inexperience. After enduring it a few times I confronted him, asked him to come outside the door and told him that I found his conduct undermining. To his credit, he apologised and never acted like that again. It was the first time in my life that I confronted authority and stopped, briefly, being a 'Good Boy'.

I also gained added confidence from finding that I could adjust to life in a large, diverse community. I remember my time in Synge Street with gratitude as a pleasant, indeed happy time. The superior was a very quiet and gentle soul who looked out for me in his vague-seeming way. As the youngest I was much teased and probably indulged. It was my task to ring the large monastery bell in the morning at 6.15, then walk up and down the corridors with a hand-bell. On the first morning I found the tongue of each of the bells had been removed (a custom inflicted on all new holders of the post), forcing me to knock on thirty or so doors, to the amusement of all. The young 'monks' had their own corridor and were a supportive mini-community. Sometimes we played soccer on a flat roof, until the superior had an understandable complaint from a neighbour one Good Friday that this was inappropriate. Normally the roof was used for the pacing up and down that formed an element of morning meditation, and I was reminded of it as the Coronavirus pandemic forced me to restrict my daily walk to pacing the terrace outside my window.

The large common room, with its range of ages and temperaments, was also a welcoming place where I learned a little more about classical music from an enthusiast who advised me on what records to buy when I got an occasional present of money. I was coached in physics and chemistry by an amiable, long-retired brother named Ryall, if I remember rightly. He used very old textbooks, which had engraved drawings as illustrations but which did their job, as I added National University of Ireland (NUI) Matriculation qualifications to my poor Leaving Certificate. This lovely old man once introduced me to a visitor as 'a relative of the founder, and a future superior general'. Three years later, on the bus home after leaving the order, I wondered if he had heard my news and was disappointed.

I also learned to enjoy the iconoclastic, anti-authority, teasing humour that I found everywhere in the Brothers. But even more congenial to me was the endless talk about sport, especially Gaelic football and hurling, fed by the weekly visits to Croke Park for which we all had free tickets for whatever was on. We walked across the city in groups and stood on the terraces at the Canal End, where I used to stand with my father at hurling matches. But in this period I remember football games best. I still have a clear memory of the soaring elegance of Kerry's Mick O'Connell in a poorly attended League game on a gloomy winter's day, and of being among the dangerously swaying record crowds later that year as Down won their second All-Ireland playing a new, fluid kind of football, the harbinger of the modern game.

I was at the centre of my own drama towards the end of my first teaching year when I was rushed to hospital and had an emergency appendix operation. Removal of the appendix has become such a routine, minor matter that it is only in recent years that I realised I may have been near death. Two things confirm the seriousness of my condition and the suddenness of my operation. I was operated on in the non-denominational (i.e. as good as Protestant) Richmond Hospital rather than the Catholic Mater Hospital or St Vincent's, and, secondly, the remarkably large and crude scar, which I still carry and have been told may be the key to recurring back trouble, the operation having severely damaged the psoas muscle. I have no recollection of the dash to the hospital or of any talk of having been in danger of death. Unlike Montaigne, whose vivid memories of a dramatic near-death experience after falling from his horse accelerated his abandonment of Stoicism and gave him a new way of writing about his thought processes, I internalised any trauma I suffered and, Stoic-like, carried on, as I had done with various challenging experiences from the time I left home. What I recall instead was my disappointment in the aftermath to realise that I would not now be able to take up the appointment to act as a steward at the High Mass in Croke Park to mark the Patrician Year, the putative 1,500-year anniversary of the coming of Christianity to Ireland. In retrospect – and in light of what was to come – this year witnessed the highest point of public approval of the role of the Irish Catholic Church, to which I was dedicated. The mass was celebrated by the colourful papal legate Cardinal Agagianian, who became a hugely popular if slightly comic figure. Hawkers in Moore Street the following Christmas, when I joined the throng of shoppers, were shouting 'Get the last of the Baluba babies! Get your Cardinal Again and Again.' The cardinal's image featured in small icons; the 'Baluba babies' were small, black, plastic dolls, and the reference – remarkably, and in the worst taste on several levels – was to the Niemba ambush by Baluba tribesmen of Irish soldiers who were part of the United

Nations intervention in the civil war in the Congo. Shocking Irish army casualties had included the brother of one of my students only a month earlier.

Instead of being part of the triumphalist Croke Park event, I listened to the Patrician mass in hospital on the radio, and later that week, still in my hospital room and learning painfully to walk again, heard the dramatic broadcast lecture by the charismatic American media evangelist Bishop Fulton Sheen. His theme, as I remember it, was on Ireland's worldwide 'Catholic Empire', greater than the evil empire (he implied) of Great Britain. It was heart-warming stuff. Sheen, who died in 1979 and was made 'Venerable' by Pope Benedict in 2012, has been in the news again of late. His formal beatification, the next stage on the road to ultimate canonisation, was postponed dramatically after charges emerged that he had covered up the sexual abuse of boys by priests in his diocese. How inconceivable such charges would have seemed in 1961.

I recently learned that the Richmond Hospital (now an 'education and event centre') had a very advanced design for a building opened in 1895 and was particularly praised for the fact that each bed had its own window. This triggered the memory that from my window I could see the entrance to the well-known 'Star of the Sea' hostel for homeless men run by the Legion of Mary, and that in turn triggered the further memory of being put in charge for a period of the Synge Street branch or 'presidium' of that remarkable Catholic action organisation which was structured on the model of a Roman legion. A yet dimmer memory (if such it be) is of a visit to one of our meetings by the Legion's founder Frank Duff, the best-known lay Catholic of the time, who sat quietly observing and saying nothing. He would no doubt have been amused, though not surprised, at the spectacle of the very young and innocent Christian Brother presiding as the much older local worthies prayed and recounted their activities, visiting the sick and alleviating poverty. It was another manifestation of the prestige of my membership of a Brahmin-like caste. This chain reaction of memories, triggered by reading a simple fact about the architecture of a dimly remembered hospital, is an example of the randomness of memory as I have experienced it, and its vast forgotten storehouse of matters great and small waiting for such a glimpse of light to illuminate them, like Derek Mahon's abandoned mushrooms straining towards the gleam of the keyhole in his haunting poem 'A Disused Shed in County Wexford'.

I still had great difficulty in walking comfortably over the following months, so severe were the effects of the operation. My pain was made worse by the fact that the first month out of hospital coincided with the community's summer holidays, spent in old coast-guard cottages in Cahore, County Wexford. There I could only look on enviously at the incessant round of games and swims, but there were compensations, especially the opportunity to visit regularly my ever-welcoming Uncle John, a curate in nearby Gorey. I saw there the same open-handed generosity that had treated me to an armful of comics in Dublin Airport, watching him give money to everyone who asked as we walked down the street. One of his regular clients, in return, briefed him about every change of film in the local cinema, where, unusually for a priest, he was a regular. Different, and to me surprising, aspects of his life revealed in those weeks were the part played by drink in the loneliness then enforced on priests, and his unexpected hellfire sermons, delivered in a powerful voice, in the beautiful parish church designed by Pugin. His conservatism was to be confirmed in the aftermath of the Second Vatican Council when he sought and received a dispensation from saying mass in English. He was also, no doubt, the source of my father's Jansenistic view on taking Communion.

After my summer of convalescence I was back teaching in Francis Street, this time taking the Scholarship Class, as 6A was called. This was comprised of boys competing for local government scholarships to secondary schools, especially to Synge Street. In this period relatively few had the means or ambition to go on to secondary education and these scholarships were critical in the later success of many boys from poor backgrounds. I had been handed another daunting task, but I was better prepared at least and some of the boys were very keen. I was still a very different teacher then from what I became after university. I was a strong Gaelic Catholic nationalist in teaching history and a devout conformist teaching religion. I doubt if I challenged my students much to think for themselves, but taught, as I had been taught, mainly with the exams in mind. But I was pleased to find, when I was invited to observe the Scholarship Class in Synge Street, famous throughout the city, that while expectations of Francis Street success were low, at least my classroom was a relatively happy and relaxed place. The Synge Street classroom, highly disciplined and focused, featured an unnerving silence; the image that stays with me is of the Brother in charge uttering the usual '*pinn síos*' (pens down) and each boy putting down his pen very slowly so as to make absolutely no noise. I think there were two or three scholarships won in my class, not bad for the school, but everyone in the Synge Street production line expected one.

Figure 34. Credit: Author

Games again took up a great deal of my energies, training teams playing in the Dublin primary leagues in hurling, and an enthusiastic athletics team which took part in various competitions the following summer. We played Artane in hurling in the windy forty acres of the Phoenix Park in a snowstorm on St Patrick's Day; we won relay medals in the Dublin Schools Sports in Croke Park in June. One of the few photographs I have from those years is with that athletics team (proudly posing with the senior relay champions cup), taken in the rudimentary Synge Street sports grounds in Dolphin's Barn (Figure 34). Among those even younger faces I almost look grown-up, and certainly pleased with myself. I am also reminded of the effort to fund the specially designed school's athletics vests worn by the boys, and of the bag of running spikes that I carried to training and competitions. And I wonder how they got on, these fresh-faced kids, those who have survived now in their seventies. I got the photograph recently from a former colleague, and even before turning to the back where he had neatly – and in Irish, as in the roll-book – listed all of their names, I had recognised many of them and remembered the uncomplicated enthusiasms of that time.

Back in the community, I studied for more Matriculation subjects, broadened my reading of novels to the Russians (Tolstoy, Dostoevsky and Pasternak) and became obsessed with the poetry of Eliot and Manley

Hopkins. I still read Eliot and Manley Hopkins and, as I nowadays re-read old favourites more than I read new authors, I have rediscovered the Russian writers through some wonderful new translations. I am struck by the fact that I resumed my reading and book collecting in Synge Street after a hiatus of three years and am sure this owed something to the encouragement of older men in that community. In the Brothers generally I encountered some gifted people but not many adventurous readers or indeed intellectuals of any kind. There was a sense, I think, that teaching was our vocation and that intellectual interests beyond that were regarded as a distraction and a potential source of unseemly pride. The few books written by Brothers at that time were credited on the title page to 'A Christian Brother' rather than to an individual. Yet despite it being a very locked in, conformist culture, I remember no adverse comments on my reading habits in Synge Street. I also began collecting records and can still visualise the record sleeves of Isaac Stern's Mozart Violin Concertos and Kathleen Ferrier singing Gluck and Handel – my earliest purchases. Music has been of ever-increasing importance in my life, at the core of the unstructured spiritual dimension that has replaced formal religion (discussed in Chapter 8). It has also offered a bridge back to my time in religious life when my musical tastes were formed.

I was, I believe, very happy and fulfilled in Synge Street, still only nineteen when I left it but already growing in experience as a teacher and developing as a person in an interesting, supportive environment. Again, I cannot resist asking myself the unanswerable question, 'Would I like that young man if I met him now?' He looks out at me from a faded photograph, the only 'portrait' of him in those years, taken by Dick Hayes, another great mentor in the community (Figure 35). I find it easier to relate to the young Brother Bosco at this stage in his life – a little more mature-looking and more confident, knowing that he has some respect among colleagues and students and has managed the challenges set for him. The photograph reflects also the happiness and camaraderie that marked those years. However, despite the poetry and the novels as well as the constant examinations of conscience and meditations, I remember my youthful religious self as still remarkably unreflective and untroubled. Had he a deeper, more reflective spiritual life? I doubt it; more a comfortable, routine one, focused on the intimate monastery chapel, but without any additional dimension, no spiritual reading (apart from poetry) that I can recall, for example, to match his literary reading. And of course life was extremely busy, between teaching and games.

Figure 35. Credit: Author

Another photograph from the end of that year is a reminder of the aspect of community living that most sustained and encouraged me – the companionship of my fellow 'young monks' (Figure 36). Taken on our summer holiday, this time in Greystones, in the swimming cove beside our lodgings, it includes Brothers from a number of communities, holidaying nearby. It is a reminder of the good-humoured fellowship that marked our lives, based a great deal on sport and 'banter' – and a resigned disgruntlement with aspects of the strict regime under which we junior religious lived. Second from the right of the middle row, I look fit and happy, and no doubt I was. At this point I had yet to feel any doubts about my chosen life; my vocation had not been tested seriously. My mood during the summer holidays that followed would be very different.

I found that photograph only recently in the course of packing for a move – to Greystones – by Clare and myself, a move much influenced by her love of year-round swimming and the attractions of that same cove. I can date the photograph roughly by my one clear memory of that holiday. Sent into the town to fetch the newspapers, I was returning across the pedestrian bridge over the railway when the banner headline caught my eye, characterising British Prime Minister Harold Macmillan's dramatic sacking of seven members of his cabinet the previous evening, 13 July 1962, as another 'Night of the Long Knives'.

Figure 36. Credit: Author

Of course, we were more than just a group of fit young men enjoying a seaside holiday, being also a privileged group of high-status young lords of the Irish Catholic universe. I didn't see it like that at the time, of course (young 'monks' were kept firmly, however kindly, in their place), but the previous two years had accustomed me to many signs of public esteem. Bus conductors issued me with free tickets, as did the GAA and the Abbey Theatre; cinema ushers guided me ticketless to my seat; parents were respectful and approving behind the famous Coombe humour; everywhere, indeed, I encountered respect. It is so difficult to communicate the extraordinary deference paid then to men and women in religious garb as they walked down a street or entered a shop. Now the few that remain, and still wear religious garb (the Christian Brothers simply wear a discreet pin in their lapels), are grateful to be ignored after the hostility that often marked the early years of the abuse scandals. I felt very sorry then for the great majority of good, dedicated people among them as I saw them sometimes flinch if I, as a member of the public, caught their eye.

Yet in the years when I was one among those accorded this widespread public approval and respect, I was also, like many young religious, male and female, exploited as much as cherished by my community. Every month I signed a form so that the order could receive my meagre pay. It identified me as a 'Temporary, untrained assistant teacher', which rankled every time I read it and was to rankle for a long time, becoming a spur to endeavour during my undergraduate years and beyond.

'Moving day' for Christian Brothers came every year after the annual retreat, in mid-August. With no warning you could find yourself, within days, in a new community. So it was, after my two happy years in Synge Street, I found myself in Tralee in a smaller community and one distinguished by its bilingual ethos. Once again I have no recollection of any upset at the move, at leaving friends and the excitements of Dublin. No doubt I saw it as both duty and challenge and, as usual, suppressed any sense of emotional cost. And again I was lucky. The community in Tralee also offered a pleasant and supportive environment, despite the eccentricities and volatility of its superior, a noted Irish-language enthusiast – perhaps even in part because of the camaraderie that developed in order to survive his sometimes bizarre rule, as had happened with the novice master in my novitiate. He took virtually no part in evening recreation, which centred on nightly card games of 'Blue Lady', the rules of which I never understood. Being no card player anyway, I was free to read my way through the house library, which had an eclectic mixture of religious works and fiction including, improbably, the complete works of D.H. Lawrence. The immersion in Lawrence that winter resulted in my never wanting to read any of his novels again, just as my childhood immersion in Dickens left me unable to face reading him as an adult. In both cases also, perhaps, there was an emotionalism, indeed sentimentalism, that appealed to me as a teenager but not later in life – at least not in terms of literature.

The monastery was an old, high house in Princes Street, long since demolished to make way for the Brandon Hotel. My room was on the top floor, as it had been at home, but this house swayed in high winds and, waking in the morning after a storm, I would find the bed had moved a distance from the wall. The house had a homely feel, a fine community room over tree-lined Princes Street, a very large kitchen garden and a housekeeper famous for her jams and chutneys. We went to daily mass in the Dominicans nearby, first looking right as we came onto our front steps to examine the mountain towards Camp in order to gauge the day's weather.

The large garden offered space for silent pacing during morning meditation, but my main memory of it is of enthusiastic explorations of the sky at night, led by one of the older monks. Again, I was the youngest, and 'minded' by some of the seniors, another of whom brought me on long bicycle rides. One day, as we came to a crossroads where some young boys were playing, he told me that we were near the scene of the infamous recent murder, on which John B. Keane was to base his play *The Field* a few years later. 'Watch this,' he said as we dismounted and walked towards the boys. He started talking to them in his practised cheery way but got no reply and the boys edged away. 'Everyone in this community knows who killed their neighbour,' he told me as we rode on, 'but no-one will speak about it, or anything else, to a stranger, much less to the Law. I'll point the murderer out to you in town some day.'

The move to Tralee didn't just mean a change of community; in a further bizarre twist to the order's notion of the duty of care it owed me I was also switched from a primary to a secondary school, teaching the lower non-exam classes. Of course, I had even less training to do this. The school, known locally as 'The Green', had a major academic reputation and some excellent teachers. It was also in a wonderful setting, in a corner of the town park, across which the Brothers strolled from their house nearby. I can't remember exactly what I taught (possibly maths, Irish and English; certainly religion) but I recall vividly the pleasure of looking down the length of the Dingle Peninsula through a classroom window. The boys were hard-working and easy to control, their backgrounds very different from my students in Dublin's inner city. One boy had occasional permission to be absent so that he could help his family bring down sheep from the mountain above Camp; some cycled long distances to get to school; most were middle-class townies. All seemed to have ambitious parents who were not afraid to call to see the teachers, occasionally, in my case, to urge the use of the strap to drive their lazy sons forward. But there were no inspections by the Department of Education (I never experienced one in my seven years as a secondary teacher, mainly, when finally qualified, in Cork city) and no requirement of detailed teaching schemes.

Having no exam classes also meant weeks of freedom in early summer, much of which I spent near the then sleepy harbour of Fenit, an eight-mile cycle away, reading, swimming and listening to larks. It strikes me, looking back, that I had a great deal of freedom all that year, to take one of the bikes, get a sandwich from the kitchen and head off for the day. On one occasion in the winter that freedom led me into a very dangerous situation. It was

Figure 37. Credit: Author

bitterly cold, and I heard that the sea had frozen twelve miles away at Camp. I cycled down the treacherous road and did indeed see the sea frozen, the small wavelets near the shore in low whorls of ice, the sand as compacted as cement. Facing the journey back as the gloom thickened, I foolishly caught onto the back of a 'scut lorry' or small flatbed truck, mercifully moving cautiously, and had a much easier journey pulled along behind it back to the town. I doubt if I reflected fully on the enormous risk to life or limb involved until years later. Perhaps it was good for me to act at times as a foolish youth rather than a preternaturally responsible adult.

The year in Tralee was unusual among those years for the visits of both my parents to the town to see me. My mother came first, by bus, and we spent a typically wet day in Killarney touring the lakes by taxi. What I think she enjoyed most were my attempts to counter the wilder fantasies of the driver as he went through his tourist patter on the local legends. A

Figure 38. Credit: Author

photograph survives of a view taken through the taxi's window with the Kodak 35mm camera she had just bought me, and in her handwriting on the back, excusing its quality, 'taken in the rain'.

Some time later Daddy drove to Tralee and we also visited Killarney, but on a fine summer's day. This jovial photograph (Figure 37) of him in his late fifties, so different from his usual persona in front of a lens, is how I best remember him, smiling at me, possibly joking at my 'foostering around' with the camera, doing 'a Paderewski'. A year later, now back home, again using my trusty Kodak, I took this photograph (Figure 38) of Mammy, unknown to her, and it too, in its peaceful stillness, is a favourite. It seems likely that those visits by my parents contributed to the reassessment of my vocation that I was to articulate later that summer to my superiors. But more significant in that regard was an experience so upsetting that I obliterated it from my memory for decades.

My early summer freedom had a consequence less pleasant than the lazy days in Fenit. Cycling there I passed by the grim buildings of St Joseph's industrial school (Figure 39) at the edge of the town, run by a separate

Figure 39. Credit: Author

community of Christian Brothers. I was largely unaware, I think, of what went on there or, perhaps more accurately, didn't want to know. Now, suddenly, I was seconded to work (and live) there for several weeks to allow some of the Brothers on the staff to take holidays. Joining me was my old friend Leo, also promoted now to secondary teaching.

My dim awareness of St Joseph's before going there probably involved little more than a sense of it as a very difficult and closed environment. I had heard grim jokes in Synge Street, 'Mind yourself or you will get sent to Letterfrack' (the most isolated of the industrial schools run by the Brothers). I have no recollection of the two communities of Brothers in the small town of Tralee ever meeting, but perhaps they did. There was a sense, I think, of St Joseph's as a kind of prison, for staff as well as for boys. After the investigations of recent years it is clear that most of the Brothers who spent their working lives in the industrial schools were dedicated and caring people, trying, without proper training or resources, to make the most of an appalling system. It must have been demoralising in the extreme. Far too many of the Brothers stationed in those grim places, however, were violent and abusive, as *The Report of the Commission to Inquire into Child Abuse* (usually known as the Ryan Report) (2009) was to show in horrific detail. Some of the worst of them spent periods in St Joseph's around the time I was sent there; I may well have been a holiday replacement for one of them. They were moved between there and other industrial schools when their abuse came to the notice of the authorities, religious or official. This abuse was also covered up by superiors, themselves often incompetent or callously indifferent, as is clear from the congregation's own records. The welfare of abusing Brothers was prioritised over that of the abused, though no help was provided for either.

As I wrote in my earlier memoir (2004), I had completely suppressed all memory of my weeks in St Joseph's in summer 1963 until I saw it featured as a centre of physical and sexual abuse in Mary Raftery's epoch-making TV documentary *States of Fear* in 1999. In my short time there I witnessed no abuse beyond the usual corporal punishment, but I was profoundly upset by the ethos of the place. In *Rebellions* I wrote:

> My clearest memory is of embarrassment at the harsh demeanour of the staff, and the cowed servility of the boys, so overwhelmingly grateful for any hint of kindness ... It was a secret world, run on fear; the boys were wholly at the mercy of the staff, who seemed to have an entirely negative view of them.

As the Ryan Report made clear, the boys I encountered were not there because of bad behaviour but because of 'destitution, homelessness, receiving alms and wandering'. They came from the poorest families, locked away and largely forgotten by the state, with the connivance of the wider community. Like the poorest boys in my primary school in New Ross or the 'penitents' in the town's Good Shepherd laundry, they were regarded as not quite human, their physical, sexual and psychological abuse somehow their own fault.

Because of the brief account of my time in St Joseph's in my memoir, I was asked to give evidence to the commission. As published in its *Report* (1, pars 451–2), my evidence of the great harshness with which the boys were treated included the view that the culture among the staff was such that 'essentially you didn't talk to [the boys] on an individual basis, because that would encourage them – that was too soft, and I was going in very soft on lots of levels'. I didn't know it then, but that view echoed the circular letter on the vow of chastity by a superior general of the congregation in the 1920s, cited earlier, condemning 'softness' or 'heedlessness or effeminacy' as dangerous in teaching. My memory, I told the tribunal, was 'simply of atmosphere, and what it was like to interact with the boys'. Their surprise at being talked to 'in a way that wasn't simply authoritarian' led them to be 'pathetically grateful' and anxious 'to form some kind of bond with you'. Overall, the response of the boys to kindness, I said, 'affected me a lot. That I remember'. Their great neediness and loneliness was corroborated by the evidence of several Brothers given to the tribunal, while some complainants also gave evidence of their gratitude for the rare acts of kindness they had received when they were incarcerated there. Leo Wright recently told me that many years later he met one of the St Joseph's boys, who told him that he remembered us well and that some of them cried when we left. Their nicknames for us were 'Brother Right' and 'Brother Wrong'. Leo also remembers the haunting responses of the boys to the query, 'Where are you from?' (a standard opening question of our early days as postulants). Instead of giving their home place, they were so institutionalised that they could only answer with the names of their dormitories – St Michael's, St Patrick's, whatever.

A distinctive feature of many of the instances of extreme abuse at St Joseph's was that they were physical rather than sexual. The worst perpetrator, given the pseudonym 'Marceau' by the tribunal, was recognised by the order before it sent him to Tralee as 'mentally unbalanced', especially due to his extreme use of corporal punishment previously in an ordinary school, whose superior wrote, 'I don't think he is fit to be in charge of boys at all.' The fact that 'Marceau' was then sent to the industrial school in Tralee, where the boys would be even more at his mercy, has to be a comment on the unconscious belief that those 'boys' constituted some kind of sub-species. It was also known that he would suffer no restraint there; the Brother in charge was described by the order's own Visitor after one annual inspection as 'lazy, disengaged and mentally slow'.

My short exposure to the darkest side of my religious family clearly shocked the very innocent and cloistered twenty-year-old that I was into suppressing all memory of it. That process probably began immediately. I have no recollection of reflecting deeply on it myself, nor, so far as I can recall, discussing it with any of the older Brothers back in my own community, to which, no doubt, I was very glad to return, appreciating its warmth and humanity all the more. In that way I became part of the conspiracy of silence that enveloped such places. But my community also included Brothers who were committed to what anyone today would consider extreme corporal punishment. Indeed, even at the time I struggled to reconcile the gentle domestic character of some colleagues in Tralee with the constant beatings I associated with them in school.

St Joseph's was, in that regard, and doubtless in others, an extreme version of a common culture, rather than a dark, completely different world. My own refusal to use corporal punishment, I may now have come to realise, wasn't simply a matter of personal preference. Instead, it reflected

Figure 40. Credit: Author

a profound disagreement with a core aspect of the culture of the Brothers. Little wonder then that I first voiced unhappiness with my vocation, and an indication that I might leave the order, in the aftermath of my time in St Joseph's. I spoke about it to the annual Visitor, one of the Provincial Council, who came to inspect each community. This must have been a very difficult decision to make, yet I remember nothing of the thought processes that led up to it, nor do I remember the interview other than that it happened and the sensible response from the kindly Visitor that I should give it another year and reflect further on it, to which I agreed.

Shortly after, I went on holiday with the community, staying at the waterside house of the order beside their school in Youghal. It was a month, once again, of remarkable freedom, much of it spent on my own, swimming at the lighthouse, taking a boat out on the estuary, reading in the garden, going (clandestinely) to the nearby cinema (the only film I remember featured Cliff Richard in the dreadful and xenophobic *Summer Holiday*), and taking photographs, now a serious hobby. A self-portrait, taken in the monastery garden, shows a more adult and thoughtful gaze, reflecting no doubt the sobering, shocking experience of a few weeks earlier and the need to confront the question of whether or not I would continue in my vocation – whether indeed I ever really had one (Figure 40). Allowing me so much time to myself may have been a considerate response by the community to my conversation with the Visitor, which would have been relayed to the superior. No doubt I did reflect on it a lot (in another self-portrait taken the same day I am reading *Gone with the Wind*!), but this process was quickly interrupted by the news that I was being transferred to a very different community, at Sexton Street CBS, Limerick.

In retrospect it seems another strange decision by the authorities. A young Brother, of whom much was expected, who had dealt reasonably well with the heavy demands made on him in the previous three years but had now indicated a general sense of unhappiness, was sent to spend his year of reflection in a big, notoriously unhappy community presided over by a superior well known for his lack of empathy, and particularly with young Brothers. Again, you wonder, what were they thinking? That they were not thinking very deeply about it may be one possibility; that they thought to put it up to me to buckle down and do what I was told rather than talk through what was troubling me, is a more likely one. In any case, I knew what I was facing from contemporaries, particularly Leo, who was now starting on his fourth year in Sexton Street.

In contrast to the quiet monastery in Tralee and the school on the idyllic green, Sexton Street seemed a big and impersonal place, physically dominated by a monumental grey Victorian building, a former orphanage, now housing the primary school. The large campus was in the course of major expansion, presided over by the bustling, authoritarian superior whose dominance of the whole enterprise was reflected in it being commonly called 'White City' after his surname. Instead of a pleasant stroll through a park, the walk to work from the large, rambling monastery involved negotiation of a crowded assembly and play area. The physical shock of the ugliness and busyness of it all was compounded by the sense of a dysfunctional community, its younger members largely ignored and almost forming a separate entity. '*Ecce quam bonum et quam jucundum, habitare fratres in unum*' (behold how good and how pleasant it is for brothers to live together in harmony) we had sung as novices. For the first time I was to experience a community in which such a spirit seemed absent. But there was also, as ever, a lot going on and I was soon happily involved in various activities, as well as teaching in the lower secondary school.

During the new school year, a strike by secondary teachers led to a picket outside Sexton Street, one of its senior teachers, Tony Bromell, later my colleague in Mary Immaculate College of Education, featuring prominently. The talk in the community reinforced the sense I had since Francis Street of a gulf between the lay teachers and the Brothers, who tended to regard them with some disdain as not being really committed, especially given their marriages and children. This was reinforced by the curious organisation of the junior secondary school in Sexton Street. There were six streams, three designated A (A1, 2 and 3) and three as B (B1, 2 and 3). Leo was 'in charge of' the three first year A classes, while I was 'in charge of' the Bs. This gave us some responsibility for timetables but also, more generally, an unstated delegated authority over the lay teachers involved. In my case these included a number of highly experienced teachers near retirement – one of whom had a great reputation in the senior school many years before, as I was to learn later from my father-in-law, a past pupil. They proved to be kindly, cynical, institutionalised men who had, understandably, lost interest in the job, in part no doubt because there was then no avenue to promotion for lay teachers in religious-run schools. Having a raw, unqualified young Brother in charge would have summed up a lifetime of disillusionment for them; and it cannot have been good for the young Brother in question.

But I had some very good students (and not all in 1B1), and again enjoyed the teaching overall. Many years later, invited to attend a dinner to celebrate the fiftieth anniversary of Sexton Street's hurling victories the year I taught there, I was asked over to the table of J.P. McManus, one of Ireland's richest men and a great benefactor of both the school and Limerick hurling.

'Do you remember me?' he asked.

'I'm afraid not,' I said, adding the standard teacher's excuse that while all pupils remember their teachers, for the latter the memory of individual students tends to blur into the mass.

'No reason you should,' he broke in, 'I was at the back of the class, 1B3, and I remember you very well.'

I waited with some trepidation for the inevitable judgement.

'I'll say this,' he said, 'you were always fair.'

'I'm very happy to settle for that,' I said, moving away as his attention shifted elsewhere.

He was like a benign monarch, holding court and dispensing the gift of noticing his subjects. This unexpected encounter, among other things, confirmed my dislike and distrust of the kind of streaming then used, which had decided in this case, as in many others, that a very exceptional boy was, in effect, a dunce.

I was invited to that dinner because I had trained the under-17 hurling team which won the Munster Championship (the Dean Ryan Cup) in 1964, thus completing a double, the seniors winning the famous Harty Cup for the first time in many decades a few weeks earlier. Some boys featured on both teams, most notably Éamonn Grimes, who later captained the Limerick senior team that won an All-Ireland (leading his old friend J.P. to name a racehorse after him). I was a fanatical coach, rampaging up and down the sideline roaring on every puck of the ball; I even insisted on a training session on St Stephen's Day, to the disbelief of the boys. However, when the team photos were taken later that summer I was excluded by orders of the superior, who by then knew I was leaving. It was a characteristically petty-minded act, which rankled, and made the invitation to the celebration dinner fifty years later, no doubt at the initiative of Leo, another stage in the healing process he has facilitated for me over the years.

Luckily you could keep out of the superior's way for the most part, and the young 'monks' had their own recreation room and were sometimes mildly subversive. It was there I first heard The Beatles, on a single smuggled in by one of my friends – another of the rare occasions during my years in religious life when the rapidly changing popular culture of the world outside briefly penetrated our enclosed world. There was great camaraderie, as in all the communities in which I lived, but here for the first time there was also evident unhappiness at the regime. I don't recall a single private conversation with the superior, but there was one upsetting public encounter. A martinet about how boys lined up for class in the yard, he pounced on one of the groups for which I was responsible, shouting not only at them but at me also. I don't remember his words, the shock was so great, but he accused me in effect of a lack of discipline and of general weakness, indeed softness in refusing to use corporal punishment; all with the clear implication that I was a homosexual, 'a nancy boy' was the phrase, perhaps. It was a small, chilling example of the relationship that could exist in the culture of the Brothers between corporal punishment, an unacknowledged sexuality, and the hidden scourge of child abuse.

Some of my most pleasant memories of that year are of involvement in the very successful camera club, begun by Leo some time before I arrived. We took and sold class photographs to fund the club's activities. I loved the magical process of developing film in the science lab and printing the black-and-white images that slowly emerged in the developing tray. More improbably, Leo (on the orders of the superior) had also started a pipe band (which still flourishes), and these two activities came together one Sunday when the band paraded across the city on its first public outing, before leading out the teams playing at the GAA grounds. My role was to capture the occasion, using the good SLR camera belonging to the club (a big step up from my Kodak). This I did with the same enthusiasm with which I had trained teams, taking several rolls of film. It was great fun, but a dampener was put on it back at supper in the monastery when the sub-superior, who was presiding, stood up and berated me for making a public show of myself and letting down the community, taking photographs like that in public. It was not an environment that encouraged the young or tolerated difference.

I had another confrontation with the same Brother some time later. I also trained an athletics team, which was entered for the Munster Championships in Clonmel. The sub-superior, who was headmaster of the senior school, refused permission for any of his students to travel, but I booked a bus and took them out of school anyway. I don't remember any row about this act of disobedience (the fact that I was leaving probably led to it being ignored), but for me it had the significance of being the first serious act of rebellion in my whole life. I was twenty-one.

CHAPTER 6

Leaving

Clearly, little of my experience in Sexton Street had given me pause for thought regarding my initially tentative idea of leaving the congregation, as voiced to the Visitor at the end of my year in Tralee. If my short time at St Joseph's industrial school brought into focus my unhappiness at the culture of the Brothers regarding physical cruelty, other aspects, particularly authoritarianism and the limits of the sense of community, impacted on me even more clearly in Sexton Street. Early in the summer I asked my parents to come to Limerick and we went out for lunch. I told them of my decision to leave, in the full confidence that their only concern would be my happiness, as of course proved to be the case. Not a hint of any disappointment or sense of worry about my future, which they may well have felt, was voiced by them, then or ever afterwards. It was an immensely reassuring reminder of what 'family' really felt like.

Whatever it was designed to achieve, the interview with the annual Visitor, who came some time later, removed any remaining doubts that I had – and of course I had some. I don't recall his name, but he was a man very different from the one I had encountered a year earlier. I can still see him, a heavyset, impassive figure who had no interest in any thoughts or questions I had and was set only on delivering a very hardline message. Well briefed by the superior, no doubt, he must have regarded me as a troublemaker, despite my record over the previous six years. The vow of obedience was absolute, he made clear, when I raised my problems with how it operated in that community, and I had to accept that fully or leave. I had realised by then that this – much more than unease at the corporal punishment ethos – was the nub of the matter for me, and that I could not accept what I was later to explain to the Ryan Tribunal was my understanding of what the vow of obedience meant for the Congregation of the Christian Brothers, 'an internal resignation of your will to your superior's. The most important thing about obedience was not what you did but what you thought.'

The fact that I found it difficult to respect the particular superior I had that year was beside the point. What I had been subjected to throughout my time in the Brothers was a very traditional monastic view of obedience, given a military twist by the then orthodox Ignatian spirituality. Other interpretations, built around a more developed sense of community, were possible and were being adopted by many religious orders, but the Christian Brothers, as part of their general and ultimately damaging failure at that time to interrogate their way of life, were rigidly traditional in that as in much else. As with hitting children, I was temperamentally incapable of being a good soldier.

Also, perhaps, my views about vocation and the religious life were too liberal and intellectual – or too precious and proud – to fit in easily to the congregation I had joined. Some years later a friend joined the Jesuits and I remember thinking, 'That's what I should have done; they would have suited me better.' Recalling this lately, I revisited the part of Joyce's *A Portrait of the Artist as a Young Man* in which the hero, having been encouraged and briefly tempted to think of becoming 'The Reverend Stephen Dedalus, S.J.', rejected the idea as a threat to his freedom. Walking by the sea, he encountered 'a squad of christian brothers' and instinctively echoed his father's prejudice against such as 'uncouth' and plebeian. Yet, immediately feeling shame, Stephen recognised 'their humble and contrite hearts' as 'a far richer tribute of devotion than his had ever been, a gift tenfold more acceptable than his elaborate adoration'. My whole approach also may have been too abstract and 'elaborate', but the notion of the Jesuits suiting me better was, like Stephen's brief flirtation, only a fantasy. As Joe Veale and others could have told me, the Jesuits would have posed largely the same challenges of obedience and of an arid masculinist culture. As it was to prove for Stephen, the vision that worked best for me ultimately was 'The University!' But in the end perhaps none of that was really crucial. Though it took me several more years to acknowledge it, my crisis was more fundamentally one of faith rather than simply of the interpretation of the vows. The religious fervour of my earlier years, with its strongly emotional basis, had slowly faded, almost unnoticed. In the end I was neither a Christian nor a Brother.

Once the die was cast, things moved very quickly. I finally had my interview with the superior, who was brusque and unfriendly and whose main concern seemed to be that I tell no-one in the community that I was leaving, which of course led to final acts of disobedience as I attempted hurried goodbyes with my friends. Furthermore, in the interest of secrecy, I was to have my trunk packed and be down in the parlour by the front door next morning an hour before the community got up. He informed me that he had confiscated the photographs, books and records in my room, reminding me that none of them belonged to me according to the vow of poverty. I don't know how my camera escaped the raid, perhaps I had loaned it to someone. I was of course very upset at such a clearly vindictive act – I had never heard of the vow of poverty being implemented in that way, and every Brother I knew had some books, and many had records.

While clearly failing in the vows of obedience and poverty, at least I appear to have had no issue yet with the vow of chastity, although that year I had my first brief encounters with young women since leaving home. This came through helping backstage for a musical in the theatre across the road but somehow connected to the school. They seemed exotic and left me tongue-tied, but, given time, no doubt that vow too would have proven impossible for me.

In leaving I was made to feel like a shameful secret, a kind of criminal, already emphatically an outsider and cast out from my second 'family' rather than simply leaving it. There was no question of leaving with its blessing. Next morning, after I sat on my own for a long time in the parlour, the sub-superior appeared, small, sleek and silently disapproving. He escorted me to the railway station nearby, bought two tickets and, after another wait, sat opposite me on the long trip to Dublin, without saying a word. In Dublin he brought me to the men's section in Clery's department store and bought me a cheap grey suit, a shoddy grey raincoat and, incongruously, a rather nice grey fedora. Did he take away my black suit and send it for recycling to the novitiate? Most probably he did. I had already left my soutane in the monastery, together with the splendid cloak, worn in winter, which I later regretted not stealing. Before he left me he opened his wallet and gave me fifty pounds – the equivalent of about one pound a month for my four years teaching, unqualified, for the order. The money would get me home, buy some more clothes, but do little to help pay for the training the Brothers had failed to even help me to begin. My trunk, as I boarded the bus to New Ross, sure at least of my welcome there, was very light, some socks, shirts and underwear, my Leaving (pass) and Matriculation certificates (enabling me to go to university that autumn), and three books I had been permitted to keep – *Knocknagow*, with its inscription by my parents; *Gerard Manley Hopkins: A selection of his poems and prose* (bought the month after I arrived in Synge Street, it has 'T.B. Ó Duinn, Nollaig 1960' written on the flyleaf); and the *Selected Poems of T.S. Eliot* (my name again is in Irish on the flyleaf – T.B. Ó Duinn, Sráid Synge 1962). Perhaps the superior felt that these religious writers might do something to help me to overcome my wayward tendencies. Perhaps they did; they are still prized possessions.

Perhaps my escort said 'goodbye', perhaps not. Was he also vindictive, or just shy? It was, of course, a thankless job, and he had reasons to disapprove of me. It was a stark contrast to the first journey I had made with that trunk, my optimism and enthusiasm buoyed up by the guardian angels of nuns to whom my mother had entrusted me. Now I had been cast into exterior darkness and had been taught the truth of Christ's metaphor about the religious vocation, so beloved of my novice master: 'He who puts his hand to the plough and turns back is not worthy of the Kingdom of Heaven' – or even, it emerged, the company of the faithful. Clearly I could no longer be judged a 'Good Boy'.

Three years later, after finishing my degree, I wrote to the provincial asking for a reference, and to the heads of all the Christian Brothers schools in Cork, where I was doing the Higher Diploma in Education, looking for the teaching hours necessary to qualify finally as a teacher. None of them replied. For those in authority I had gone from 'Brother' to non-person, a failed investment. But this rejection and obliteration turned out not to be true of the Brothers I had known, as opposed to the authoritarian organisation I had left. As I was to discover many years later, I became part of their very intense, tenacious and kindly collective memory, as did all who had spent meaningful time among them. The ghostly presence of Bosco Dunne (Tomás Bosco Ó Duinn) lingered for them, as indeed it did in some respects for me.

Even more than that of the town I grew up in, the world of the Christian Brothers I left in 1964 is a vanished world. Its monasteries have been largely abandoned; its schools staffed entirely by lay teachers. This decline was accelerated by the abuse scandals but had been in process from the 1970s as Irish society became ever more secular. Worse than the loss of their houses and schools has been the loss of reputation, the virtual obliteration of nearly two hundred years of achievement, something that must be felt terribly by its elderly survivors who had given their lifetime in service to the ideals of Edmund Rice. They were badly served, in my view, by the leadership of their congregation, which proved too rigid and conservative to adjust not only to the modern world but also to reforms in the wider church, and in religious life. The individual Brother was often poorly supported in terms of the role assigned him, and in his own self-development. The many kindly, idealistic and talented Brothers I had known deserved so much better.

As I revised this chapter, Irish newspapers carried coruscating criticism of the Christian Brothers because of the congregation's conduct in a new phase of the scandal of child abuse in its schools and institutions. In attempting to evade its agreed responsibility to compensate its victims for abuse that has been verified by the courts (as all other religious orders in a similar situation have done), the leadership of the Christian Brothers, after decades of obstruction and of denial even of admitted abuse, has now implemented another abhorrent and cynical legal strategy in High Court litigation, to make it virtually impossible for victims to obtain the compensation due – despite the congregation's great wealth. In refusing to nominate a senior member to act for the whole in such cases, as every other order concerned does (a nomination necessary because such religious bodies are not recognised legal entities), the leadership is forcing every claimant to summons every individual surviving Brother in Ireland, at enormous cost of time and money – and above all of mental suffering. As one of the victims has put it, this further extends and compounds their experience of abuse.

It must be immensely distressing also for the innocent, dedicated Brothers being subjected to this, their own version of abuse, nearly all elderly, often ill, already carrying deep scars from the abuse scandals of the past. I have not had the opportunity to speak to any of them about it, but it is easy to imagine their distress. Throughout the account above of my years with the Brothers the leadership's repeated failure in their duty of care towards us has been emphasised. It is distressing and scandalous to see that this continues in relation to men who have given a lifetime of service to the congregation.

PART TWO

Learning to Adapt: The 'Good Boy' in later life

Introduction

Unlike many who left the Brothers without qualifications, I was lucky that my parents were able and willing to put me through university so that I could qualify as a teacher, something I was desperately anxious to do. While comfortably off by the standards of the time, they had little to spare in either income or savings, and I had five younger siblings. I had long been sheltered from the practicalities of life, and it was only years later that I realised that coping with my sudden re-appearance not only involved considerable sacrifices for my parents but impacted also on my brothers and sisters.

I have written an account of my university training in *Rebellions*, initially as an undergraduate at University College Dublin, later as a postgraduate at University College Cork, and finally at Peterhouse, Cambridge. So I became a qualified teacher at last, starting at second level but for most of my career as a teacher of history in University College Cork. Unlike many academics, I have always regarded myself primarily as a teacher, with research and publications being mainly by-products of my courses rather than the main focus. Training as a historian, together with some new and challenging life experiences, changed me over time from being religious, nationalist and conformist in my thinking to being independent-minded, a rationalist and sceptic, and ultimately a humanist. It also gave me a new confidence that helped me to break gradually, at least in my professional life, from my 'Good Boy' persona, of being over-anxious to please and fearful of conflict. Indeed, my writing, from the beginning, tended to be argumentative and unorthodox, while at the same time attempting to win over the reader, if not quite with charm then with an effort at engagement, even a style. This transformation took time, and for many years there was a clear divergence between my rather over-assertive academic/literary persona and my still over-emollient interaction with those closest to me.

In the months after I left the Brothers I picked up the threads of my old family life, going with them on the annual holiday to Duncannon, a gentle, relaxed re-introduction to living in the secular world. In this small seaside village, that life now revolved around the tennis club and pitch and putt course, and in that environment I met a family, relatively new to the village but with whom some of my siblings were friendly. The only girl of the family was Mary, a clever, vivacious sixteen-year-old, and we were married five years later. I brought to marriage the same fatal combination, as I see it now, of confidence and ability to manage life, a lack of emotional maturity, especially an inability to deal well with conflict or difference, and a determination to make all rough paths smooth. My time in religious life was not the best preparation for the give and take required in the intimacy of a marriage. We had two much-loved daughters but were unhappy, and separated after fifteen years. Since then I have been able to work out a better balance with a new partner, and later my wife and colleague, Clare. We have two grown-up sons, who together with my daughters, and a grandson, have done so much to make my old age a very happy one.

The chapters of autobiography that follow are organised thematically and often digressively, rather than using the narrative approach of Part One. They are essentially extended essays on my thoughts and experiences in adult life. In the first of these I attempt to understand the impact on my personal life, and especially on my relationships, of the basic habits I absorbed in childhood from my mother – and that she had learned as a child in managing her alcoholic father. In the second I trace my gradual estrangement from Catholicism and embrace of a form of humanism, which owes much to the thinking of Montaigne, especially in his later essays. The third looks in more detail at the ways in which I have been changed by my academic training, and considers my experiences of teaching and research. I developed a new sense of vocation, this time as a historian, mainly of Ireland during a period of historically conditioned conflict which involved for me a rejection of nationalism and new understandings of Irish history that are complex, inclusive and based on a wide range of sources, some of them unconventional. That approach also reflected my early training in University College Dublin, part of the National University of Ireland that has been my community for nearly fifty years, as student, academic, faculty dean, and ultimately a member of its Senate. So this chapter also includes my experience of and response to the current utilitarian threats to its traditional culture of liberal education and academic independence.

I was able to retire early, and used this great privilege to develop a new academic interest, art history, getting my main initial training through involvement with major exhibitions in the Crawford Art Gallery in Cork and carried on through research projects to the present time. Retirement and the gradual onset of old age also gave me more time to read widely and the incentive, intensified by the challenges of a global pandemic, to return to memoir-writing. This time the focus has been not on locating myself in history (as attempted in *Rebellions*) but on trying to understand myself and my life better, and more honestly, as I face death without the comforts of conventional religion. These are some of the themes of the later chapters, mainly written in Greystones, a small town beside the sea to which Clare and I moved at the height of the first Covid lockdown and which has provided a fresh new environment for these re-examinations of my life, helped greatly also by my engagement with the essays of Montaigne.

CHAPTER 7

Personal Life

It struck me, after it ended, that I had embarked on my marriage in a highly romantic and naïve state of mind – just as I had set off a decade earlier on my religious adventure to join the Christian Brothers. Many couples, of course, begin their relationship in the same way but, nowadays especially, come up against the many compromises and adjustments involved in learning to live together and the hard realities of trying to set up in their own home. Neither applied to young professionals like us over fifty years ago. So affordable were new homes then we were able to buy, straight away, a fine suburban house, near the school where I taught, for three times my entry-level salary, with the help of a small local authority mortgage. And of course the idea of living together before we married never occurred to us – nor to anyone else we knew. Ireland was still a very Catholic and a very conservative country in 1969, in total contrast to the contemporary Californian Hippy scene or the counter-culture of 'Swinging London', about which we heard so much. If we had lived together first for a while, as is the norm now in no-longer-holy Ireland, I think it likely that we would never have married, such were the problems simmering under our romantic carapace. In love with love, we didn't really know one another, and when we began to as newly-weds we both shied away from confronting the fact that in fundamental ways we were not suited to one another. My 'Good Boy' persona contributed greatly to this. Also, in the Ireland of that time, having married and without the slightest idea that we might ever be un-married, any thought of dealing with problems may have seemed less urgent, or even, given that there was no obvious sign of crisis, to be unnecessary.

In a more open, mature relationship, our problems might have been resolved, with help, but we were blinded by love and not at all mature, despite appearances to the contrary. After we got engaged, Mary's kind, courteous father had a serious chat with us, asking that we consider waiting for a few years, pointing out that we were very young and perhaps implying that we were also rather immature. Later, when we went back over his arguments, we were particularly amused at the idea that we might be too young to get married. After all, Mary was then twenty and I was twenty-five! On some levels indeed I seemed the younger one, more immature emotionally, still far from processing my experiences in religious life, but able to manage everything practical with great aplomb – or so it seemed. It is very hard, nigh impossible now for me to get any clear sense of my mind then, of who I really was. Leopold Bloom, remembering his early times with his wife Molly, years after the death of their son and now obsessed by the fear of her infidelity, ponders, as he travels his familiar haunts looking for business:

> I was happier then. Or was I? Or am I now I? Twenty-eight I was. She twenty-three ... Can't bring back time. Like holding water in your hand ... Just beginning then.

Our beginning lacked realism, not that we were dishonest, but that we were unreflective and didn't face up to what was involved. We were very kind and affectionate to one another and very supportive. Mary put on hold the law degree on which she had embarked so that we could go to Cambridge for me to do a PhD, and she worked to help support us there. The surprise (our relationship being, as it remained, largely a platonic one) of finding, a few months after our arrival in England, that she was pregnant transformed our lives and made our financial situation precarious. The arrival of our daughter revealed how badly prepared we were to cope, especially after Mary developed a serious, long-term post-natal depression. And so, as many do in such a situation, we focused on our beloved baby and on managing as best we could, beset by money worries, ignoring the problems encountered by us as a couple and individually, including the need to get help for her depression, with which, instead, we rather grimly coped. Years of that pattern, more entrenched after we returned to Cork and had another wonderful daughter (and another happy distraction), meant that everything collapsed when we finally had to face the reality of our relationship (when Mary shocked me by telling me she had long been suicidal), and we separated. The words of the then current Abba hit about a divorce in the group – 'Knowing me, knowing you/there is nothing we can do' – was wide of the mark in terms of our knowledge of each other, but it seemed an appropriately sad background song for the end of our marriage, just as 'Lara's Song' from *Dr Zhivago* had been the saccharine signature tune of its romantic beginning.

Looking back over my life there is much that I regret (such as not having tried harder to relate properly to my mother; or not keeping in touch with people who were good to me), but the one thing about which I have long felt a deep sense of guilt was the breakup of my first marriage, nearly forty years ago. Guilt isn't necessarily the right response to such a complicated, messy tragedy, but everyone I know who has gone through such an experience (as so many of my romantic, early-marrying generation did) has felt it. An enduring sense of failure is more accurate, perhaps. John McGahern put it devastatingly well in his memoir: 'A divorce is like a death, but instead of that inevitable end, the person we have loved stands there as a living reproach of deep failure.' So much is invested in marriage that this sense of failure is similarly magnified. In so far as I remember it at this remove, and trying to penetrate through the obliterating emotional storm it turned out to involve for us, I didn't feel guilt at the time so much as a great loss and sadness. Once mooted, our separation seemed inescapable, and nobody's fault. We had been very much in love, very romantic, no doubt with unrealistic expectations. When, after fifteen years of marriage, we had to face the fact that, despite our two adored daughters, we were both profoundly unhappy, we couldn't in the end see how to change that. I had long been in denial of my own unhappiness – that wasn't who I was – until confronted by the full extent of hers. We talked endlessly and I think honestly in the months before I left. However, part of what we discovered was that such mutual understanding as we had from the start had evaporated. We learned that you can live for many years with someone you love, and suddenly find that you are strangers.

Looking back, remembering how idealistic and in love we were, I feel sad at our naïveté, each carrying unacknowledged burdens from our pasts – me maimed by a damaging family and religious upbringing and a misdirected sense of responsibility, she by a very unhappy childhood, the sources of that unhappiness never really explained, probably never adequately explored. In my mind it had come to be connected somehow to her grandmother, who lived with the family during Mary's childhood and teenage years. I remember vividly my only meeting with this very old lady (very much a *lady*), stiff-backed on a chair and dressed in black (from early on I conflated this memory with Whistler's painting of his mother). It was the summer when I had first met Mary and I was there, clearly, to be vetted by her grandmother as to whether I was a suitable escort for her at the local dancehall. I found her 'gran' a very powerful, scary person, as she was in part for Mary also from early on when her cot was put into her grandmother's room to help with the old lady's fear of the dark. She became probably the biggest influence on Mary's early life, and not a very healthy one to judge by her memory of lurid stories about ghosts and death. When recounting these stories Mary rejected any notion that this experience had been damaging, but I wondered then, and more so as our world collapsed and she was so resistant to discussing her problems. It also strikes me now that Gran's husband was another glamorous, bad alcoholic and that similar destructive coping habits must have been some part also of Mary's inheritance.

As I have come to understand it, ours was the mutual attraction of two needy people – her need for security meeting mine for managing life without conflict. This came to mean that in our marriage Mary and I had lived out two mutually destructive roles. She lacked self-confidence and seemed happy to depend heavily on me; I 'solved' all problems and carried nearly all burdens, and was stupid enough to think I was a good husband by doing so. Instead I enacted another, and deeply undermining, version of the 'Good Boy', failing to confront our emotional problems before it was too late. Each of us, inevitably, over time became resentful of our roles, but each was also very slow to understand that, or the inevitable unhappiness that was developing. When that did become clear, initially I felt bewildered and lost, but ultimately I was helped to some self-awareness and understanding of what was happening through working with a sympathetic but also challenging psychologist, recommended by a friend – the beginning of an ongoing process of which this memoir is a part. When I left the marriage, part of my state of shock and upset came from the realisation of how little I understood myself.

While Mary initiated the breakup, she soon came to reject the whole idea and became angry and hostile. This was understandable at the outset, as she was very upset, and I accepted a lot of the blame. Sadly, however, as one of her brothers warned me had been true of her since early childhood, she was unable to let go of any strong sense of hurt and loss, and this endured for the rest of her life. As well as its impact on our future relationship, especially our mutual commitment to co-parenting, this deep-seated, disabling mindset, seemingly ineradicable, was to continue to prove a great source of sadness and difficulty for her in sustaining a range of relationships. Even now, after all the years that have passed, and remembering how profoundly her liveliness, intelligence and affectionate nature affected me when I first knew her, I am immensely saddened by how unhappy her life turned out to be, especially now that I better understand in my own case how a psychological pattern developed in early childhood can prove destructive. In her case it proved to be a pattern impossible to break, or even to confront. I wasn't very surprised at her unwillingness to seek professional help as our lives fell apart. She had been terrified always at the idea of working with a psychologist, due to her fear, as she put it to me very early on (possibly in the context of her grandmother's stories), 'of what might be discovered, that I might be thought, and even be, insane'.

The early years of separation proved particularly difficult and were especially hard on the girls, not just in dealing with our breakup but in coping with their mother's anger and unhappiness and with the extent to which it came eventually to be deflected, however unwittingly, onto them. They kept the deterioration of their relationship with her from me for many years in order to protect me, but I should have noticed and asked harder questions – a great regret now. For many months, initially, I collected them from school every day and stayed with them in the house until Mary got home from work. Every day they then had to witness her vehement anger at my leaving, as if for the first time, again and again, and the terrible toll that took on me. In the end I couldn't cope, and came to be afraid of meeting her, and of being in the house, or even on the phone. My health suffered badly, from exhaustion, depression and panic attacks. But much the hardest thing for me was the extent of my separation from the girls in those years and the enduring sense of loss in relation to their childhoods, even the memory of which became, and has remained, partly obliterated by the trauma involved. There was a sad symbolism in the demolition of that house some years later by the bank next door, which bought it at an inflated price in order to extend its premises. On the other hand, that sale enabled each of us to buy our own house, and to that extent, at least, to move on.

I can now understand Mary's anger better, at least my role in it. I had done so much to establish and constantly reinforce the role of being her rock, her defence against a threatening world. To avoid facing problems, especially any that might involve emotional confrontation, I had been, often to an extreme degree and at great cost, the manager and smoother of all practical difficulties, something on which she came to rely. In leaving, I had, she felt, abandoned my role and betrayed our bargain. Much of the time, she would point out, we had seemed, and even were, happy, and enjoyed each other's company and our life with the girls. When we separated, close friends were disbelieving. Indeed, it was true that our unhappiness was hidden, never discussed even by us until the end. By then there was no doubt in my mind that our marriage had broken irretrievably, and our years of emotional storms after I left only confirmed that. But of course this is only my attempt to understand what happened between us and is narrowly focused on my 'Good Boy' theme. It is the story that best explains what happened, from my perspective, and the story also perhaps, as it developed over the years, that I could live with, and survive.

Mary's death ten years ago brought it all to the fore again, and brought only a limited, sad sense of closure. As her relationship with her daughters deteriorated further in her final years, she took refuge more and more in a group of intensely loyal friends, many of whom she had met when she gave them encouragement and help with their problems from behind the counter of the small shop she had opened when she had felt unable to continue practising law – a kind of informal Citizens Advice Bureau. They had admired her undimmed vivacity as much as they did her generosity and kindness. They were prominent at her funeral, after which an old friend, who had both loved her and thought her self-destructive, said to me, 'Mary had a great capacity for friendship, and for unhappiness.' At the crematorium some of us noted the contrast between the rather mute sadness of those who had been closest to her, but were later alienated to one degree or another, and the more vocal sorrow of those who had loved her but never had that love tested. I will always be haunted by the sadness and the lack of fulfilment in her life, but I no longer feel responsible for that.

Our daughters have long reassured me that it was not my fault that it all went so wrong, that I should not feel guilty, and yet I have had to live with the fact that I contributed greatly to Mary's unhappiness and to theirs. You have to live with the consequences of your actions, however unintended and unexpected. I had believed, for example, and not unreasonably, that Mary would adjust, have a successful career in law, and eventually re-marry; that we would co-parent the girls without any friction and stay friends on some level. The fact that none of this happened may have owed something to the fact that by leaving, I had further undermined her confidence, never very great. She had great opportunities to rebuild and take control of her life but continued to experience difficulty in taking and sharing responsibility. Years after our separation she ended a relationship in which she professed to be very happy, 'for the sake of the girls'. Perhaps she could not risk disappointment again.

But I also had to learn how to forgive myself, not be too hard on the unhappy person I was all those years ago and instead to have self-compassion as well as compassion for others. This is what I have come to see and identify with in Rembrandt's eyes, in his self-portraits in old age. Such sadness as is involved in past mistakes, just as in diminishing powers, has to be accepted as part of the life we have lived, but should not cast too dark a shadow over the inexpressible joy, as subsequently came to me, of being alive, in the world, in love again and happy. That is what I also take from Montaigne, to learn to leave the irrecoverable past and its guilt behind and to focus in old age on the present, on how 'to pass pleasantly and not laboriously what time I have left'.

* * *

I am lucky to have a very happy second marriage (and the love of my two sons to add to that of my daughters) in which I have learned, with help from Clare, a different way to relate, to be less managing, more willing to accept difference, to express the true range of my emotions, to be mutually supportive. It is impossible of course to fully escape from what Montaigne called the 'ruling pattern' established in childhood, but it is possible, with help, to modify its harm. Yet, no matter how much I wanted to, especially knowing how important it was to Clare, I proved incapable of abandoning my 'Good Boy' persona in relation to my mother. I could not tell her about my new relationship. Initially this was simply a powerful, even a panicked, instinct. In trying to understand it, I looked closely at my relationship with my mother, probably for the first time. What was I afraid of? All my life she had been loving and supportive of me. What I slowly came to recognise was that behind her normally calm, emollient exterior was a very powerful personality, shaped, I came to believe, by a childhood coping with her father's alcoholism and the collapse into poverty that was threatening her family. I had long known that her religious sense was both intense and rigidly orthodox, and from early on I had hidden from her my loss of religious faith by continuing to go to mass on visits home. Now this inability to challenge her on something so fundamental was extended by the realisation that she would see my relationship with Clare in terms of the same religious absolutes, that I was breaking God's commandment and that of the church. The thought of challenging her on that made me paralysed emotionally, but also panic-stricken. I had, perforce, told her about my marriage breakup, and she was sympathetic, blaming Mary (of course), and always hopeful of a reconciliation. But I simply could not cope with telling her that I was in a new relationship. This instinctive fear (indeed, to my mind the certainty) that she would withdraw her love if I told her must have reflected a powerful unstated feeling from childhood, one intuited rather than the result of anything I remember her saying or doing.

However, that intuition appeared to be validated when, discussing it with a sibling, I was told that Mammy, not long before, had turned a much-loved nephew away from her door after she learned that, many years after his wife had left him, he was living with another woman. A fervent, very conservative Catholicism had long been Mammy's emotional refuge, her point of certainty in the world, and she told him that his defiance of church teaching seemed to her a betrayal that she could not accept. Years earlier we had all seen how such rigidity could extend beyond the moral sphere to protecting the near-sacredness for her of the romantic myth of her old family home, and the deified father. She stopped speaking to her brother Jack after he sold Ballymacar, where he had long lived and farmed but had no son or daughter who wanted to take it over. His crime was to have sold to a neighbour rather than to someone in the wider family (though no-one wanted it, or was in a position to buy it). She also forbade all of us to have any contact with Jack, though we were all fond of him and he had built a house near her. It was disconcerting to see how her personality, usually so emollient, switched to a stubborn hostility to her hitherto beloved brother. But even such warnings should not have deterred me from facing up to telling her about Clare.

Some years after Daddy died Mammy had opted to move into a nursing home, carefully chosen by herself, an assertion of her independence as well as a reflection of her fear of living alone. There, she was initially very active and sociable, before she had a number of strokes, the last one robbing her of speech and, to a degree that was difficult to judge, the ability to understand all that was said to her. While it thus became easier than ever to hide my situation from her, even after Clare and I had a son, I felt increasingly unhappy about doing so, not only because of the shadow it cast over our lives but because I also felt bad in terms of my own self-respect. Before her strokes I had resolved at each visit that I would tell her, and failed. Finally, after our son was born, I took the advice of a friend, 'Just tell her, or you will never forgive yourself.' And so I did, emphasising that I was very happy and that she should not worry about me any more. She smiled her charming, warm smile, but of course I had no idea how well she'd heard or understood me. Insofar as I was doing it for myself, what I felt was less relief than a sense of desolation, to think that I could only be honest with her now, in *extremis*, when I had nothing to fear. I knew that she loved me very much, and I should have been able to trust in that. So negative was my own internal response to having told her in that way that I wiped all memory of it, until Clare gently reminded me as I tried to write about this whole profoundly upsetting experience.

Feeling so very conflicted, so ashamed of such apparent moral cowardice, utterly sympathetic to Clare's inability to understand my dilemma fully, I was, I believe now, paralysed essentially by the emotional climate that had made me a 'Good Boy'. How the intuited fear of losing my mother's love could have such devastating power over me – in my otherwise confident and successful mid-forties, decades after I left home, having had minimal contact with her for many years, and with all that was at stake for Clare and me – I still do not understand. Did something traumatic, and later entirely forgotten or suppressed, happen in my early childhood? Or could I have absorbed so elementally and deeply her emotional state, despite having no memory of it ever being articulated? Neither question seems capable of an answer.

I can only compare this devastating fear to my equally paralysing and ongoing experience of acrophobia, an anxiety disorder involving intense fear of heights. When our boys were small we all went on a guided tour of an elaborate, easily negotiated cave system in the south of France. The well-signalled highlight was an enormous cave known as 'The Cathedral'. We entered through its narrow opening, only to find that it brought us in at roof level, onto a platform a hundred feet or more over the floor. The platform had secure railings, as did the long row of steps to the ground, but I was frozen with fear, even terror. It was not possible to go back, and so I could only hold on to the wall, my back to the drop, and feel my way, holding its rough surface, as I inched down the steps. I would have done anything to have it otherwise, aware of how much my reaction scared my young sons, but there was no way I could manage other than how I did. Even now I can still be paralysed by such fears, even when faced with some far less dramatic challenge.

If I couldn't fully understand my inability to tell my mother, how much harder it was for Clare, especially given the fact that, with her characteristic honesty and openness, she had told her parents some years before that she was going to Cork to live with a separated married man who had two children, and she had faced their very understandable and vehement opposition. It was very hard for her to accept finally, which she did, with great generosity, that this was something I simply couldn't do, despite the threat involved to our relationship. This was the most vivid and bewildering instance of the maiming caused by my 'Good Boy' persona, and it brought me close to an emotional breakdown.

The sense of crisis involved only began to end for me with Mammy's death a few years later. We, her children, were all there, around her bed in the nursing home for many days as her body slowly closed down ('cell by cell' was how her doctor put it), in what seemed a final glimpse of her powerful, stubborn personality. We had long been used to her inability to speak, and indeed in recent years our uncertainty about whether or not she could even hear or understand us. But we talked and joked and laughed as if she could, rehearsing many of her stories, recreating the outgoing, loving personality that was virtually always to the fore, and the great camaraderie and affection between us that had always delighted her.

Talking among ourselves later, we all saw her death as a relief from the sadness and suffering of her later years, starting indeed with her fear and loneliness living at home after Daddy's death, years during which she had often expressed the wish to join him. However unwillingly, her death was for me some relief from the sense of failure and guilt that I have been able to articulate and understand only now. Attempting to do so is, perhaps, the main reason that I have written this memoir.

My father's death twenty years earlier had involved relatively uncomplicated feelings for me – memories of a relationship of love, support and humour, and a sense of loss that will always endure. Not long before he died we had gone for a pint and discussed Mammy's falling out with her brother and her vehement injunction that none of us were to talk to him. I proposed to Daddy that I would call to Jack's house and then tell her, urging her to accept the situation. He smiled sadly at me, and said, 'You will find that there is no point in taking your mother on about something like that.' Then, as later, it proved indeed to be something I couldn't do. Perhaps we both loved her too much to risk upsetting her, or simply lacked her strength of will. My early unconscious conditioning proved too great an obstacle to any attempt to establish an adult relationship with her.

* * *

Despite the deep sadness and trauma that has at times marked my life, I am very aware of how privileged and happy overall it has been, and inevitably in old age I sometimes ponder what use I have made of whatever gifts and opportunities I have had, what have I contributed, and failed to contribute, to the world – a rather romantic, even grandiose question, of course.

I take some consolation in the fact that I was a teacher for over fifty years and tried to help thousands of students to think for themselves and to develop a love of learning. My teaching, at whatever level – primary school children to postgraduate students – was, I like to think, marked also by a strong sense of empathy, and this, as some have told me, was a help to them. As a historian teaching and writing in a country and at a time when people were prepared to kill in defence of a particular view of the past, I tried to fulfil my civic duty by informing not only my students, but a wider audience, of the need to understand and acknowledge the complexity of our history and challenge the simplistic, polarising nationalisms that have promoted violence and division.

While reasonably happy to have been able to make some positive contributions, hopefully, in such areas, my romantic nature has never quite let go of the thought of a parallel universe in which I could have made more dramatic and heroic interventions, an echo of youthful dreams of saving the world, riding a white horse like a missionary priest in one of my mother's pious magazines.

But, more realistically, there is also a regular sense of guilt at not giving back more and not helping to tackle society's problems beyond the comfortable confines of the classroom or the study.

We are constantly, and often graphically, made aware of the lives of appalling misery endured by so many in today's world. Television nightly brings us scenes of the devastation of war, of famine, of forced displacements, our screens filled with the traumatised faces and skeletal bodies of small children, of abused women, of distressed men, deprived of any ability to provide for or safeguard their families. Often the horror is so extreme that it is impossible to watch, and instead I look away, even change the channel, upset, feeling powerless.

Yet, I have reacted often in the same way in my own environment, where I could engage directly and help. Walking through the small, friendly city where I long lived, I would fail to engage properly with the people begging, often living on the street; even when giving them a few coins I didn't look them in the eye. Sometimes a young man begging reminded me of one of my sons and I gave extra, but again without engaging in any personal way. I felt guilty, but also, it may be, fearful of such reminders of the fragility of our comfortable lives. For that reason too I have often found it hard even to look in a normal manner at people I passed in the street who had major disabilities. I had great admiration for those who did engage with our homeless, our addicts, our incapacitated, especially the young people I saw hunkered down, talking to such afflicted people in laneways or in shop doorways while I passed by hurriedly, helplessly, almost in a panic. It was much easier to answer remotely the appeals of charities and aid agencies coping with homelessness, famine or war, however selectively and inadequately, but shouldn't I at least engage more? Why such an emotional reaction?

Sometimes I think of the romantically inspired effort I made, age fourteen, to join the work of the Christian Brothers in the slums of India (or so I imagined it), and the contrast with my comfortable life as a teacher in middle-class Ireland. Or I think of one of my sisters who spent years living among one of the poorest peoples in Africa as a nurse, several days' journey from the nearest hospital. These are the kinds of dramatic sacrifices that appealed to my romantic nature, but I have avoided even the mundane. My oldest friend stayed in our home town and became a successful businessman. His recent death has left a great hole in my life. We met for lunch a few times a year, often followed by a walk. These were lovely occasions, reflecting a friendship of over seventy years. Our chat was often interrupted by my friend's phone ringing and his dealing with urgent requests for help from poor people in the town whose circumstances were well known to him as an active member of a charitable organisation, quietly helping those in need. I admired him greatly for that while also feeling guilty each time, remembering that I confined my giving to donations and avoided such direct contact with the poor and unfortunate – something I remembered again at his crowded funeral mass and its sense of a grateful community.

There is, no doubt, a strong element of selfishness in my failure to engage, but also occasionally what I can only describe as an instinctive emotional recoil, a kind of squeamishness, amounting at times to panic. When I was a child I once (only) went fishing at the river with my friends – just a line and hook, with a worm attached to it. When a small eel took my bait and I hauled in the line until he was out of the water, I became very upset and threw the line, and the wooden frame on which it was wound, into the river together with the poor fish, which probably died a more cruel death as a result. I appear to have had the same reaction often as an adult when confronted by human suffering. I doubt if I would have lasted a month in India. My rejection of corporal punishment as a young teacher, described earlier, may have had an element of idealism, but it also included the same overwhelming squeamishness and sense of panic at the prospect of striking a child. To be as charitable as possible to myself (as, of course, I should be), I might categorise this failure to engage directly with social problems as an excess of empathy, a disabling emotionalism.

This also extends to my domestic life, which features regular, sudden, mercifully short-lived outbursts of weeping, for example while sharing something I had read that moved me, or some memory, happy as well as sad. I have regularly broken down momentarily when speaking at memorial services and at weddings. It is as if I have a simmering emotional reservoir, just below the surface, ready to gush forth at the slightest provocation. Family and friends are indulgent, indeed often amused, and I have felt particularly embarrassed at times when 'tearing up' over someone I didn't even like. No doubt psychology could offer erudite explanations, but I have never been tempted to inquire, especially as I have my own, relatively benign hypothesis, that it may be connected with the suppression of emotion in my childhood as a 'Good Boy' and in my years as an obedient young religious. It would also appear to be connected to the regular sense of guilt I feel, whether in relation to things done in the past or things omitted, whether in the private or in the social sphere.

* * *

Montaigne's upbeat rejection of guilt or repentance initially seemed unrealistic, even facile to me, and it took a little from the appeal of his essays, but over time I became persuaded by his argument and embraced it as offering a useful corrective to my maiming religious upbringing. Montaigne's appeal lies partly in his regular, cheerful admissions of faults and weaknesses – his idleness, lack of seriousness, and above all his lack of consistency, his going along 'befuddled and staggering, with a natural drunkenness'. Gradually the reader learns that in fact Montaigne does not see these characteristics as faults but simply as his nature, indeed as human nature. His commitment to 'publishing and accusing my imperfections', but without any sense of guilt or repentance, he explained late in life by reverting to the Stoic influences of his younger days. Montaigne was not a systematic philosopher (more a chronicler of his own thought processes), and his essay 'Of Repentance' frames his argument within two apparently contradictory descriptions of himself. The first reflects the fact that 'the world is but a perennial movement. All things in it are in constant motion.' His writing therefore 'is a record of various and changeable occurrences'.

The second self-description is based on the seemingly contradictory idea of a strong, unchanging core. He claims that because he has harmed nobody, 'my conscience is content with itself', which is good, because 'Vice leaves repentance in the soul, like an ulcer in the flesh'. But he distinguishes 'vices that take us by surprise and towards which we are swept by passion' (especially illicit sex) from 'those which by long habit are rooted and anchored in a strong and vigorous will' and these latter 'cannot be denied'. In their case, 'Repentance is nothing but a disavowal of our will and an opposition to our fancies ... It makes this man disown his past virtue and his continence.' Virtuous souls may be incited to do evil, but 'we must judge them by their settled state, when they are at home'.

And so he cannot 'imagine or conceive' feeling the need for 'repentance', citing 'the Stoic precepts, which indeed order us to correct the imperfections and vices that we recognise in us, but forbid us to be repentant and glum about them'. Repentance 'does not apply properly to the things that are not in our power; rather does regret'. He may 'condemn and dislike my nature as a whole' and ask God to pardon 'my natural weaknesses', but, he claims, 'my actions are in order and conformity with what I am and with my condition. I can do no better.' At the end of this comforting analysis he cheerfully gives himself what the Catholic Church would call 'general absolution'.

> In all affairs, when they are past, and however they have turned out, I have little regret. For this idea takes away the pain: that they were bound to happen thus, and now they are in the great stream of the universe, and in the chain of stoical causes. Your fancy, by wish or imagination, cannot change a single point, without overturning the whole order of things, and the past and the future.

This startling final claim – that to challenge anything in our past conduct that relates to our core nature is to attempt to overturn 'the whole order of things', including 'past and future' – is an extreme statement of his case, but his use of the basic Stoic argument, that we can do nothing about the past and can know nothing about the future (other than the inevitability of death) and so must focus on coping as best we can with the present, accepting our nature for what it is, does make guilt and repentance largely redundant, indeed an unnecessary self-indulgence – 'your fancy, by wish or imagination'. Central to Montaigne's Stoicism is his avoidance of such self-indulgence and of 'sudden agitation'. He attributes this to being 'nearly always in place, like heavy and inert bodies'. It is such emotional stability that I have often lacked. I am not a natural Stoic, but have benefited from Montaigne's advocacy of it.

Though he remained a practising Catholic, Montaigne has no echo here of Catholic teaching on sin and repentance, with its emphasis on individual guilt, beginning with sharing in the 'original sin' of Adam and Eve. For me, Montaigne's appeal to Stoic principles echoes the sense of liberation I felt as a young teenager when (as detailed earlier) a priest in a talk went to some lengths to establish, on sound theological principles, that it was virtually impossible for us to commit a mortal sin. Not feeling overwhelmed by guilt over things that are fast receding into the past, about which you can do nothing, is also liberating, although clearly, as I have found, a difficult thing to learn. So is the idea of living in the present, treating ourselves 'a little more tenderly' and learning 'how to enjoy our being rightfully' (not being 'repentant and glum') – as he sums up his basic philosophy in his great valedictory essay, 'Of Experience', to which I will return.

CHAPTER 8

Spiritual Life: From Catholic to humanist

Two of the books I was allowed to take with me from the Christian Brothers have remained an important, if disintegrating, presence on my shelves throughout the intervening six decades. If, as I speculated above, I was allowed to keep them because each has a strongly religious, indeed Catholic or Anglo-Catholic element, the fact that I have continued to dip into them regularly and sometimes engage with them more intensely may vindicate the thinking of the Brother who spared them to me. They are part of the overarching spiritual dimension that connects my earlier with my later life; J.S. Bach's choral works have the same meaning for me, among others.

Both of my survivors are books of poetry that is challenging, erudite, and still to me often mysterious. The challenges in the poetry in *Gerard Manley Hopkins*, which I got as a Christmas present in 'The Penguin Poets' edition in 1960, lie mainly in his intoxicating style, his attempt, as he described it, to create an 'inscape' that would fuse the beauty of what he observed with the thought this inspired, through a free-flowing (but also often dense), musical use of language. Because of their extraordinary beauty and the thrill of recognition that they produce, many of these poems have long been part of my mental furniture, particularly in their responses to the natural world, which may begin or end with reference to the divine but become consumed also by the human attempt to capture the experience. Thus, in the first verse of 'The Windhover' (1914), dedicated 'To Christ our Lord':

> I caught this morning morning's minion, king-
> dom of daylight's dauphin, dapple-dawn-drawn Falcon, in his riding
> Of the rolling level underneath him steady air, and striding
> High there, how he rung upon the rein of a wimpling wing
> In his ecstasy! Then off, off forth on swing,
> As a skate heel sweeps smooth on a bow-bend: the hurl and gliding
> Rebuffed the big wind. My heart in hiding
> Stirred for a bird – the achieve of, the mastery of the thing!

The challenges posed by the other surviving volume, T.S. Eliot's *Selected Poems*, bought two years later, were more intellectual and cultural, particularly in 'The Waste Land' (1922), long the iconic poem of Modernism and a key text for my generation, with a particular appeal perhaps for someone trying to free himself from a rigid traditional view. Here, instead of one-dimensional orthodoxy, was a myriad of voices, a sometimes bewildering mixture of literary and artistic reference points, and instead of religious certainties the sense of a chaotic world, emerging from the horrors of a world war and threatening the loss of individual identity. It dazzled and mesmerised, even when I found some of it impenetrable, as I still do. I have no doubt that it influenced me in my attempts to develop new cultural roots, but would find it hard to explain precisely how, beyond, possibly, the embrace of uncertainty. There were aspects of Eliot that I found, and still find, off-putting – an intellectual coldness, his occasional displays of antisemitism and misogyny. I much preferred the opening poem of the collection, 'The Love Song of J. Alfred Prufrock', with its humorous evocations of the insecurities and humanity of a modern 'Everyman', not unlike those of Leopold Bloom, the true hero of *Ulysses*; both also echo the playful late humanism of Montaigne.

On a bright autumn day in 1987, however, I found a very different T.S. Eliot. Exploring the countryside near Cambridge, Clare and I followed a narrow byroad to Little Gidding, dimly remembering its association with Eliot. He had visited there fifty years earlier, attracted by the story of the radical lay religious community that had been established in this hidden place, the site of an abandoned medieval village at 'the world's end' in the early seventeenth century (their impulse similar to that of Eliot's Puritan ancestor who emigrated to New England some years afterwards). The Little Gidding community later gave shelter to the fugitive Charles I and as a result was raided by Cromwell's troops. Four years after his visit, in the midst of the London Blitz, Eliot wrote 'Little Gidding', which in 1944 became the final poem of his *Four Quartets*.

We found, seemingly unchanged, what Eliot had found, the medieval manor house, which had been restored by the community, as had the small medieval church, with a single tomb in front of it. When we arrived (the sole visitors in the hour we spent there), the church door was open and inside the spare, silent interior, on a wall rack, were some copies of Eliot's *Four Quartets* and a box for payment. Hitherto unknown to me, this little volume was to become a significant influence on my first memoir, begun a decade later, especially its meditations on memory and history. Now, in this, my second attempt to understand my life, *Four Quartets* has acquired a new significance, particularly for its reflections on 'Time present and time past'.

Eliot was a deeply religious poet, and *Four Quartets* included an effort to understand how Christian belief could be brought to bear on the crises of his middle years, including, on a personal level, the failure of his marriage and his guilt at the treatment of his wife, his inability to sustain an older but ongoing relationship, and his struggles with autobiography. More generally, these poems reflect on the inhumanity involved in social change and the devastating war he was experiencing first hand as an air-raid warden during the Blitz. He had become an Anglican (and, on many levels, a very English American) in the mid-1920s and was staunchly orthodox in relation to its core doctrines. However, the religion of *Four Quartets* is less that of orthodox Anglicanism than of medieval mysticism, long a part of his search for a personal spiritual transcendence. But there was also a marked humanist dimension to these poems.

Shortly after his conversion to Anglicanism Eliot wrote a number of articles on humanism, by which he meant rational, critical thought which is essentially secular. The first argued unsurprisingly 'that humanism is, in the end, futile without religion'. Subsequently, however, he warned of 'the danger, a very real one, of religion without humanism', which can help to keep it from degenerating into superstition. However, a broader, less intellectual humanism, one that reflects on human experience in its own terms, is key to the appeal of much of Eliot's poetry, including *Four Quartets*, balancing the mysticism that he proposes as the core of a transformative Christianity. However, while the humanist experiences are graphic and memorable, the religious element, in contrast, is often knotted and obscure. In the first poem, 'Burnt Norton', for example, haunting evocations of a failed love affair, the sorrow of childlessness, the bleakness of human life among 'the gloomy hills of London', provide the matter for meditations, including on the writings of St John of the Cross. Even to the diminishing number of readers, like myself, with some background in these mystical writings, their meaning here seems even more elusive than in the originals. What entrances the reader instead, and is never forgotten, are the autobiographical elements, like his account of a visit to the garden of an abandoned country house with the woman to whom he professed love but failed to commit to in the end:

> Footfalls echo in the memory
> Down the passage which we did not take
> Towards the door we never opened
> Into the rose-garden.

While Eliot continued to understand his life in terms that combined Christian thought with memoir, my spiritual journey has involved the fading of religion as the human came more clearly into focus.

* * *

Reading not only Eliot but a wide range of modernist literature (as well as history) may have contributed to the realisation in the decades after I left the Brothers that I no longer believed, not just in the dogmas of the Catholic religion in which I grew up but in the existence of a god, any god. This was such a gradual process that, when I finally declared myself an atheist (to friends at least) in my late thirties, it seemed to me unsurprising, and I gave it little thought. I had also reflected little initially on any sense of loss that might have been involved in my slow retreat from religion. In commenting on a draft of this chapter, my friend Terry O'Reilly enclosed an excerpt from an account by the philosopher Anthony Kenny of a conversation he had with two other 'lapsed Catholics', one being Graham Greene. As they discussed why it was that those converts who have given up their faith often feel such a great sense of loss, Greene quoted from Arthur Hugh Clough's poem 'Easter Day': 'We are most hopeless, who had once most hope/And most beliefless, that had most believed'. Perhaps reflecting the relative shallowness of my faith, I didn't experience Clough's rebound of hopelessness or despair. Instead my sense of loss was more specific, occasional and limited, mainly the loss of the comfort of ritual.

At funeral masses for loved ones, my parents in particular, I have been struck anew by the consolations of religious belief and solemn ritual for those of the bereaved who have faith, but without wishing I was still one such. I have felt no desire to join in the familiar responses, and have even positively resisted the reflex of doing so. At humanist ceremonies in crematoria, in contrast, I have felt their lower impact as ritual, even as I empathised with their greater concern to honour the singular aspects of a human life. My distance from the faith that had so long defined me has also been evident in the fact that I have no memory since leaving it of wanting to pray when dealing in my own mind with bereavement, trauma or crisis, no matter how extreme my upset, and it has been extreme at times.

I have learned that atheism is not simply a negative; its corollary, that the individual takes personal responsibility and relies on human understandings and consolations rather than on a notional all-powerful god, is a positive strength – although it may also appear rather arrogant to some, a minor echo of Satan's justification for rebellion in Milton's *Paradise Lost*.

Humanism – by which I mean principally this foregrounding of the human and the individual – is, of course, an ancient way of thought (Eliot denied it was a 'philosophy'), particularly well developed in the Renaissance, drawing inspiration from Classical antiquity, and popularised by Erasmus, who (within a Christian framework) stressed the power and importance of rational thought and scholarship, individual self-development and peaceful co-operation based on empathy with other human beings. Among its later devotees – and an important conduit for its influence on our time (including on me) – was Michel de Montaigne, also well read in Classical texts but less focused on the intellectual qualities of being human, and more ostensibly secular. In his later essays especially, coming to terms with old age, he went beyond the largely passive Stoic view of a heroically borne death as the aim and the ideal. Instead he turned to Epicurean writers, especially Lucretius, and their humanist stress on heroic living rather than dying, on the enjoyment of the body rather than its mortification, and the embracing of life rather than death.

When I went to university, a few months after I left religious life, I became a student of history. In the process I learned less about the past than about a different way of thinking – empirical and sceptical – which was fundamentally humanist. This resulted in a rebellion against nationalism in parallel with my estrangement from Catholicism – the twin pillars of my cultural formation, the twin orthodoxies of my early intellectual life. That estrangement was gradual, and initially focused on loss of belief in the teachings of the church, and ultimately in the very existence of a god. Alienation from the institution developed at first from my experience of its control of education, and then from the harm arising from its influence and control of so many aspects of Irish life and on the personal lives of individuals, even those of other religions and none. The scandals in recent decades in relation to clerical sexual abuse and, more broadly, the treatment of the vulnerable, especially women and children in Catholic Church-controlled institutions, finally revealed the extent of the evil involved, and also the complicity of the state.

I have never been a member of a political party but have voted always for Labour, in large part because it has been most vocal on the need for politics to be secular. My political epiphany came as an undergraduate, in a crowded Liberty Hall listening to Noël Browne at his most passionate and mesmerising argue that Ireland would never be truly independent until the control of the Catholic Church over education and health was ended. Twenty years later I was also very impressed by a key book, *Church and State*, by my colleague and later friend Des Clarke, a philosopher at UCC, which made an equally passionate but also forensic case for their separation. My own low-key political activism has been confined to the human rights struggles, as I perceived them, for the rights to abortion, divorce and gay marriage. While the ultimate victories in these areas through popular referenda involved marked positive advances in the secularisation of Irish society, Noël Browne's plea is still far from fully achieved in either education or health, as conservative, over-cautious politicians lag behind a transformed public opinion.

These questions of religion and politics also arose in my academic work. It may be possible to be Catholic and nationalist and a good historian, as my late friend Brendan Bradshaw showed, but, as I often argued with him, the acceptance of two sets of dogma as frameworks of analysis has to limit the range of understanding and interpretation. Scholarship has to be open-minded and transcend dogma, whether secular or religious. The idea of 'Christian humanism' illustrates the same problem of limitation. My friend Terry queried why I contrast humanism so strongly with religious belief, as 'in your understanding of humanism I can find nothing incompatible, for instance, with my own religious faith'. I know that he is both a very committed humanist and deeply Christian. However, while much humanist thought can be compatible with Christianity, the reverse may not hold for many humanists. Having rejected the Christian explanation of the world and especially the Catholic versions, an entirely secular humanism is *all* that I have by way of spiritual resource and consolation. Indeed, my understanding of humanism is shaped significantly by that rejection and is marked by the lack of a divine framework and of a belief in an after-life. The human and the temporal mark the boundaries of my spirituality, in contrast to those of the Christian humanist.

I learned also that history-writing, like life in religion, is communal by nature, but instead of all assenting to the same inherited 'truth', each historian's contribution to the collective forms part of a complex, cumulative understanding of the past, a web comprising individual threads in tension, pulling in different directions. That understanding is in constant flux, responding to new material, new interpretations and new contexts that add new meaning. There are no agreed or fixed truths. Thus, my academic training and practice not only made me a particular kind of historian but also an empiricist, a sceptic and a relativist, and in the face of that combination, whatever shallow religious sense remained to me was quick to dissolve.

With its emphasis on rational thought and debate and its encouragement of human empathy, my academic training and experience also led me to be a humanist in the broader sense. As such, my engagement also with music, literature, art and nature has resulted in the development of what might be called a secular spiritual life, that is, one involving a different kind of transcendence than religion offers, infusing such engagements with a sense of wonder, of beauty and of enhanced understanding. This is to *experience* humanism rather than to read about it, making it a matter of practice rather than of theory. It has come increasingly into focus for me with old age, as an answer to the inevitable questions arising from the rejection of religion: Facing death, what can replace its consolations? Believing that there is no afterlife, that this life is all that we have, what can help us to live it meaningfully, and then face annihilation? The best way to prepare for death, Montaigne believed, was not to focus on it but to live life as fully as possible. The enjoyment of a broadly spiritual humanism, as I am attempting to describe it, is a major element of that approach for me. The range of its consolations are immense, but here I want to write about three specific transcendent and illuminating pleasures that have preoccupied me in recent times: music, nature and re-reading favourite fictions.

* * *

Music, long an obsession, became ever more important and focused on during the isolation imposed by the pandemic. For a large part of every day I listen to music. To be more accurate, I have music playing. Mostly, it is in the background, when I read or write, with intervals when it snares my attention and I stop to listen to a passage before re-immersing myself in other things. Sometimes I sit down, simply to listen, perhaps to something that is new to me, drawn to my attention through hearing it on the radio or at a concert. I listen almost exclusively now to what is still often called 'classical' music, carrying old connotations of snobbishness though it has long been music of wide popular appeal and now relates to one popular form among many. As indicated here and there in this memoir, elements of such music have featured in my life since childhood and my growing focus on it simply reflects a deepening attachment over time, connected in part to its relationship to my academic research but also to ageing and its tendency to turn the mind to reflection. Mostly nowadays I listen to solo instruments or chamber ensembles, ranging from early music to that of the late nineteenth century. As I write now, for example, I am 'listening' to Stefan Isserlis play Bach Cello Suites, one of a number of versions that I have, its quietly reflective tone suiting my Monday-morning mood, a contrast to the excitement of Pablo Casals' version, reflecting his discovery of this 'lost' music, which I prefer at other times. Every note is familiar, yet I never tire of it.

Sadly, however, I remain largely ignorant about the music I listen to, and in particular about its technical aspects. It is a mysterious, haunting language, endlessly fascinating, despite the fact that I have no real understanding of why it moves me in the different ways that it does. I can come out of a concert and express strong views, about the balance in a trio or the unaccustomed speed of a favourite movement, but can be still unsure of basics, such as the operation of changes in key. I have found a limited way into its mysteries through reading about the historical contexts of favourite works, especially by musicians and musicologists. Recently, I listened carefully to the nine pieces by Beethoven, through which Laura Tunbridge constructs a multi-faceted biography (*Beethoven: A life in nine pieces*). At present I am reading the dense, yet thrilling study of Bach's choral music – now the music most important to me – by John Eliot Gardiner, which is full of technical analysis as well as historical context but done so engagingly as to make my ignorance seem irrelevant. But for the most part I am content to let music surround me and wash over me, unanalysed, as I do with the skies over the sea on my daily walks. At its most elemental, perhaps, the appeal of great music is experienced through the senses. One of the most poetic evocations of this is the response of Proust's narrator in *In Search of Lost Time* to listening to the septet by his fictional composer Vinteuil:

> The multiple sensations of light, the airy sounds, the noisy colours which Vinteuil sent us from the world in which he composed ... something which I could compare to the perfumed silk of a geranium.

I have to confess to still listening to music mainly on CDs. While helping with our house-move lately our sons, each very involved in his own music genre, smiled at my careful packing of discs and their later shelving. That is all so outdated and unnecessary, they reminded me – again. Streaming on Spotify can give me all the music I will ever need on my phone or computer – no clutter. But I like browsing the shelves, looking for something I heard last night on radio, or being reminded of pieces I loved but haven't played for a long time. Above all, my own small collection, gathered over many years (some of my CDs replacing recordings I had originally on vinyl or on tape, or successively on both) is a record of my musical journey, part of my life history. Thus, for example, my vinyl collection, such as it was, contained mainly operas and symphonies, both now represented very poorly among my CDs, as they came to seem in old age too declamatory and loud for reflection; my tapes had little of Johann Sebastian Bach, now among the composers best represented on my shelves, the one with the greatest range and humanity.

So is it possible, given my musical illiteracy, to put into words what it is I am responding to in my favourite music? (Perhaps it is futile to try, as Montaigne appears to have concluded.) As with reading literature, my response, I believe, can best be described as humanist, being focused on the particular *voice* of the composer (or of the instrument, as in the case, for example, of the 'human'-seeming cello), because, even when they have a vast range, composers seem to me to have characteristic voices. This may be a crude measure, but I often pick out a CD (as I pick out a book) to match the voice I want to hear. There is, for example, the solemnity (even when joyful) of J.S. Bach, the intensity of Beethoven, the vivacity of Mozart and the poignancy of Schubert. But it is often voices *within* the music and their interaction that are most important, and most reflect human dialogue. For example, the complex interplay between violin and piano in Beethoven's violin sonatas, and the even more complex conversations within his quartets, seem to resonate with thought as well as feeling. The attraction of a particular mood can also be important, the mood of dancing in Mozart, the plangent mood in Schubert and Fauré. The attraction for me of the plangent I think of as inherited from my mother and her love of the nostalgic and the dying fall in Irish songs. Its ultimate expression, perhaps, is the Chopin Étude that I first knew through the sentimental song based on it, in English 'So Deep is the Night', made famous by Richard Tauber but which John McCormack also recorded late in his career. It was perfect for his 'tear in the eye' repertoire of popular song. Perhaps the increased attraction of such music is a further reflection of ageing.

What I enjoy most when I listen, or half listen, to music can best, if loosely, be called *beauty*, by which I mean something ineffable, sacred, an uplift of the spirit. It is the defining feature of the whole remarkable range of Bach's music, from the complex, dramatic choral works to the contemplative works for single instruments, cello, violin and piano and organ. Of course it is present in all great music and can be manifest in many ways, often unexpectedly, like in Mozart even at his most light-hearted. It is what I reach for when I put on slow, reflective piano works like the Nocturnes or Études of Chopin, or the Sonatas of Beethoven, or Schubert. So much of what is spiritual for me in music nowadays relates to its encouragement of meditation, or at least of thought and of daydreaming.

My current musical tastes were, of course, formed by earlier experiences. The fact that my historical research has focused mainly on the late eighteenth and early nineteenth centuries helps to explain my interest in the music of that time. My childhood training in church music, greatly intensified when I was a religious novice, proved an *entrée* to early and baroque music. My current saturation in the choral work of J.S. Bach responds to those early experiences and creates a musical continuity to my life. It is now an established Sunday-morning ritual to play a Bach choral work, almost a secular version of attendance at Sunday mass in early life. And indeed some of my favourites are masses, one, *Mass in B Minor*, even called 'The Catholic Mass' by musicologists, while recently I found a CD of 'Bach's Lutheran Masses'. His debt to Luther was profound in terms of folk culture as well as religion, or, more accurately, the role of folk tradition in religious music. He attended the school that Luther had attended two centuries earlier, and a key part of his early musical experience came from a traditional hymnal put together by Luther, for whom music was a major key to prayer, as well as to education. There is a dramatic, popular core to Bach's Cantatas, composed for specific occasions in the liturgical calendar, based on the marriage of music with biblical texts. This sense of drama is still part of their appeal to modern audiences, who are moved by the delineation of joy, or sorrow, though they may lack easy access to the German biblical texts, or the Lutheran tradition.

Some of Bach's Cantatas can be described as 'secular', because written for non-religious occasions, but for him all of them were both religious and secular, all profoundly human, speaking to the human condition. Thus, whole sections of his rousing *Tönet, ihr Pauken*, the most joyous music I know, composed in honour of the electress of Saxony in an attempt by Bach to gain court favour, were re-used by him in the *Christmas Oratorio* a year later. So, while I enjoy the echoes of my Catholic background in listening to these sacred works, my spiritual benefit from them can be described nowadays as secular and humanist rather than religious and doctrinal – though Bach might have disputed the distinction.

* * *

Another example of the secular spirituality that consoles me – and a contrast to the exquisite and moving human inventions of music – is our response to the natural world that surrounds and sustains us. For most of us in the West this response is still heavily conditioned by the Romanticism that swept Europe from the end of the eighteenth century, best represented still for my generation in its promotion by Wordsworth as a kind of secular religion. The ecstatic emotionalism of his youthful identification with nature has little appeal for me now, compared to the mature, reflective view he was to develop 'in lonely rooms' and 'mid the din of towns and cities', during which

> I have learned
> To look on nature, not as in the hour
> Of thoughtless youth; but hearing oftentimes
> The still, sad music of humanity

It was in the context of that 'still, sad music' that he remained

> A lover of the meadows and the woods
> And mountains; and of all that we behold
> From this green earth; of all the mighty world
> Of eye, and ear, – both what they half create,
> And what perceive; well pleased to recognise
> In nature and the language of the sense
> The anchor of my purest thoughts, the nurse,
> The guide, the guardian of my heart, and soul
> Of all my moral being.

This is to experience nature as consolation and inspiration, as well as transcendence, for the human spirit.

It is my good fortune to live now near the sea, and emerging from our small town to the water's edge, finding myself again under the vast canopy of sky, facing the romantic vista of greater Dublin Bay from Howth to Bray Head, across the ever-changing colours and textures of the water is a daily experience of spiritual uplift and endless fascination. Clouds, in their constant movement, speak to our sense of transience, but also of energy, as John Constable showed in his cloud studies of the early 1820s. My own 'studies', as reflected in my 'smart' phone 'Gallery', also record fascination with their shapes, shifting compositions and moods, their natural 'abstract' art.

But I am just as absorbed and nurtured by many of the less operatic manifestations of nature, and particularly wildflowers. To quote Wordsworth again,

> Thanks to the human heart by which we live,
> Thanks to its tenderness, its joys, and fears,
> To me the meanest flower that blows can give
> Thoughts that do often lie too deep for tears.

Of the little I learned as a trainee religious, what has stayed with me as a regular practice is the aesthetic and philosophical pleasure of picking and arranging flowers. Sixty years ago, as a novice, I shared for a period the task of gathering and arranging flowers for the chapel altar. This was made easier by access to a large walled garden, including a glasshouse with its benches of flowering potted plants, best remembered being a rich array of azaleas. But my favourite memory involved wildflowers. One day, on the eve of a major feast, my co-worker and I found the garden gate locked, its key mislaid, and so we had to improvise. Remembering that the woodland nearby had masses of bluebells, we gathered armfuls and some foliage to support and complement them. As I remember it, the novice master was appalled at the garishness of the display, although the idea, no doubt, came from the tradition of a 'May altar' in Catholic classrooms in honour of Christ's mother Mary, which often featured bluebells. One of my mother's favourite hymns began, 'Oh Mary, we crown thee with blossoms today/Queen of the Angels and Queen of the May', and there is a long tradition of the use of flowers in Catholic ritual.

A second education in flower-arranging came through the habit of picking wildflowers on walks with Clare, and later our sons, arranging and re-arranging them as a bouquet as I went and tying the final ensemble with a stalk of long grass. Put in water in a small glass, they often outlasted and outshone the more colourful cut flowers from the garden or the florist, their dying a fading away rather than the collapse of the larger garden varieties. I still make wildflower nosegays on the increasingly rare occasions when a variety of flowers and grasses offer. Nowadays I do it with a twinge of conscience about biodiversity loss, assuaged by only picking where there is profusion and limiting myself to one or two samples of each plant.

I have a sense of the gathering and arranging of bunches of wildflowers as a creative exercise, expressive also of personality, and connected to the business of writing – collecting and arranging material, and tying it all together in a way that gives meaning. Montaigne, in drawing together his myriad quotations from classical writers, was sometimes defensive about the process, at one point using the analogy of the flower bouquet: 'I have gathered a posy of other men's flowers, and nothing but the thread that binds them is my own.' But without the thread there is mere collecting, not thought or aesthetics.

Wildflowers, like birds, have ancient origins and have long been treasured for their beauty or their medicinal value and, as their names often indicate, their connection to folklore. Nature poets, notably John Clare, experienced them as triggers of memory and communicators of moral lessons. Of modern poets, their great celebrant is Michael Longley, who is an old friend. His response to them, like John Clare's, is complex. Schooled by botanist and artist Raymond Piper, he is interested in their taxonomy; he is also bewitched by the poetry of their local names; he sees the solace they give in sorrow, and their celebration of life. In one of his best-known poems, consoling his child after the murder of an ice cream man during the 'Troubles', 'I named for you all the wild flowers of the Burren/I had seen in one day', which he then does for us also, five lines of names made poetical. Welcoming his baby grandson on his first night at his remote cottage at Carrigskeewaun, he tells him, 'I have picked wild flowers for you, scabious/ And centaury in a jam-jar of water/That will bend and magnify the daylight'.

A seeming contradiction in loving flowers so much that you pick or cut them and bring them indoors for your pleasure, is that by doing so you kill them, and perhaps cause them suffering, as some scientists now believe. So there is an argument for enjoying – and leaving them – where you found them. But there may also be an argument for honouring their beauty by arranging and displaying them indoors, and learning from them. Perhaps the main thing you learn from arranging flowers in a vase is how fleeting life and beauty is. Take tulips, cut while still in bud: they show us a whole life cycle over a week, each phase having its own beauty – the opening of the flower and the slow revelation of its colour and form; the beauty and perfection of the fully opened flower; the even greater beauty of its dying, especially in the older varieties with large blooms, each petal a palette of modulated, bruised colour tones, like smudged pastels, as they die. This phase evokes sadness, as well as appreciation, a reminder of mortality and old age, which also has its beauty. I visited the great essayist Hubert Butler not long before he died at ninety-one. Even more handsome than in his prime, his frailty was belied by eyes the colour of cornflowers, and a hard-won serenity.

Cork's riverside lake has an island where herons nest, and a steeply banked slope on one side which each spring has a dazzling display of daffodils, 'beside the lake, beneath the trees', like where Wordsworth saw his famous 'host of golden daffodils'. Every year when that slope had turned yellow, after weeks of anticipation, as buds hinted at what was to come, I, of course, remembered that poem as I walked the path. It is beautiful and haunting, but it also strikes me as transparent, and one-dimensional; the flowers are 'jocund company' making the poet 'gay'. Even when recalled 'in pensive mood' the response is the same: his 'heart with pleasure fills/and dances with the daffodils'. I prefer Robert Herrick's 'To Daffodils', written nearly two hundred years earlier, its then modish melancholy a contrast to Wordsworth's later untroubled romanticism. I am, perhaps, a melancholic romantic. For Herrick the daffodils, with their brief season, are a reminder of the transience of life: 'We have short time to stay as you,/We have as short a spring;/As quick a growth to meet decay as you or anything./We die/As your hours do, and dry/Away/Like to the Summer's rain.'

Daffodils not only die quickly, they do so without grace, simply withering to a papery rustle, drained of colour. Cut when in bud and arranged in a vase, their sudden, vivid bloom lifts any room, but their equally sudden decline results in an unrelieved, depressing ugliness. They are better left in the ground, where their natural decay is softened by their slower-dying leaves.

Matching my daily shock and pleasure at the moment of arriving at the sea's edge is the earlier daily re-acquaintance during summer months with the wildflower meadow, with which we have covered most of our back garden. It is a dense mini-wilderness of vetches, clovers, poppies and other plants I have yet to identify, alive with many kinds of insects and bees, with drifts of tall marguerites and even taller plumed grasses towering overall. If the seascape is my cathedral, this is my modest side-chapel or hermitage. It is a small token of support for the biodiversity threatened by climate change, while being also a sustainable source of wildflower bouquets. Its beauties will all fade and die in intermingled phases during the autumn, the ground cleared and raked to encourage next year's growth, which will start hesitantly and patchily before thundering again into its full glory. It is thus a sermon on transience, as is the ebb and flow of the tide, as powerful as any in the Bible. This morning, walking our stony beach with its percussion and swoosh of low-breaking waves, I remembered a Shakespearean sonnet I learned in my Christian Brothers school many decades ago when others now dead walked this beach and doubtless remembered these same lines. They come unbidden, and mostly accurately (I checked), a hard-won product of my often-brutal schooling.

> Like as the waves make towards the pebbl'd shore,
> So do our minutes hasten to their end.
> Each changing place with that which goes before,
> In sequent toil all forward do contend.
> Nativity, once in the main of light,
> Crawls to maturity, wherewith being crowned,
> Crooked eclipses against his glory fight
> And life that gave does now its gift confound.
> Time doth transfix the flourish set on youth
> And delves the parallels in beauties brow,
> Feeds on the rarities of nature's truth,
> And nothing stands but for his scythe to mow:
> And yet to time in hope my verse shall stand,
> Praising thy worth, despite his cruel hand.

* * *

Noting the transience of life and historic time is one of the melancholic pleasures of old age for the historian, so wonderfully captured in the writings of W.G. Sebald, in his great novel *Austerlitz* particularly, making him one of the great chroniclers – and humanists – of our age. When we had finally moved house we liberated our books from the boxes in which they had languished for six months and put them, haphazardly for now (and still!), on shelves. It was a great pleasure to look over them, to be reminded of what we had been missing. They were the chosen ones, the survivors of a painful cull of all that we had accumulated over the years, the main criterion for retention being that they were the books we were *sure* we would re-read, either for their academic or literary value or simply the pleasure of re-acquaintance. My particular contribution to our reduced collection reflected the fact that my reading tastes, like my taste in music, have tended to show a growing preference for low-key works, conversational fictions exploring ideas or memories, the great contemporary exemplars for me being Marilynne Robinson, Javier Marías, Jenny Erpenbeck, Julian Barnes, and in Ireland the often-mischievous erudition of John Banville and the powerful plainness of Colm Tóibín. However, I don't read or re-read as some kind of intellectual or autobiographical exercise. Reading fiction has been, above all, a source of pleasure, comfort and stimulation throughout my life. Beauty, empathy and intelligence in writing are great gifts, and sitting quietly with a novel, new or familiar, is a pleasure – sometimes even an excitement – that only increases with age.

Recently, for example, in our excellent Village Bookshop I bought John Banville's newly published and greatly anticipated *The Infinities*, which he has declared to be his final novel of what may be called a literary kind. I was reminded of the day nearly forty years earlier when in Dublin and, on my way to the Cork train, I called in to Hodges Figgis, the wonderful bookshop that has since crossed Dawson Street to larger premises. In my wallet was an unexpected cheque given to me the previous evening after I gave a lecture somewhere on some difficult, knotted problem, long forgotten. On impulse I bought the recently published *Kepler* by John Banville in hardback, a rare extravagance in my then very straitened circumstances. I read it – or rather, gulped it down – entranced by the language as well as its vivid portrayal of Renaissance science and the struggle of a genius to develop complex theories in the midst of a chaotic life. I finished it fifteen minutes from my destination, then immediately started again on page one, shaken. Can it really be that wonderful? Of course it is, a view confirmed by subsequent re-readings and my renewed pleasure at the richness of its language, particularly in its evocation of the physical world, light, skin, oranges in a pewter bowl. Ever since then I have bought each Banville novel as soon as it appeared and have continued to be entranced by the language and, over the more recent series of novels, by his portrayal (shot through with a mordant sense of humour) of the thoughts and feelings of the ageing male. We are close in age. He provides a challenging balance to the upbeat view of ageing in the late essays of Montaigne.

It was a surprise for me to find, as we unpacked our books, that the writer I most wanted, indeed needed, to re-engage with first was the German W.G. Sebald, though he had long been a great favourite. Why, I wondered, was it his voice (in translation) that I most wanted to hear (those are the terms in which I felt it) in the circumstances in which we found ourselves, in a new place, during a time of plague? It is a very particular voice, melancholic, dreamlike, retrospective, digressive, yet also passionately engaged. His writing combines past and present, history and autobiography, with a serendipitous curiosity. As with Montaigne, whose essays I doubt I will ever finish re-reading, I felt strongly the sense and comfort of a re-acquaintance with a wise, ever-provoking old friend, first encountered when accompanying him (in literary terms) through an East Anglian landscape (*The Rings of Saturn*, 1995), a landscape with which I was acquainted a little, as he evoked and ruminated on many layers of its recent and distant past. And so I re-read all of his books in the first weeks in our new home, in between intense bouts of emptying boxes and filling shelves, drawers and cupboards. With their haunting evocations of transience, their often-blurred focus on discovering meaning and identity and their eclectic reading of arcane texts, they fitted my own sense of introspection and helped me to settle and adjust to a seismic change in my life. It was, of course, change freely chosen, unlike that experienced in many of the lives he chronicles (*The Emigrants*, 1992; *Austerlitz*, 2001), shattered by the Second World War and its aftermath, the time into which we were both born, he later than me but right at the heart of that apocalyptic conflict, not, as I was, at the margins.

As I engage happily with my new environment, walking daily by the sea, I have enjoyed equally the pleasure of 'strolling' along my still jumbled books, lighting on one here and there, sometimes disappointed (why on earth did we keep that?), more often delighted and finding things I had forgotten. I have recently settled on re-reading another fascinating series of writings in translation, this time by the enigmatic Spanish novelist Javier Marías, in particular his trilogy (but written as one novel) *Your Face Tomorrow*. His hero/narrator Jaime Deza is a sophisticated intellectual, adrift in London after separating from his Madrid-based wife Luisa, 'so as not to be near her, when she is slowly distancing herself from me'. His remarkable gift as a 'translator or interpreter of people' leads to his recruitment by a shadowy British intelligence agency, and on one level it is a spy novel, focused not on action (though there are some graphic episodes) but on the ethics of surveillance, and thus a novel for our time. The entire work is in tune with Montaigne's ambition 'to follow a movement so wandering as that of our mind' and to describe it 'in the airy medium of words'. In an interview Marías said, echoing Montaigne, 'I don't write to gain time: I write in order to lose it, to feel it, to feel it pass.' The novel combines an inner monologue with a series of conversations as Deza tries to come to terms with ageing, his father's memories of the Spanish Civil War and those of his Oxford mentor of the Second World War, the unexplained breakup of his marriage, questions of guilt and responsibility raised by his surveillance work, his preoccupation with the precise translation of languages, and with human psychology. It is a dense work, demanding close attention, and you may ask, 'Why read through its thousand-plus pages again?' (and that despite having it in badly produced paperbacks, already falling apart, and with crammed pages of small print). One reason was the urge to renew the effort to understand better its underlying themes and arguments, but the principal pleasure was that of re-acquaintance with another mesmeric voice, sinuously layering description and reflection, effortlessly carrying the engaged reader through lengthy digressions, ultimately to new, still shadowy understandings, rather than resolutions. Reduced to its various elements it may appear conventional enough and possibly boring, rather than being, as it is for me at least, fascinating, opaque, clever and amusing. Its guiding literary spirit, perhaps, is Laurence Sterne's *The Life and Opinions of Tristram Shandy*, which Marías translated into Spanish at the beginning of his career and has declared his favourite book, by which he means *his* translation, 'my Tristram Shandy'. His early death, announced as I revised this text, was felt as a personal loss.

So, that is what matters most to me now in my reading and re-reading, the distinctive, engaging, questioning voices that I enjoy and trust, humanist voices that expand my ability to make sense of my life, of my sense of history. It is hardly accidental that so many of the novelists and poets that I most often re-read nowadays – Banville, Manley Hopkins, Eliot, Tolstoy, Sebald, Marías, Longley and Heaney – can be categorised as ageing males, who echo my preoccupations with memory and mortality.

That is also true of my most intense experience of re-reading (after Montaigne's *Essays*), that of Proust's *In Search of Lost Time*. (My fondness for Marías has a lot to do with his often-observed similarities to Proust.) In 1992, on my fiftieth birthday, I bought as my present to myself the splendid six-volume edition just published by Chatto & Windus and, as the title page puts it, 'Translated by C.K. Scott Moncrieff and Terence Kilmartin. Revised by D.J. Enright' (and thus having, as Marías might argue, a multitude of 'authors'). I already had the original Scott Moncrieff translation, here supplemented by some new or corrected material from the recent authoritative French edition. It is regarded more than ever nowadays as itself a great *English* literary masterpiece. I had occasionally looked into it, like a nervous swimmer putting a tentative toe into a cold sea. This new, much lauded edition convinced me to engage with Proust properly; I was,

I told myself, finally old enough to take it on. It turned out, of course, to be a great (if sometimes confused and confusing) pleasure, so much so that I began it again on my sixtieth and on my seventieth birthdays, each time taking longer to get through the six volumes but each time also finding new, hitherto unexplored pleasures, like its romantic sense of history or its often savage humour.

I have started it again now to mark my eightieth birthday – aware that the perennial question – will I manage to finish it? – has an added, difficult-to-ignore context this time, which has caused me to wonder why I was committing to this literary challenge again, facing over three thousand pages and two thousand characters (it helps that most of these demand little attention) and learning to negotiate once more an obsessively introverted and often unsympathetic social world. After just a few chapters the answers become clear again. The language is wonderful, so rich in its spirals of simile and metaphor, in its endless digressions, prose so unlike any other. The main characters, their stories and interactions have an endless, often repellent fascination, but also, in their essences, a deep familiarity. Above all, for me, his is the most mesmerising and enjoyable of all literary voices, and the core of the novel is not the story but access to a questioning, well-stocked mind in constant motion – as Montaigne also proposes to give us (though Proust evinced little interest in Montaigne). A favourite example of the unexpected juxtapositions that mark his ruminations on time and beauty occurs in his account of 'Madame Swann at Home'. She hands him her jacket to carry as they walk, and he is mesmerised by the care and detail of the work on the inside, not normally visible – only to switch halfway through the sentence to comparing this feature to an aspect of medieval church carvings. No other writer so often stops the reader in his tracks, forcing a re-reading, savouring a passage like this brief extract:

> In the sleeves of the jacket that lay folded across my arm I would see, and would lengthily gaze at, for my own pleasure or from affection for its wearer, some exquisite detail, a deliciously tinted strap, a lining of mauve satinette which, ordinarily concealed from every eye, was yet just as delicately fashioned as the outer parts, like those Gothic carvings on a cathedral, hidden on the inside of a balustrade eighty feet from the ground, as perfect as the bas-reliefs over the main porch ...

With Proust we are on a voyage through time, not just his own time, though that is captured brilliantly, but the nature of time itself, navigated most memorably by the illumination of that rare form of memory that is triggered by the subconscious but based above all on a conscious retrieval of memory – of a society as well as an individual. It is one of the greatest of humanist texts, an attempt to understand, above all, what it is to be human, its characters and situations far more universal than suggested by its aristocratic and bourgeois settings.

Such are some of the sources of spiritual nourishment and consolation that make the experience of old age more meaningful and enjoyable for me. Music, reading and responses to nature are among the articulations of the human which, combined with rational thought and discussion, offer more meaningful ways of being in the world, in my experience, than those prescribed by the coercive abstractions of religion, especially one that is clergy-dominated. For some, humanism may appear a catalogue of self-indulgence, especially when, as in my case, it involves the resources of a privileged life. It has long been dismissed also as so lacking in structure, rigour and clarity as to be unable to rival religion. Yet, its openness to individual experience and its emphasis on individual understanding and responsibility can demand more attention than the imposed obedience and routine observance that often distinguishes religious practice.

CHAPTER 9

Working Life

Many years ago, when faculty dean, I was asked at short notice to give a talk to a group of visiting American primary school teachers. Having nothing prepared, I began inevitably by talking about my own experience. This is my memory of what I said.

> I began teaching at primary level, and found it fascinating, but also exhausting – teaching every minute of the school day, stuck with the same class, and with no free time. So it was a relief when I switched to secondary teaching, changing classes regularly during the school day, which also had one or more free periods. But of course there were other burdens, particularly the relentless pressure of preparing for state exams. When finally I switched to university teaching I felt I had the best of all teaching jobs, with relatively few hours in the classroom and no discipline problems. Of course there were new demands, not least in devising courses and preparing lectures, resulting in much longer working weeks than I had ever experienced before. But overall, as far as teaching goes, I know that I have the easiest job and you have the most difficult.

This, of course, was rather shameless playing to the gallery, but it did also reflect my experience in teaching at all three levels, one unusual among academics.

Teaching has never lost for me its initial sense of being a vocation. When I was a very young and untrained member of a religious order, teaching in a number of its primary schools (in which, like Montaigne in his time, I frequently heard 'nothing but cries, both from tortured boys and from masters drunk with rage'), that vocation was one of *instruction*, above all in religion but also in what was generally perceived as *knowledge* at the time, primarily of facts, often reinforced by rote learning (although all teachers realise, as Montaigne put it, 'To know by heart is not to know'). Once I had been to university, had learned to think critically, and became a qualified secondary teacher, that sense of vocation changed to one of challenging students to love learning for its own sake, and to think for themselves. It was about opening rather than filling their minds, about realising potential and not enforcing conformity, about preparing for life, not just for exams. The teacher's main duty to the student, Montaigne believed, is to 'teach him to know himself'. This is – or should be – also true of university teaching, which will be my focus in what follows, having dealt with my earlier experiences in detail in Chapter 5.

At the end of John Williams' bleak masterpiece *Stoner*, the eponymous hero, an academic Stoic whose life had been a catalogue of disappointments – a failed marriage, a failed career (at least in terms of reputation), and years of bullying by a colleague – had to endure a retirement event, and at the end of insincere speeches wishing him well, felt obliged to answer.

> He got to his feet, and realised that he had nothing to say. He was silent for a long time as he looked from face to face. He heard his voice issue flatly. 'I have taught —' he said. He began again. 'I have taught at this university for nearly forty years. I do not know what I would have done had I not been a teacher. If I had not taught, I might have —' He paused, as if distracted. Then he said with finality, 'I want to thank you all for letting me teach.' He sat down.

I identify with William Stoner on a number of levels, but above all in his sense of teaching being that which most defined him as an academic and was the true measure of worth, not reputation for published work, which during the course of my career became the main criterion in the modern university (though nowadays often trumped by the ability to attract research funding and media attention).

For many years, when asked, 'What do you teach?', my automatic response has been, 'History'. But of course no-one *teaches* 'history' or indeed any other humanities subject. Some basic knowledge is of course important, but only as a basis for something else. Knowledge, as such (e.g. of facts), is better acquired by reading. What teaching can do is offer guidance on how to respond to what you read. As Montaigne advised his ideal tutor on how to educate his aristocratic student, 'Let him be taught not so much the histories as how to judge them.' Fundamentally, all you can teach or, more accurately, communicate is a number of the key understandings that you have gained as a researcher and writer. 'This subject is very important'; 'this debate is really interesting'; 'any worthwhile explanation will be complicated'; 'your interpretation is valid and valuable, once supported by the evidence'. In other words, history teachers are only as good as their ability to communicate their own passion for the subject, their commitment to objective analysis and their sense of the complexity and nuances of the sources, including their resonances in the present. In these ways they can help to develop the critical faculties of their students, their ability to think for themselves, and that is the goal.

When I was an undergraduate at University College Dublin I was influenced in particular by two contrasting lecturers. One, a low-key, intense woman, Maureen Wall, gave wonderfully coherent but dense lectures based on her ongoing research; the other, Robin Dudley Edwards, a flamboyant, celebrated man near retirement, roamed widely and serendipitously, drawing on decades of reading and reflection, often ignoring the announced topic. Both, however, communicated the same thing: that history is fascinating and difficult, and open to different interpretations. Even as first-year undergraduates we were encouraged to regard ourselves as historians too, part of their community, entitled to our opinions once backed up by evidence and argument.

I was very lucky to have been exposed to that view of what university teaching could do, and that sense of it as a collaborative enterprise. The courses I devised over the years that I thought worked best involved close reading with small groups using primary literary texts, or paintings, which could enable dialogue with students and were crucial to the research and writing I was doing at that time. For example, an undergraduate course I enjoyed particularly was based on shared readings of key novels reflecting colonial experiences – Joseph Conrad's *The Heart of Darkness*, James Joyce's *Ulysses* and Chinua Achebe's *Things Fall Apart*. In art history, likewise, I encouraged close 'reading' of eighteenth-century Irish landscape paintings in terms of colonialism and class. For many mainstream historians such texts and images were controversial as sources because they lacked the kind of empirical evidence available in the contemporary records of 'fact' that they normally used. My belief was that, read sensitively, taking account of their contexts and the literary or artistic conventions involved, they can offer valuable evidence about contemporary thought and culture. Certainly students responded to them, often to a very high standard. Some even developed research interests and later published books on the poetry, novels and art to which they were introduced in these undergraduate courses. Shared, close engagement with primary material, and the challenge of high expectations, offer the most rewarding teaching environment.

Such encouraging responses to small-group undergraduate teaching have also offered some compensation for the poor, often uncomprehending responses of many students to large, often compulsory survey courses. Many academics would admit that this kind of teaching experience could be tedious and discouraging, demanding a strong sense of commitment and some inventiveness if one is to continue to try to engage. In my early years lecturing in UCC I shared such a two-hour lecture in a BA survey course with my head of department, John A. Murphy, with him taking the first hour. As I waited outside the crowded lecture theatre to take over I would listen mesmerised to his finale, often a poem, theatrically declaimed, or the verse of a song sung with melodious exuberance. As he came out I would get a friendly 'Off you go', which also seemed to me to say, 'Match that!' and I would go in and give my carefully scripted lecture, which I was aware might appear pedestrian by comparison. My approach, confident in having a script, was to focus on my delivery, not to appear to 'lecture' in the sense of declaim or impose from above but to engage by using a conversational tone, to draw my listeners in to engage with the argument rather than push them to accept a particular answer. This was my version of 'performance' throughout my academic career.

Teaching, I had realised from early on, was a form of acting (this may also be true of aspects of the 'Good Boy' persona), and my basic training had been by a master who later had an important career in Irish theatre. As mentioned earlier, Barry Cassin, an actor then in his thirties, came most weeks to the novitiate to take us for elocution lessons. He was the only secular figure we met over the course of that intense, enclosed year, his exoticism accentuated by his colourful clothes and theatrical persona. But what impressed me above all was his use of the voice, his ability to modulate it and project it in myriad ways, all demanding attention. Montaigne had also learned this by experience, writing in his last essay on how he uses his voice:

> The tone and movement of my voice express and signify my meaning; it is for me to guide it to make myself understood. There is a voice for instructing, a voice for flattering, a voice for scolding.

And, he might have added, a voice for controlling. Once, bringing a bus full of conference attendees to the dinner I had arranged, the convivial mood was spoiled by the disruptive antics of a graduate student I knew, who had little social sense. I stood up and spoke a few mild words in a low, cold voice, very different from the expansive one I had been using all day. People strained to listen, the student apologised, but the mood in the bus became sombre. Going into the dinner an old friend said to me, 'I didn't know you could be that scary.' I smiled, and remembered my old teacher.

The problem of making crowded survey courses engaging for students is ever greater in the modern university with its very high numbers, many students pushed by our education system and parental expectations into following courses for which they have little aptitude or enthusiasm. Large classes and overloaded, over-ambitious courses alienate many students, and some barely survive, if that. Standing in front of such classes in the years before I retired, it had been hard not to feel discouraged, aware that the exams at the end would almost certainly reflect failure in my teaching more than success, the least ambitious students regurgitating garbled versions of what they half-heard at lectures. I was, I think, judged to be a 'good lecturer', well prepared and challenging, but this traditional system often left teachers as well as students drowning. On the other hand, even 'weaker' students could show real engagement and make interesting, sometimes surprising, contributions in their chosen specialised options courses. Some younger colleagues were developing different approaches in my final years of survey-course teaching, operating in a seminar rather than lecture format and using the new technology – all very exciting and progressive, but too great a challenge for me at that stage. I was stuck on 'talk and chalk'.

The odd circumstances of my early life meant that I started teaching before I was eighteen; I stopped fifty-two years later. When I took early retirement from the university aged sixty-one I continued teaching part-time, offering a final-year degree course in my new research area of art history. When I finally gave that up at seventy I suffered real anxiety that I would find it very difficult to stop, having for so long identified myself as being, above all, a teacher. But I found instead that there was relief rather than trauma or regret. I told concerned friends, 'No, I was glad to stop. I'd got bored listening to myself,' and there was some truth in that. I knew that on a good day I could still do it well – helped by the fact that each of my lectures was now built around a PowerPoint presentation with slides of paintings to engage the interest, even if the words failed to do so. Acting requires a lot of energy, and while Barry Cassin was to keep working into his ninetieth year, in his final decades he was mainly a director. I too ran out of steam and was glad finally to stop and focus on research and writing, while still enjoying the chance to tread the boards now and again giving the occasional invited lecture, still in thespian mode.

* * *

Before looking at my research and writing, and their relationship to my teaching, it may be helpful to explain how I see the nature of history as an academic discipline, and the role of the historian. On the face of it, he/she has an impossible task. The past is, in absolute terms, irrecoverable and thus unknowable. Even the best-documented event can be described or analysed only partially, and many key events have little contemporary documentation. That for the bloody battle for New Ross in 1798, I pointed out in *Rebellions*, would fit into one of the shoe-boxes in my parents' shop. Sometimes, watching a documentary on an archaeological dig, I find myself smiling as large hypotheses are proposed on the basis of small remnants of surviving material. But then, I remind myself, all historians have to hazard an explanation of an event or even a society on the basis of incomplete data. Even when there is extensive documentation, assessments of its biases and randomness raise further questions that admit of no complete answers. Finally, the personal perspectives and values of the historian, and the slippery nature of language itself, all raise yet more obstacles to understanding 'what happened'. Every generalisation is problematic and involves forcing recalcitrant material into neat formulations. As Montaigne pointed out in his praise of Tacitus and his preference for trying to understand the private motivations of important individuals rather than the actions of the state, 'All judgements in gross are loose and imperfect.' My focus on non-standard contemporary evidence, such as literature and art, was an attempt to expand our historical understanding beyond that based on official records and other narrative accounts.

The task of the historian is to research and evaluate all available sources for the subject in question and, grounded in them, to give an opinion as to what happened and what motivated the historical actors involved. The key word is 'opinion'. While there are, of course, verifiable facts, there are no truths in historical explanation, only hypotheses, more or less informed, some commanding widespread approval through the range and deployment of the evidence on which they are built. Usually too, each hypothesis is shaped by knowledge of others already in existence; it joins in a debate, and once published may help to advance that debate further, depending on the judgement of fellow practitioners about the quality of the research and analysis. Over time, all such hypotheses are fated to be eroded, many even obliterated by the blizzard of new research and analysis, based on more extensive records, or new emphases or forms of understanding. History-writing, like the computer on which I am writing this, has a built-in obsolescence. Over a lifetime of publishing most of us become familiar with the pattern, reminiscent of Lewis Carroll's disappearing Cheshire cat, whereby something we published is noted and debated in the texts of colleagues for a decade or more but then gets relegated to the footnotes of the next generation and to the bibliographies of the one following, before disappearing altogether, leaving only a dim memory, like the smile on Carroll's cat, possibly to be followed up by researchers of the future. Historians ought to be humble about their opinions and tentative in asserting them, but of course we tend not to be, having invested so much in them and having been trained to argue for them.

What can also make historians over-assertive is a belief that the analysis being put forward about the past has relevance to some passionately held opinion about the present nature of their society. This may be true particularly of writing history of and for divided communities, like those of the island of Ireland. While it may be at odds with a strict view of their professional training, Irish historians, like those of Poland or India for example, can feel the need to also contribute to contemporary debate, rarely directly but by challenging the myths on all sides that contribute to division and violence and by demonstrating the complexities revealed in contemporary sources. But then, all history-writing is inescapably political and opinionated, no matter how much historians strive for neutrality. This has certainly been true of my work, which has clearly been shaped by my background and my experience of my time and place, as well as by the surviving evidence for whatever topic I was researching and the current state of the debate about it. My short study of the ideology of Wolf Tone, for example, published in 1984, was based on an outline analysis of his writings, which I believe has stood the test of time, but its opening chapter also connected his legacy with 'reminders of contemporary tragedy and horror', clearly referring to events in Northern Ireland. So, I cannot follow Montaigne, who lived and had an active political role at the interface of a long and vicious religious civil war, when he wrote, perhaps tongue in cheek, of his surprise 'at what little cost to the repose and tranquillity of my life I have passed more than half of it amid the ruin of my country'. I found the cost – but also the opportunities and obligations – of such a situation to be considerable.

* * *

What historians choose to research and how they publish their findings could be a study in itself. Early research topics often come from PhD supervisors, and many scholars are so taken with that area and the questions it raises that they stay with it throughout their careers. Others come to lose interest in their early research, or even to dislike it intensely, and develop new interests, inspired perhaps by a particular book, or intrigued by a new controversy, or tempted by an enterprising commissioning editor. Having acquired the taste for change, many will continue doing so, and in the process may make important connections between their various interests. I have belonged to the second category, but from a particular combination of interests and influences my choices could be considered marginal and even a little eccentric, at least in terms of mainstream Irish historical scholarship. My chosen research areas over a lifetime were poetry in Irish from the seventeenth to the nineteenth centuries, Irish fiction from 1800 to 1850, the 1798 Rebellion, and Irish art from 1750 to 1850. There were interesting connections to be made between them, the most important for me being the Irish experience of colonialism, for most of that time a deeply unfashionable topic. The marginality of what I published was accentuated by the fact that it was mainly in article or essay form and in academic journals or conference volumes – the kinds of publication that one study suggested had an average readership of less than ten for each article! As it turned out, I was more comfortable with what is essentially the essay form, rather than in attempting large over-arching narratives or extensive, sustained analysis. Those published essays, like the lectures that foreshadowed them, have tended to be provocative pieces, designed to stimulate a response and to have interdisciplinary appeal. But why did I make the choices, and take the approaches that I did?

Some of the background factors involved have already been touched on. Being born beside the ruins of a Norman tower house, spending my early life in a house built just before the 1798 Rebellion and in what was originally a Norman town that was long bilingual (for centuries even trilingual), having a mother immersed in family lore and being aware of significant historical ancestors, having an intensely nationalist education in the local Christian Brothers school, made even more intense by the seven years I spent in that order, where I also developed a sense of vocation about teaching that was to last for fifty years and strongly influence my work as a historian – all of these influences certainly played into my academic work, though mostly in ways impossible to describe adequately or to quantify.

My university education, and the political environments in which it happened, reveal more tangible influences. The fact that I did my undergraduate degree in history in University College Dublin, and at the time of the fiftieth anniversary of the 1916 Rising, influenced my choices and attitudes more than anything else. My teachers were strong advocates of the German model of empirical research, established by the generation of Irish historians that came to the fore in the new Irish state in the 1930s. Based on principles of 'scientific' history, that approach challenged the nationalist mythologising of the Irish past. The fiftieth anniversary of the 1916 Rising offered an important opportunity to a number of my teachers to carry that challenge further. In a series of key articles (based on ideas initially developed in undergraduate lectures) they undermined the heroic nationalist narrative that had developed about the rising and had become the founding myth of the state. In particular, the belief that the rising was a popular revolt by the 'nation' was shown to have little basis, and instead to have been a coup, stage-managed by a very small, unrepresentative group, the 'military council' of a secret organisation. They had no democratic mandate but arrogated to themselves the leadership of the virtual 'Irish Republic' and with it the right to inflict mass violence on their community. I was a second-year undergraduate in 1966 and was profoundly affected both by the crude nationalism of the official commemoration and by the startling new arguments of these historians, particularly Maureen Wall and Kevin B. Nowlan (both traditional moderate nationalists). It is hard, after decades of so much innovative historical research, to recapture the sense of how radical and liberating their revelations seemed to us then. Outside the university, however, an extreme version of traditional nationalism soon gained a significant impetus from the eruption in Northern Ireland of what became known euphemistically as 'the Troubles', and this became the background to my teaching of history in a secondary school in Cork.

In Cork also my academic training entered a whole new phase, from doing an MA (part-time), supervised by Oliver MacDonagh, an Irish historian but a British history specialist with a major international reputation and great range and sophistication. He suggested that I write my thesis on the political ideology of the great Liberal prime minister W.E. Gladstone and he afterwards encouraged me to go on to do a PhD. Initially the plan had been that I would go to Yale, where Oliver had recently been a visiting professor and been very impressed by the development of interdisciplinary approaches to historical research, especially in combination with literary studies, in which he had a particular interest. With Oliver's support I was offered a place in Yale but eventually turned it down, mainly because the American PhD system meant beginning with several years of intensive coursework before I could even begin a thesis. At thirty I felt I couldn't afford such a leisurely pace, and, besides, I had already done a major thesis for my MA.

So I went to Cambridge instead, attracted by the contrasting great freedom and informality of its approach to doing a doctorate. But I still aspired to using Yale-style interdisciplinary approaches, only to find that the Cambridge history faculty wasn't quite ready for that, being at the time dominated by an ethos of historical research that proved antithetical in general to my interests. My topic (expanding on my MA thesis), focused on an analysis of the debates on the 1886 Irish Home Rule Bill in Westminster in terms of conflicting views of empire. Unfortunately this clashed with the new orthodoxy, which downplayed the importance of ideology, insisting that all domestic political developments, and the relationships with subordinate peoples in the empire, could be explained almost completely in terms of pragmatic transactions among and between elites. Ideas, the new orthodoxy asserted, were simply tools used as weapons in such practical politics; no-one believed in them. My genial PhD supervisor, Jack Gallagher, a major figure in this movement, was critical of any general use of 'imperialism' and came close to proposing that there was, in fact, no such thing as a 'British Empire'. (When he rejected a draft chapter I showed him on English nationalism as the core of British imperialism, it was on the grounds that neither term was meaningful. Had he lived to witness the debate over Brexit he might have changed his mind.)

In the end my PhD thesis, in arguing for the importance of complex imperialist ideologies on both sides of the home rule debate, was in large part a critique of this anti-ideology approach, often called 'high politics'. Ironically, this historical orthodoxy itself contributed significantly to a new ultra-Tory ideology that influenced Thatcher. Rather as Keats portrayed the Biblical figure of Ruth, 'in tears amid the alien corn', I soon fell out of love with my research and with British history and finished the thesis rather grimly and pragmatically; I never tried to publish it. In particular, I was unhappy with the limited range of source material and interpretation I was allowed to use – the use of literary stereotypes, for example, or a comparison between attitudes to Irish and Indian nationalism were vetoed as 'not really history' by the History Faculty Board – or so Gallagher told me, perhaps mischievously. Instead, having joined a Department of Irish History I moved to working on Gaelic poetry and lost sight of the fact that my Cambridge experience was significant in my later commitment to using non-standard sources and in my focus on Irish history as being, above all, colonial. But the Cambridge orthodoxy about empire became influential in writings on Irish history also, for example those on the colonial 'plantations' in sixteenth- and seventeenth-century Ireland, which some new studies robbed of ideological meaning and reduced largely to the pattern of population movements and business transactions. (That would have been impossible if the Gaelic poetry of the period was considered.) It can also be seen in the ways in which the use of 'colonial' to refer to the admittedly unusual case of Ireland in the following centuries was frowned on. The Cambridge view of interdisciplinary approaches to historical research was also to be the norm among Irish historians up to relatively recently. And so the battles I had begun in Cambridge were to continue throughout my career.

As had been the case after my BA, I was eager to get back to teaching, little anticipating in the beginning that the main driver and shaper of my future research and writing would be my teaching rather than my PhD, especially in developing courses for specialist undergraduate seminars. I based these on sources that I could explore with the students, and these became, in turn, the focus of further research, and ultimately writing – which in turn fed into further development of the courses. This is rather too neat a formulation for a process that came to reflect both teaching and research impulses in an interactive, ongoing relationship – a process common among academics, of course. What was unusual in my case was that in my teaching I moved away completely from my PhD work, and less because I had become disillusioned by it than because of the nature of my initial academic appointment.

When I applied for lectureships in University College Cork I was deemed appointable for one in the Modern History Department and another in Irish History. Because I could also offer a course in a new interdisciplinary programme through Irish I ended up in the latter, and that changed the trajectory of my academic work completely. In Modern (notionally non-Irish) History I would have lectured and published in the area of my PhD; instead, under pressure to develop a course through Irish quickly, I turned to the political poetry of the seventeenth century, which had long been an interest. It also offered the possibility of working through a series of texts with the students, using easily available scholarly editions, with translations. This course was then the basis of my first publication, an article in *Studia Hibernica* (1980), 'The Gaelic Response to Conquest and Colonisation: The evidence of the poetry'. This was a short, broad and rather brash survey, deemed useful by the editor, I imagine, as the first of its kind, and based, as I pointed out, entirely on edited versions of the poems published over previous decades and hence relatively superficial in terms of understanding the original manuscript sources. My modest disclaimer did not save me from the ire of some Gaelic scholars over many years. However, the first and most devastating critique came from my then graduate student Michelle O Riordan. When I read it first, in a draft chapter for her thesis, I could only applaud. Since then, over some one thousand pages she has developed with ever-broadening, interdisciplinary scholarly sophistication a rich, complex reading of the material that I had sketched in twenty-two pages, in an article that, Cheshire Cat-like, still has a presence in her bibliography. I have thought this story worth rehearsing, not in order to claim spurious credit for her scholarship but as an example of scholarly interaction, part of the process by which history gets written and transformed. It also illustrates the synergy between teaching, research and writing that has marked much of whatever contribution I have made.

I published a number of other articles on the politics of Gaelic poetry in rather obscure places. A feature, perhaps only visible to myself, that now strikes me about them all is that I identified strongly with the material on a personal level. I remember the emotion in my own voice when delivering a paper in Edinburgh on 'Voices of the Vanquished: Echoes of language loss in Gaelic poetry from Kinsale to the Great Famine', later published in the first issue of the *Journal of Scottish and Irish Studies* in 2007. I included a large number of quotations from the original poems and was deeply affected by their poignancy. I thought of collecting this series of essays in a short book, but in the end didn't have the confidence to do so given the notorious negativity of much Irish-language scholarship, already experienced in the response to the *Studia Hibernica* article. Of course the standard of these essays was not such as would be expected in a specialist Celticist publication, but they had worthwhile arguments to make, and not only for historians. Perhaps I should revisit the idea.

My lack of confidence in this regard may be more widely shared, given the continued resistance of most historians of the early modern and modern periods to using Irish-language sources. There have been some encouraging recent exceptions, but most works on this period are still written with little if any reference to Irish-language sources, and especially to the complex development of a bilingual society over several centuries which was central to Irish cultural development. The wider context of my experience of bilingualism is dealt with in the next chapter.

My location in the Irish History Department also resulted in my developing in parallel a seminar course on the early nineteenth-century novel, covering Maria Edgeworth, Lady Morgan, Charles Robert Maturin, John and Michael Banim and William Carleton. Edgeworth's *Castle Rackrent*, a remarkably dense, complex and comic short novel, had long been a favourite, and when I used it in teaching for over a decade I found something new to explore every time. The much longer (often three-volume) novels by the other writers I used proved also to be rich and challenging as historical as well as literary sources. The acquisition by the UCC Library of a new American series of facsimiles of nineteenth-century Irish novels made the development of the course feasible. I enjoyed enormously working through these texts with students, and many of them got a lot out of it also, some going on to publish significantly in the area.

Once again I published a series of articles in hard-to-find places, for example on landlordism in Edgeworth, on bilingualism and Catholic middle-class insecurity in the Banims, on representations of language, history and O'Connellite politics in Morgan. Again, I considered using these essays as the basis of a book, and this time had made considerable progress when I abandoned it. Why? In part it was because I became discouraged. My text had grown gargantuan, over-ambitious and convoluted; it bored me, and I came to imagine that it would also bore readers – certainly historians, and also literary scholars, though for different reasons. Some years earlier I had published a survey and ideas piece on Irish Romanticism (not unlike the first essay on Gaelic poetry) which was being widely cited at this time (helped by the fact that it was included in a Cambridge University Press volume). The essay form had far more appeal to me and seemed more effective in communicating ideas.

I had also grown dubious about using literary theory, now increasingly esoteric and anti-historical. Years earlier I had prefaced a conference volume I edited (*The Writer as Witness: Literature as historical evidence*, 1987) with 'A Polemical Introduction: Literature, literary theory and the historian'. It urged my fellow practitioners to engage with new developments in literary studies; it was politely (and understandably) ignored by most of them and used as a stick to beat me with by others. I learned a great deal from literary theory, which I still find useful, but in terms of promoting my views on Irish colonial history it had become a blind alley.

Some of the same resistance emerged in relation to the new approaches to colonialism that had featured in all of my writings on literature. My use and understanding of colonialism in the Irish case is very different from the nationalist view. My research, in both Irish- and English-language sources, had revealed it to be not simply a matter of 'conquest and colonisation', of brute force and heroic resistance, but a multi-faceted process of interaction over centuries that produced – as well as conflict and polarisation – a hybrid and, for a long period, bilingual culture. My interest in approaching colonialism in this way was also influenced by international scholarship, particularly that of Frantz Fanon, Edward Said, Ashis Nandy and the work of Indian historians connected to the *Subaltern Studies* journal. Irish historians generally have tended to regard such 'post-colonial studies' as not sufficiently empirical, or simply as a focus for theoretical excess, but at its best this multi-disciplinary approach offers insights that can enrich our understanding of Irish experience.

By now I had also become involved in what became known as the 'revisionist' debate. When my generation had come on the scene as academics, the spurious claims made by and about the 1916 leaders had been taken over not just in a fudged manner by the state but explicitly by a terrorist organisation, the Provisional IRA, pursuing what was in large part a murderous civil war, again in the name of the virtual 'Republic'. Given its own valorisation of the traditional view of 1916, this was a claim that the Irish state found difficult to challenge. It was left instead to historians and some cultural and political commentators to continue to revisit the sources and reveal, in ever more detail, what the complex realities of the Irish Revolution (as it is now popularly and inaccurately called) and its historical hinterland had been. For some nationalist scholars and politicians, such research and writing involved a betrayal (some of my early essays were cited in those terms) and they labelled the historians involved as 'revisionists', a term which I, like most of my colleagues, regarded initially as meaningless; revising current historical understanding in the light of new evidence and perspectives is, after all, the basic job of every historian. But I ultimately came to accept, even to 'own' the term for a while, as standing for an important scholarly project and a challenge to a compromised establishment view. While I was in the 'revisionist' mainstream early on with the very short book on the ideology of Wolfe Tone (arguing that he was neither a nationalist nor a radical in the modern senses of those words but a 'colonial outsider'), my challenges to nationalist orthodoxy were largely oblique, arising from studies of literature and art.

'Revisionism' ultimately became a cliché and a thinly veiled term of abuse, even among some historians who for a short time called themselves 'post-revisionist' – that is, more enlightened, more positive about nationalism. The 'revisionism' debate, conducted initially in *The Irish Review* when I was an editor of that interdisciplinary journal, produced some valuable re-evaluations of attitudes to the Irish past but it had little impact ultimately on Irish history-writing. Few historians advocated even a modified revival of nationalist interpretation, and anti-revisionism was essentially a fashionable, short-lived cultural trend promoted by an influential literary and media coterie led by the Field Day movement. Our understanding of Irish history did change radically in the decades following, but this owed little either to Field Day or to critiques of nationalism like mine. Instead, the opening up of major new areas of research, especially women's history (greatly expanded by my former graduate student Maria Luddy) and local history (led by the History Department in Maynooth), transformed the profession. This change is particularly clear in the way the past came to be commemorated, especially in the 'Decade of Commemorations' programme covering the period immediately prior to the 1916 Rising and its aftermath.

My third major research focus was also a product of particular circumstances (as was the case with my final area of research – art history, covered below in Chapter 11). I had no intention of getting involved with anything connected to the bicentenary of the 1798 Rebellion, until my seriously ill mother, who took a great interest in it, suggested that I might write something on her great-great-grandfather, killed (according to family tradition) in heroic circumstances by the military at the battle for New Ross. I was happy to promise to do a small article, perhaps for the *Journal of the Wexford Historical Society*, but some years later I ended up instead publishing a book, a substantial volume, *Rebellions: Memoir, memory and 1798*. It is not a conventional monograph but is experimental in form and writing. The first of three parts is a memoir of my background and life ('here is the historian'), the second is an analysis of previous interpretations of the 1798 Rebellion, especially that of the government-sponsored bicentenary ('here is his view of the debate he is joining') and the third a detailed micro-history of the battle for my home town, New Ross, on a key day of the rebellion, 5 June 1798 ('here is his version'). Writing it posed interesting challenges (it also put me in the eye of the 'revisionism' storm), and the response of readers (considered in an added section in the second edition), the great majority of them non-academics, has encouraged me in this new attempt at memoir-writing and reflection.

Academic historians, on the other hand, tended not to engage with the book, indeed to ignore it, perhaps because it breached too many traditional scholarly conventions and was *too* 'revisionist'. Most important, perhaps, was a view that the severity of my critique of some fellow historians for their contributions to the official bicentenary of 1798 had breached some unwritten code in relation to academic debate, despite a tradition of robust disagreement in the profession. More simply, colleagues may not have wanted to take sides. Although it became clear over time that most of them agreed with my analysis (which, remarkably, has never been challenged seriously during the intervening twenty years), virtually no-one was prepared to say so publicly, despite heavy attacks on me in the media.

Catriona Crowe's thoughtful review of *Rebellions* saw it as the work of an 'increasingly beleaguered' or 'embattled' historian. For her, this extended beyond my isolation during the bicentenary year (which had been very evident), and she sees in the memoir element a man 'who moves through his life at an angle to things, solitary, interrogative, often doubtful, sometimes enthusiastic'. Coming back to memoir-writing now, twenty years later, I recognise this description more than I did initially. In the intervening time I have tended to become ever more withdrawn from the community of historians, less deliberately than through a succession of events – mainly my early retirement from full-time teaching, which coincided with a move to a different research area, art history; our relocation to a small seaside town, which removed me from a university environment; and finally, the intensification of seclusion for us all due to the pandemic. I have not been unhappy with my somewhat solitary academic state; indeed, it seems to suit me. It is tempting also, in terms of this new attempt at memoir, to see my commitment to pushing out the boundaries in relation to sources and approaches in research, and my tendency to energetic debate in print, as, in part, a rebellion against the conformity and orthodoxy of my upbringing. Clearly, as a historian at least, I came to be regarded by some as not quite a team player, not an academic 'Good Boy'. If that is the case it can perhaps be seen as part of the long and necessary process of freeing myself from an emotional legacy that has done me much damage.

I documented in *Rebellions* how the bicentenary of the 1798 Rebellion was hijacked to support the political agenda of the Irish government in relation to the peace process in Northern Ireland, and thus its very bloody and sectarian nature downplayed. Any apprehension I had that this might be repeated in the new 'Decade of Centenaries' (from 2012) was quickly dispelled, however. A very different approach was taken by the state, which appointed a large, representative panel of historians, the Expert Advisory Group on Centenary Celebrations, under an experienced and knowledgeable chair. This has shown itself to be committed to taking account of all traditions, groups and areas – developing a complex, cumulative and, as it turned out, massively 'revisionist' narrative (exemplified in the best-selling

Atlas of the Irish Revolution) that has gained almost universal approval. In its 'Initial Statement' the Advisory Group laid down as a basic principle what I think can fairly be read as a tacit acknowledgement of the mistakes of the 1798 bicentenary as I had represented them.

> Commemoration should not ignore differences and divisions. The goal of inclusiveness is best achieved, not by trying for an enforced common interest or universal participation in commemorations ... Whatever the challenges that may arise in developing commemorative arrangements, there should be no attempt to contrive a historical or retrospective consensus about the contemporary impact and legacy of divisive events.

The remarkable flood of scholarly publications associated with the Decade of Centenaries, with local studies and the experiences of women to the fore, may have vindicated the so-called 'revisionist' enterprise and underlined the fact that it was always the mainstream, but it is undoubtedly true that the appeal of the old heroic mythologies remains strong in popular consciousness, as academics marking exams by the less-engaged history undergraduates often ruefully attest. Looking over the tables laden with new academic centenary histories in a Dublin bookshop, I was struck by the inclusion of old-fashioned popular 'histories' on a table nearby with their traditional parade of 'martyrs' and binary stories of English perfidy and Irish virtue. There will always be a market for such pieties, particularly as the most vocal of the self-proclaimed heirs of the 1916 leaders, the Sinn Féin party, moves inexorably to power, with the support mainly of young voters who have no memory of the 'Troubles' and little sense of Sinn Féin's philosophy of 'armed struggle'. There is still a long way to go.

Thus, as a historian I have been, above all, a teacher, whether of students or the history-reading public (*Rebellions* sold very well, and finally gained me a substantial audience), but I have also seen myself as a writer, and as such interested in language, style and experimentation. This was a hallmark of the work of Oliver MacDonagh, my first research supervisor and a major influence, and for many years afterwards a great friend. The work on administrative history for which Oliver became – and remains – well known internationally was written in conventional form and language; only the ideas were startlingly new. For his prize-winning book of essays *States of Mind: A study of Anglo-Irish conflict, 1780–1980* (1985), he developed a very different essayist style and language, influenced strongly by his literary hero, John Henry Newman. His two-volume popular biography of Daniel O'Connell had a human, empathetic, even autobiographical quality, while his book of essays on his favourite novelist, Jane Austen, combined her distinctive, mordant style with his extensive knowledge of the period in which her novels are set, to wonderful effect. He too professed a fondness for 'the essay kind of book', which involved for him 'the sense of circling the wagons, shooting arrows from different directions, rather than a bull-headed direct assault'. He was a great scholar who also wrote for fun, and as a challenge. He was unfailingly encouraging to me, even when a little appalled, in professional terms, at my writing a memoir. Yet in his final years he was persuaded to write a series of short childhood memories which captured the exuberant enthusiasm of the boy he had been. I included them, together with autobiographical elements in some of his talks and writings, in *Looking Back: Living and writing history. Oliver MacDonagh 1924–2002* (The Lilliput Press, 2008). I miss his aerograms from faraway Australia, every inch of their flimsy paper used, regularly finishing letters by continuing all around the margins, in true Victorian fashion.

Such then has been my experience and my practice, at an angle for the most part to mainstream history-writing and sometimes at the margins. This is not to express regret or disappointment. Teaching and writing Irish history has been a privilege, a passion and a pleasure, particularly during a time when the public need for greater and more complex understanding was so important. But it has also been stressful at times and it ultimately became more adversarial than was comfortable for me. In recent decades I have withdrawn gradually from the more contentious debates and focused on researching and writing on Irish art, *c.*1760–1860, which offers fascinating new challenges and a supportive, less febrile environment (see Chapter 11). My sense of history as a vocation remains, but the urge to communicate and persuade is less powerful now. I no longer teach courses, but I continue to see research and writing as teaching by other means. I have continued asking the same basic question: 'How did Ireland's experience of colonialism shape its culture and politics?' That has been my main contribution to Irish historical research, in my view. I have only one answer to that question, repeated in one context after another: 'Colonialism in Ireland, as elsewhere, produced a complex hybrid culture, and not the binary opposition beloved of nationalism.'

Years ago I heard a story about Albert Einstein, which I hope is true, though I have failed to track down its source. Asked by an eager young researcher, 'When you get a new idea, do you write it down at once, so that you don't forget it?', the great man replied, 'You will be doing well to get even one new idea in your lifetime. When that happens, you will never forget it, but will keep repeating it.' This has certainly been true of my 'new idea' ('new' in terms of Irish history-writing at least), and I have some hope that it will finally attract more attention. Certainly, in their embrace of complexity and openness to ideas from other disciplines, some of the younger generation of Irish historians offer that hope.

* * *

Historians ultimately lose the arguments they engage in, their work rendered obsolete or absorbed in the great churn of overall debate as new evidence and new perspectives come to the fore. Far more serious is the threatened loss of the bigger battle for academic values and freedoms in our universities, which was a major focus for me during my final years in academic life. The university, whether as an ideal or specifically University College Cork or the National University of Ireland of which it is a part, has been a major part of my life as student, teacher and academic for nearly sixty years. It became, in effect, my new community after I left the Christian Brothers, and much of my life has been spent arguing for the principles that have long been held to define it. Whether at departmental, faculty, university or national university level, I have opposed policies that have seemed to me to be authoritarian, that is, going against the spirit of community that should be at the core of academic life, but was coming increasingly under threat in the decade before my retirement.

The fundamental principles which defined my professional life were articulated most memorably by John Henry Newman in *The Idea of a University* in the late nineteenth century, and it remained the classic defence of academic values against the swelling tide of utilitarianism for my generation. It was a set text when I studied English as a first-year undergraduate at UCD. While I soon forgot the detail of Newman's argument, its basic message had strongly informed my undergraduate experience and has continued to resonate. Newman believed that a 'liberal education' should be the distinguishing feature of a university, its core value being the proposition that 'knowledge is capable of being its own end'. Such an education was a training of the mind to produce 'a philosophical habit' in relation both to learning and to life. The contemporary enemy for Newman was the seemingly all-powerful 'philosophy of utility', according to which the university's role would be the provision of 'professional' training, its focus 'instruction' rather than 'education', its 'knowledge' applied to specific practical ends.

Newman's viewpoint may appear to many nowadays to be a very idealistic, even romantic one, but it held sway for over a hundred years and met with serious challenge in Britain and Ireland only with the expansion of the global economy and the associated massive growth of universities towards the end of the twentieth century, when the feared 'philosophy of utility' finally came to dominate university life and culture. It is often categorised as 'the managerialist revolution', by which business models replaced the academic, as governments insisted that the economic value of the university to society should be the priority while at the same time cutting their financial contribution to university budgets and demanding radically increased student intake. Over time universities have been forced inexorably to fund themselves more, to view their undergraduate students as customers, their postgraduates and junior staff either as generators of research funding or cheap labour as undergraduate teachers. Staffing in non-academic administrative areas increased dramatically, while academic posts declined relative to student numbers. Decision-making became top-down; consultation, while still often emphasised, became token; appointments and promotions were determined increasingly by administrators and based on a record of fundraising more than by proof of academic ability.

In the frantic efforts to replace public funding with self-generated income, the modern university is driven to monetise everything, including learning and reputation, even in the humanities. Recently, strolling around my *alma mater*, University College Dublin, in its current suburban, business-oriented manifestation, so different from the crowded city-centre buildings of my undergraduate experience, I was struck by the insistent reiteration, on buildings, on colourful publicity hoardings and in the bookshop, of the spurious claim that James Joyce was un undergraduate at UCD from 1898 to 1902. As is well known, and documented in its official history, UCD was founded in 1908, six years after Joyce graduated from University College, then part of the Royal University. 'The Royal' was a university only in name, being the examining (and partly funding) body set up by government in 1879 to serve the old Queen's Colleges, and the Catholic University, founded by Cardinal Newman, later re-named University College. This was the university that Joyce attended, staffed mainly by Jesuit priests and wonderfully described in *A Portrait of the Artist as a Young Man*. It became University College Dublin (and a significantly different institution) as part of the new federal National University of

Ireland in 1908. So a more complex story then, but one hardly beyond the wit of a university to tell simply: 'James Joyce was a graduate of University College, formerly the Catholic University founded by Newman and later part of University College Dublin.' The connection with Joyce is real and important but should not be based on a deliberate historical inaccuracy by a great university, as UCD is.

The 1997 Universities Act further transformed the Irish universities on the utilitarian lines that were anathema to Newman but were already the basis of new third-level institutions. I was one of the few senior staff at my university who attempted, without success, in the years immediately before my retirement to modify the radical effect of that revolution on academic culture and structures. Most professors decided to keep their heads down and focus on safeguarding their own fiefdoms (I was not a department head and could hazard more). At the same time I was involved in related battles in the Senate of the National University of Ireland and published my account of them in the NUI centenary volume that I also edited. These battles may be of little interest now to the reading public, and in any case they were lost and the university as I knew it was utterly changed, perhaps forever. Already, the majority of current academic staff have never known a university based on a true sense of a community of scholarship, ruled by consensus and academic values, and so they don't miss it. But for those of us who were lucky enough to experience it, that traditional university, despite its inequalities and conservatism, can now seem a lost golden age. That sentiment can only warrant a pitying smile as an old man's lament to the promoters and supporters of our brave new world. The old system – hierarchical, dominated by overwhelmingly male professors, resistant to interdisciplinary developments – certainly needed major reform, but this was already well under way even when I joined the academic staff at UCC. Admittedly it was happening unevenly across the system, and some professors continued to run their departments in traditional dictatorial fashion and to act like feudal lords on university bodies. As departmental structures changed, I experienced some aspects of both old and new, but was lucky, even as the most junior member of my initial department, to be involved in decisions about staffing and course changes; I was put on faculty committees and felt a valued part of the academic community. Years later I was persuaded to take on successive terms as faculty dean, largely in order to be involved in the accelerating process of reform in the university. In my final years, just before the full extent of the utilitarian revolution was made manifest in the '97 Act, UCC academics, after a long process of consultation and debate, produced a major reform programme. It was utterly different in spirit to that soon to be imposed from the top as government policy, in which the whole system of consultation with academic staff was bypassed, its structures retained as window-dressing only. As outlined earlier, the university is now, essentially, a business, its values utilitarian rather than academic. Presidents are appointed to be chief executive officers, operating through a new layer of middle management, who make the key decisions about funding, curriculum development and staffing.

This account would, no doubt, be challenged by contemporary university hierarchies, but for many of my generation it would be difficult to exaggerate the scale of the transformation and loss that has occurred in universities in the past decades, and all too easy to be pessimistic about their future. However, universities have adapted to radical challenges and changes over centuries and found new ways to articulate academic values – and preserve their autonomy. They can, hopefully, do so again, when the limitations of the new utilitarian model and its narrowly conceived academic programmes become clearer. But those who believe in traditional academic values can – and should – also fight for them now, and especially for the humanities, under threat worldwide, which most exemplify and depend on them. While the process of radical change cannot be reversed in any foreseeable future, it might be modified by restoring to the foreground some of the core principles now threatened by total loss – and by arguing for them not only by quoting Newman but by appealing to the utilitarian, economic value of degrees in the humanities. This is not a new idea. Thirty years ago deans of arts faculties (including myself), in seeking to defend our already embattled degree programmes, ran publicity campaigns pointing, for example, to the fact that of the chief executive officers in the top one hundred companies in the United States at the time, far more had a degree in classics than had a master's in business administration; that the critical, analytical skills learned by humanities students were crucial in business, and adaptable to the rapidly changing business environment in ways that degrees designed to serve current technologies and business practices were not. It is a case that should be made again, but more forcefully and professionally.

Likewise, scientists, many of whom are frustrated by the dominance now of applied research, could do more to show the proven economic value of 'blue sky' or primary independent research. More broadly, universities can and should make the case that their academic independence would result in an enhanced economic contribution to the state. Politicians and business leaders have shown little understanding of the traditional strengths and full potential of universities, and universities in turn haven't done enough to educate them, in part because universities' own leadership nowadays comes increasingly from business-inflected backgrounds, and they feel that they benefit from the top-down rather than the communal model. A crucial, and as yet unacknowledged, challenge for university 'leadership teams', as they are now called, is to re-learn the strengths of the former ethos and systems only recently abandoned and to fight for the re-instatement of academic freedom, of knowledge for its own sake as the best basis for applied knowledge, and of the university as, above all else, a community of scholars.

CHAPTER 10

Language and Identity

'Irish Catholic nationalist' seemed a simple, unproblematic identity when I was a child. As a young adult, however, as detailed elsewhere, I rejected the concept of 'nation' as a romantic construct used to enable power and justify the unleashing of death and destruction; Catholicism I also came to regard as more about abusive power than spirituality, and thus both key aspects of my early sense of identity collapsed. This process involved for me a sense of liberation. Like Joyce's hero in *A Portrait of the Artist*, and doubtless just as pompously, I had freed my 'soul' from the 'nets flung at it to hold it back from flight ... nationality, language religion' – only in my case not from 'language', which remained for me a powerful but complicated source of identity.

I also, in time, came to reject simplistic appeals to 'the Irish people', not least when tossed about as if a self-evident descriptor by some historian colleagues. Like fellow county man Colm Tóibín, I came to realise that I don't really understand what it means to identify even with 'Wexford people' – only knowing, like him, the people of my home town, and then only in a historical, nostalgic sense rather than the modern, multi-ethnic reality, a place where I know virtually no-one.

What has it meant for me, then, to be 'Irish'? When I was a postgraduate student in Cambridge in the early 1970s I was a regular attender at the informal seminar on British history, held in the hospitable rooms of George Kitson Clark, a leading expert on my research area. Immensely affable, Kitson was in the habit of asking one or two of those who had spoken after the paper to stay back at the end for a whiskey. He had the vaguely patronising fondness for Irish people then very common in Cambridge, despite the 'Troubles' in Northern Ireland. On the second of these occasions he murmured thoughtfully, as he re-filled my glass, 'Not very Irish, are you?' – citing, as an example of what he meant, several colourful as well as articulate students who had made a mark in the seminar in previous years. The implication clearly was that I seemed to him more 'English' than 'Irish'. Feeling obliged to protest the genuineness of my Irishness, I pointed out, by way of possible explanation, that I came from the area where the

Normans landed in the twelfth century. 'Ah,' he said, 'that could be it.' This has stayed with me as a subtle articulation of the English stereotype of Irish natives, ubiquitous since the Norman period and that can be summed up ironically as 'Oirish', the enduring popularity of which can be seen in recent years in the number-one BBC comedy series *Mrs Brown's Boys* and, more subversively (perhaps), in some of the plays of Martin McDonagh.

The most radical effect of colonialism on Ireland was linguistic – the slow replacement, over centuries, of Irish with English, involving several phases of bilingualism when both languages were used at the same time, strongly influencing one another. That change involved various and often important elements of linguistic insecurity, famously articulated by Shakespeare in the angry outburst by the Irish Captain Macmorris in *Henry V* (1599), beginning 'What ish my nation?' He was rejecting the stereotype of the Irish as not only wild and ignorant, but also disloyal to their English, Scots and Welsh allies in the faltering war against the Gaelic Irish. The allies were all described as 'nations', still used in the Latin meaning of a race or tribe of people who share a common origin and speak the same language. But Captain Macmorris, an Elizabethan soldier of Ango-Norman origins but part Gaelicised, had a linguistically mixed background and was likely be insecure in his own identity, especially when in England, and hence, perhaps, the incoherent anger of his short speech. Shakespeare rapidly moved on to other things as the Irish wars faded as a public concern, and he never tried to answer Macmorris' question.

Indeed, when Seamus Heaney took it up nearly three hundred years later in the poem 'Traditions', as part of an exploration of the linguistic element in English colonialism in Ireland, he too avoided an answer to 'What ish my nation?', beyond quoting Leopold Bloom in James Joyce's *Ulysses* who, after suffering racial abuse for his Jewish background from an ultra-cultural nationalist, answers the question, 'But do you know what a nation means?' with 'A nation is the same people living in the same place ... Or also living in different places.' Asked by his chief nationalist tormenter, 'And what is your nation if I may ask?', his response is, 'Ireland ... I was born here, Ireland', before going on to reject 'Force, hatred, history, all that'.

Bloom is attempting a new, pragmatic meaning of 'nation' based on the happenstance of place, and away from the version of the traditional markers of race and language, accepted by Macmorris and now represented by 'The Citizen'. Bloom's is a radical rejection of the stereotype, and now, a century later, one perhaps even more appropriate given Ireland's multi-ethnic, multi-linguistic population. I grew up with the nationalist version but have long favoured Bloom's, while going further and rejecting all versions of 'nation' as meaningful descriptors of 'identity'. Language has still some importance in how I define my sense of identity, but my journey in that regard, like that of the country as a whole, has been difficult and confused, marked above all by a linguistic insecurity, which is a version of what has been there since Shakespeare's day.

In a key scene in *A Portrait of the Artist as a Young Man*, Stephen Dedalus, an undergraduate at what was still, essentially, Newman's Catholic University, had a conversation with the Jesuit dean of studies, 'a poor Englishman in Ireland'. Stephen, a brilliant but tortured intellectual from a poor background, began with great confidence and scholarly brio, only to feel insecure and inferior in relation to what was his birth language, and indeed his only language, when the dean queried his use of the Dublin colloquial word 'tundish' for 'funnel'. Suddenly, Stephen's sense of intellectual superiority was confounded by the realisation 'that the man to whom he was speaking was a countryman of Ben Johnson', in other words that he came from a culture regarded as superior as well as dominant. Articulating to himself what was the great cultural trauma of the Irish experience of colonialism, Stephen realised:

> His language, so familiar and so foreign, will always be for me an acquired speech. I have not made or accepted its words. My voice holds them at bay. My soul frets in the shadow of his language.

My soul has also fretted in the shadow of a language, Irish, another 'acquired speech', but one that I had partly lived through in my formative bilingual years, after which, like Stephen, I lost confidence in my ability to use it in what was perceived by the guardians of the language to be the proper manner, that is, like a 'native' speaker on the western seaboard, like Tomás Ó Criomhthain or Máirtín Ó Cadhain.

There was no Irish-language tradition or competence in my family background. My reasonably well-off Dunne and Rice ancestors were almost certainly bilingual in practical dealings into the early decades of the nineteenth century but predominantly English-speaking at home. My parents had no sense of Irish, beyond some words in colloquial speech. My experience of learning it in primary school was the negative one of most people my age, although I had been keen to follow a foundation course on the radio for a while. My relationship with the language changed with dramatic suddenness when I joined the Irish Christian Brothers aged fourteen and found myself doing the entire school programme through Irish. The fact that I took the lead in an Irish-language play four months after I left home would suggest that I took to it with new enthusiasm and quickly acquired some fluency. I became bilingual in effect, and this was reinforced throughout my seven years with the Brothers, their community life, as I experienced it, also having a strong bilingual element. And of course I taught Irish as an unqualified teacher in their primary and secondary schools. This bilingualism seems, in retrospect, to have been my greatest cultural gain from those years, and it still shadows my life, even though for years now I rarely have had occasion – or the confidence – to speak Irish.

That early experience helped to determine my choice of subjects when I began an arts degree in University College Dublin. I did Irish in first year, planning to do it to degree level, combined with English, my favourite teaching subjects (and those that would be most in demand when I could finally apply to schools as a qualified teacher). But I did not continue with Irish beyond first year, and the possible reasons for that may help to explain my gradual disengagement from the language during my years as an academic – and its problematic nature in relation to Irish identity. At the time I tended to blame the professor of Irish in UCD, a very prominent Irish-language scholar, Tomás de Bhaldraithe, who could be abrasive and undermining towards those whose Irish wasn't up to his standard. I don't remember being targeted specifically by him but I do remember the collective sense of embarrassment and unease when someone (often a young nun) was in the firing line.

My sense of what he wanted from us was *vernacular* Irish, or *canúint*, as spoken by native speakers in the remaining Irish-speaking areas on the western seaboard. That was also to become, and remain, my sense of the standard among Irish-language academics, and I knew I couldn't meet it. I had good, even excellent 'school Irish', but without the benefit of immersion in the living Irish of a *Gaeltacht*, or Irish-speaking community – such as de Bhaldraithe (who grew up in Dublin and had changed his name from Waldron) had experienced in Connemara – I could never achieve real fluency. When I did finally spend a few weeks in the Kerry *Gaeltacht* some years later I never felt a similar expectation about my Irish in speaking with local people. Indeed, I recall a number of companionable evenings in Ó Catháin's pub in Ballyferriter spent talking to a local farmer, Muiris Ferritéir. Remarkably, in an area with no hurling tradition, he was a great fan of the Wexford hurling team that I had followed with my dad, and Muiris had often travelled the long miles to Dublin to see them. I could speak to him in Irish unselfconsciously, and he just wanted to talk about hurling.

It would be easy, of course, to blame de Bhaldraithe – my version of Joyce's dean of studies – for my enduring lack of confidence about speaking Irish, but I know that he was a symptom, not a cause, his expectations being common throughout the education system and indeed among the shrinking community of Irish speakers outside the *Gaeltacht*. A core aspect of the Irish nationalist response to colonialism from the early years of the Irish state, the ambition and the attempt to reverse centuries of Irish-language decline in a short period, was based on the belief that it had been imposed from outside by imperial policy rather than being primarily the result of socio-economic and cultural stresses, which dictated individual Irish choices over generations. The assertion that Irish had remained *the* 'national language', and the foolish assumption that this could be demonstrated and enhanced through the schools thanks to an innate language memory that would make it easy for students to learn it, led to counter-productive programmes and teaching methods. Even when I was trying to teach Irish to fourteen-year-old inner-city Dubliners sixty years ago it was obvious that this policy was not only delusional, but harmful. In retrospect, my whole experience of Irish, and that of generations before and after me, was to be stunted by its recruitment to a narrow nationalist agenda that was linguistically illiterate and nostalgically romantic.

Even though I hadn't qualified in Irish in my degree, my still-functioning bilingualism was crucial in my subsequent appointment as a secondary teacher to Coláiste an Spioraid Naoimh, a dynamic new school in Cork. In the middle of my interview its headmaster, unsure about my competence in Irish, and given that the advertised post included teaching it, suddenly switched languages, and because I was able to respond reasonably well, gave me the job. A decade later my continuing ability to impress through Irish proved crucial in my appointment to a lectureship in history at University College Cork, despite my having spent many of the intervening years in Cambridge, occasionally experiencing Stephen Dedalus' linguistic insecurity about 'English' English. As well as lecturing in history, I was deemed suitable to teach a final-year seminar course through Irish for a new interdisciplinary degree, *An Léann Dúchais* (crudely, 'Native Learning'). I did this for a number of years, lecturing on the politics of Gaelic poetry from the battle of Kinsale to the Great Famine as a source for our understanding of early modern Ireland. As outlined earlier, this led to a series of articles, still ongoing, that use Irish-language sources and have a focus on bilingualism, which I believe to be a crucial, and too little regarded, key to understanding Irish history in the colonial period, and down to modern times. It may be worth noting that these articles have made little impact on either Gaelic scholars (perhaps as not being sufficiently scholarly) or my fellow historians (perhaps as being outside their expertise, a straying into notoriously combative territory). Whatever the reasons, I think it may illustrate a scholarly divide that is damaging to both; of course, it may simply be that these articles were not considered to be very interesting or persuasive by either side.

I had many excellent students in my course on Gaelic poetry, some of them native speakers, and I remember no sense of inadequacy in lecturing through Irish. The course also brought me into the ambit of Irish-language scholars in other departments, some of whom became friends. Yet, so far as I remember, we always spoke in English in social situations. I was encouraged to frequent the Irish-language common room, *An Seomra Caidrimh*, for coffee, but after a few visits I stopped using it. I remember telling myself that I disapproved of the concept of such a 'common room', but I knew even then that what I really felt was the old inhibition, the sense that I didn't belong, that my Irish was not good enough. No colleague ever consciously gave me the slightest hint of such a judgement; everyone was very welcoming and encouraging. But, *I knew* – or so I felt, the old voice still resonating in my head.

One day during those years I walked down a corridor in University College Galway with the ebullient Gearóid Ó Tuathaigh, the most fluent conversationalist I have ever met, his words emerging in torrents, but also in perfect paragraphs and bristling with ideas. We were speaking in English, but various people as we passed spoke to him in Irish and he switched effortlessly from one language to the other and back again. Not for the first time I envied the bilingualism of UCG and wished that it could also be more a feature of my own university. Not for the first time also I wondered to myself why I did not switch to Irish in the course of this and similar conversations, as I could easily have done; indeed, why I contributed nothing to such attempts as there were to make UCC more bilingual, why I lacked the confidence to do so, as it seems to me now. This has been to my great loss and regret, instead having, through lack of use, allowed my facility in Irish to wither after I stopped giving that course. Years later, invited to appear a few times on a book programme on the Irish-language TV station TG4, I felt profound embarrassment at how halting my Irish now was. Driving to the studio I remember rehearsing an excuse for my

Gaeilge bacach, ceal cleachtadh (maimed Irish due to a lack of practice), but the station's staff were so welcoming, especially the programme's host, the encouraging Páraic Breathnach, that I put my inadequacies to the back of my mind and stumbled painfully through.

While my spoken Irish has continued to deteriorate, I retain a shadowy, diminishing bilingualism in my head, regularly coming up with the Irish version when searching for an English word, and even finding that I had used verses or sentences in Irish when drafting lectures or essays. When writing about ageing, in Chapter 12, for example, I carried around in my head for days a nostalgic poem by Douglas Hyde, empathising with his contrast between his youth and his old age (*Do bhí me luath, 'nois tá mé mall* [I was once swift, but now am slow]) but not with his rather pointless wish to be *arís óg/Sa ghlean inar tógadh mé* [again young in the glen where I was raised]. Likewise, sitting on a calm spring evening beside a small harbour, it was Máirtín Ó Direáin's 'An tEarrach Thiar' that came to mind:

Toll-bhuillí fanna
Ag maidí rámha
Currach lán éisc
Ag teacht chun cladaigh
Ar ór-mhuir mhall
I ndeireadh lae;
San Earrach thiar.

Irish endures, a shadowy but somehow crucial presence in my day-to-day life as well as in my memory. My only engagement with it now, other than in doing research, comes through reading occasional articles in *The Irish Times* and the often excellent programmes of quiet, reflective conversation on TG4 – both a source of pleasure, but also inducing a sense of loss. This sense also ran through Gaelic poetry from the seventeenth century on as more and more Irish speakers changed to English and were denounced for this by poets, themselves bilingual. Most vehement was Dáibhí Ó Bruadair, who, in lamenting how '*mórchuid d'fhearaibh Éireann*' (most Irishmen) will speak no language other than '*gósta garbh-Bhéarla*' (the ghost of a clumsy English), combined the sense of insecurity about both languages that is a major legacy of Ireland's colonial experience.

I have long been fascinated by the decision made by some academics of my generation and earlier, who were brought up English-speaking, that they would only use the Irish version of their names, thus, in effect, taking on new personae, even perhaps re-making themselves. It seemed to signal, in part at least, a determination to be recognised as fully a 'native' speaker. If I had continued with Irish as an undergraduate, perhaps I would have done the same, reverting in effect to the secular aspect of my self-identification in religion. T.B. Ó Duinn was on the flyleaves of the books I was allowed to bring home from the Brothers; T.S. Ó Duinn on the books I had beginning first year in UCD (Seán replacing Bosco). That was my sense of identity before being disenchanted by Irish and enthralled by history as an undergraduate. When I published my first article (ironically it was on Gaelic poetry) years later it was as T.J. Dunne, which was dropped for all subsequent published work in favour of 'Tom Dunne', perhaps unconsciously a colloquial attempt to appeal to readers.

The idea of Tomás Seán Ó Duinn as a lost identity or *alter ego* is a beguiling one and has some validity, but that loss need not have been decisive in terms of practising bilingualism. This I could have learned from my colleague, and later dear friend, John A. Murphy, who retained the English version of his name despite growing up in an area where Irish was still widely spoken, and beginning his professional life as Seán A. Ó Murchú when a secondary teacher in Farrenferris, and indeed publishing his fine two-volume survey of European history for schools, *Stair na hEorpa*, under that name. Yet he became and remained 'John A. Murphy' from the time he became an academic in UCC, taking the opposite course to many of his new colleagues, who had changed to using the Irish version of their names exclusively. But this had no effect on his *use* of Irish. He remained fluently and often vociferously bilingual. This was most dramatically manifested in his parallel life as a singer, in which he kept expanding on his repertoire of songs, especially in Irish. I remember an occasion, for a celebration of his birthday, well into his eighties, when he learned a very long and complex *sean-nós* song in praise of Napoleon. He died only recently, having asked, perhaps mischievously, that his gravestone should simply give his dates and the comment, 'He sang'. Had he thought of it, he might well have added an Irish version, 'Chan sé'. I plan to have no grave, and hence no gravestone for some future melancholic romantic, fond of searching through old graveyards as I am, to find and ponder, 'I wonder what did he do?' – the query John A. was addressing. On my imagined stone I might, in emulation, suggest putting 'He taught' under my name and adding below it, 'Mhúin sé', and 'Tomás S. Ó Duinn. D'éag 1964' (died in 1964).

Remembering that early sense of the impossibility of acquiring 'proper' Irish, of learning, in effect, to sound like a Blasket islander or a Connemara fisherman, I was amused not so long ago to hear an Irish-language academic bemoan the problem of dealing with the influx of students from the ever-growing numbers of Gaelscoileanna (newly established secondary schools whose teaching and ethos is through the Irish language). While some come from families with standard Irish, most do not, and have developed an entirely new demotic *canúint* or vernacular in their enthusiastic efforts to operate through Irish in the playground as well as the classroom. A mixture of Irish and English and lacking many of the elements of traditional grammar and syntax, it had been stoutly defended by some of its speakers as proper Irish when they went to university – or so I have been told. Perhaps their lecturers and professors may henceforth have to spend more time in the Gaelscoil playground than in the fast-disappearing *Gaeltacht*.

Left to evolve naturally in a bilingual context, as seems to be happening in an accelerated way in the new all-Irish schools, rather than being canonised and calcified as it was by state policy in a mistaken effort to preserve and 'revive' a traditional monoglot version, Irish might now be spoken much more widely, though transformed into a modern urban vernacular which would be producing its own rich literature. In the end, I don't blame de Bhaldraithe for my flight from Irish, which was due principally to my own failure to overcome the sense of inadequacy that official 'Gaelgeoir' attitudes induced in many people. The success of the new Irish-language schools is remarkable, especially given that many parents are choosing to educate their children through a language they themselves do not know, cutting themselves off from sharing meaningfully in the experience of homework, for example. Factors such as smaller class sizes in the new schools are often cited, but there has to be also an inchoate sense of connection with the language that, in many instances, transcends their negative experiences. Over many decades, even as its use declined in traditional Irish-speaking areas, goodwill towards Irish has been evident in many surveys, but so has negativity about the methods and attitudes involved in teaching it. In a sense, a majority of Irish people may subconsciously feel, as I do, locked out of a lost linguistic world, a shadow world that haunts our own.

My sense of identity nowadays is more European than Irish, even though I lack the strong local, historical and linguistic connections long associated with identity in 'nation'; being, as a European, a native of the periphery, which was outside most of the great events and movements that defined European history, and being unable to speak any of the continental languages. So why am I happy to identify strongly, even enthusiastically, as a 'European'? Perhaps because 'European' was an identity freely chosen (in a series of referenda) rather than inherited, one offering new hopes and horizons in place of the romantic, small-minded and fractured version embodied in the Irish state. I was attracted by its broader and more meaningful sense of 'community', a shared identity, committed to collaboration, to the expansion of identity rather than the introverted, confrontational, atrophied tradition that Irish nationalism had in common with most European versions. The EU is a powerful symbol of co-operation between countries which had a recent history of wars; it transcends the power of traditional nationalism, diverting it into broader and more challenging channels. It is, indeed, a union of nations that have chosen to pool their interests, prioritising pragmatism over romantic ideology. I relate to the symbolism as well as the practicality of the common currency, weights and measures, and to the reach and ambition of its cultural programmes. Indeed, it has many faults, inherited from the older nationalisms, but also a growing tradition of debating and confronting them.

As will have been clear in earlier chapters, I identify strongly with European culture, especially its literature, music and art. While I cannot read the originals of the books I read, I have access to them through the growing availability of translations, one of the greatest contributions to the expanding development of a European culture. It is simply a different version of access and identity. My sons speak a number of the main European languages but read relatively few of their books in the original. Their sense of identity comes from the experience of speaking the languages and living in the cultures. Perhaps the greatest regret about my early education is that I had no opportunity to learn French or German, being confined instead to one dead language, Latin, and a 'native' language, which few people learned well and most never used after finishing school. Despite the goodwill towards Irish and the remarkable enthusiasm for Irish-language schools, it remains (and is likely to continue) a shadow language, of largely sentimental value. One of the tragic aspects of this is that it results in a less distinctive version of our European identity, which is mediated through English.

Many years ago, as part of the attempt to improve my Irish, I stayed for a few weeks in the house of Máire Breathnach, near Ballyferriter. Also staying with her was Micheál Ó Dubhshláine, the principal of the one-teacher school in nearby Dúnchaoin, recently appointed by the community after the Department of Education had ordered the school closed. He was my age, and also an outsider, a native of Kildare. But he had lovely Irish, and was to become an important writer in the language. He also loved 'classical' music, especially what Máire called, with a fond dismissiveness, '*an ceol Gearmánach sin*' (that German music), her term for his records of Beethoven symphonies. I remember being amused at what seemed her parochialism, but I was wrong. She spoke from the secure, separate identity of another great European language. I knew Beethoven through English and didn't for many years think of him as German. I would have a different and perhaps better sense of European identity as an Irish speaker. I would certainly have been more reminded of Gaelic Ireland's long and important connections with Europe.

The position of Irish within the European Union is a contradictory one, echoing its position in Ireland post-independence. It became an 'official' language of the union in 2007 at the insistence of the Irish state (thereby creating a large number of posts for Irish translators and interpreters and strengthening the position of Irish in the universities), yet Irish is also widely recognised (though not officially) as one of the union's endangered 'minority' languages. Hopefully the extensive European research and policy development being done in that area will ultimately benefit Irish and, if we can finally face up to the realities of our linguistic past and present, perhaps even lead to the adoption of bilingual policies in Ireland – ultimately the only salvation of Irish – and bring our lost shadow world into the light.

CHAPTER 11

Semi-Retirement

When I told friends and colleagues that I planned to retire at sixty-one, some wondered if it was a good idea; wouldn't I get bored? Or, worse still, age more quickly? My response was that I was not retiring to stop working but to change to work I preferred, to free myself from the grind of full-time teaching, from dealing with some difficult colleagues and from the demands of the ever more intrusive university bureaucracy. Far from accelerating ageing, I hoped retirement would rejuvenate me by giving me a fresh start and fresh challenges. These mainly involved writing projects, some in art history but also non-academic writing, to date two different experiments in memoir-writing. In an earlier chapter I discussed the sense I sometimes gave people of being an academic loner, somewhat at odds with my discipline and with the changes threatening the traditional university. Retirement – more accurately semi-retirement – was an opportunity to be an unattached 'independent' scholar, a status I had often envied, and hoped might suit me better.

However, the future I hoped for also involved 'retirement' in the sense of an expansion of time, not only to pursue other things but at times to do nothing in particular, time to stop being constantly busy and active, time to think and to look around me, time to enjoy life, not least the sense of being alive, and time above all to understand myself and my life experience better, the need for which will have been apparent to the reader of the earlier chapters.

If you understand 'memoir' in terms of an exploration of your life largely through your memory (which is how I understand it), as opposed to contextualising or 'improving' your memory by supplementing it with the historical record, you have to accept its fluid, changeable nature. A memoir, so conceived, is a record not of the past but of a present, which is in constant transition. Memoir involves an interaction of past and present, a matter of how you remember an elusive past in an ever-changing present. This makes memory a difficult and often frustrating tool to use. It cannot be forced or summoned at will but only encouraged and given room to expand. Retiring, and thinking of writing a different kind of memoir, needed a new mindset, a different start to the day than a dash to the desk or the teaching room or the meeting. Strolling, daydreaming and not having a strict schedule were crucial to this process – facilitated by the need to walk an active dog.

Now the family's chauffeur and chief shopper, my early-morning routine began with dropping my wife off near to her work, and our sons to their school, after which I drove to one of Cork city's most magical places, the Marina, a tree-lined walk to Blackrock, beside the tidal river. Just off it is a path around a small lake (known, mysteriously, as the Atlantic Pond), with a wooded island at one end home to eight or nine nesting pairs of grey herons. There I walked with our lovely, if often infuriating, black-and-tan terrier, Bobby. The lake had a varied bird life: mallard ducks, swans, small white egrets, moorhens, coots, occasionally widgeon and teal, and marauding visiting cormorants. I became an avid, if ignorant, bird-watcher, finding it fascinating and relaxing, emblematic of a new life, more contemplative, less driven. A little poem learned in primary school had asked, 'What is this life, if full of care/We have no time to stand and stare?' Now, for the first time in my life, I took that time, ignoring for a while the desk waiting for me at home, or the shopping list in my pocket.

While Bobby explored, begged food off passers-by and chased the occasional duck, I stood and watched the intensely busy life of mallards and their remarkable flying speed, or a pair of swans bringing their almost fully grown offspring on a practice flight – taking off, 'running' on the water at one end of the lake, filling the air with the excitement of their beating wings, landing three hundred yards away after a low flight, with thrilling deceleration, before settling demurely, their wings now set to sail on calmly. But above all I watched the herons.

However, before all that, on the way to the lake, I would pass a thorn bush, and very often, a few feet away, level with my head, I would find a robin, head cocked to one side, looking at me – and whistling. One morning I whistled back. His head cocked the other way and he replied. This exchange, regularly repeated over months, could go on for a minute or two, and always left me smiling, and foolishly pleased, as if I had been granted an interview with some important dignitary. Our whistling, I thought, was an acknowledgement; we each recognised the existence of the other. To misapply Descartes: 'a robin saw me, therefore I am'.

Of course, Descartes would never have said any such thing, one focus of his vehement disagreement with Montaigne being the latter's persistent speculation about 'this equality and correspondence between us and the beasts', on the basis that all were sentient creatures. Montaigne's curiosity extended to regular efforts to see the world from the perspectives of societies different from his own – like 'cannibals', for example – but also those of animals, dogs, horses and, most famously, his cat. Raising the question of how humans can know 'the secret internal stirrings of animals', he used his own domestic situation. 'When I play with my cat, who knows if I am not a pastime to her more than she is to me?' In a later edition he added, 'We entertain each other with reciprocal monkey tricks.'

On the mornings I communicated with the robin I was particularly alert to the magic of the herons when I turned the corner. My first instinct would be to look at the wooded island, where the nesting pairs might be visible before the summer foliage got too dense. Each nest was a large, untidy construction of small branches, some of them probably very old, held together by their guano (and smelling to high heaven, the experts say), refurbished every year to repair storm damage. Usually there would be a number of these fascinating birds on my side of the bank, parading slowly on their long ungainly legs, watching the water, or standing statuesquely, stock still, ready to strike. Most remarkable was their imperturbability, their apparent lack of fear at your approach; then, when they deigned to notice you, their languorous flapping of large wings and a veering sideways drift, before soaring up, folding their awkward frame into a neat, aerodynamic shape, suddenly looking like something prehistoric, a survival of the age of the dinosaurs. Recent research has shown, indeed, that all birds evolved from dinosaur ancestors, but the heron's way of standing, walking and flying perhaps best fits the popular sense of what a flying dinosaur might look like.

They have extraordinary flying skills and surprising manoeuvrability, best seen in spring when they are working on renewing their nests, ferrying thin branches a metre long or more from the island below them or from the further banks, stripped from saplings or found on the ground. Landing on a slender, swaying branch near the nest where the female waits, calling impatiently, the male is transformed from an ungainly provider into a graceful balletic dancer, to transfer the building material to the waiting beak. Every time I saw this was a thrill and another minor miracle. Montaigne, in the same vein, wrote a lyrical description of how swallows build their nests, seeing it as an example of 'how much superiority the animals have over us, and how feeble our skill is to imitate them'. And of course birds are a far more ancient species than we are.

Scientists believe that modern birds evolved from dinosaurs during the Jurassic period (165–150 million years ago), millennia before humans evolved. Thinking about the birds, as well as looking at them, can give the historian a deeper sense of historical time. The ancestors of the heron were building their untidy nests and prospecting for fish in whatever version of the Lee valley existed long before the first human settlers came. Likewise, the distinctive flight paths of swans in Cork city, moving every morning from the river to a number of inland lakes, may replicate those of their ancestors, when there were no humans to see them. A geologist told me once that if the history of the Earth was to be represented by the line of a marathon, some twenty-six miles long, the history of human life on Earth that we have records for would be represented only by the last foot. Working, as I also am these days, on a study of Irish landscape art from 1750 to 1850, I am acutely aware that this is a minutely small area of human inquiry and, furthermore, that my limited contribution to understanding it is bound to be superseded in a relatively short time. We historians could acquire some valuable perspective by talking to robins and looking at herons.

Despite the pleasure of such leisurely early mornings, they also reinforced my sense that I don't like being idle for long; it makes me feel restless, and vaguely unhappy. In particular I need, it seems, a reason to go to my desk every morning, with a project on which to focus. Of course, nowadays I don't start so early or have the energy to stay so long – and some days I am happy to keep away from the desk altogether. I am very privileged to be able to continue with research and writing after leaving the university – the materials and facilities I needed are still just as available to me, not least membership of its library and its ever-expanding digital resources. This good fortune was brought home to me when talking to a recently retired colleague whose whole research career had been lab-based and who had to vacate his workspace almost immediately on retiring. 'There are many brilliant young scholars impatient to take my place,' he told me. He had set up a workroom at home but could only write up his final findings. After that there would be no more new data. He was becoming a keen golfer.

In the years before I retired I had been frantically busy – a factor indeed in the decision to go early. On top of my teaching, I was dean of a large faculty for six years, making me also a member of an intimidating number of university committees, more being added during a period as a member of the university governing body. For a variety of reasons, I did not make a quick or full transition to a life of daydreaming, study and writing when I stopped teaching full-time and attending college committees. Indeed, if anything I seemed just as busy for some years, involved for example in helping Cork University Press to survive a difficult financial crisis and continue publishing, and being active in the Senate of the National

University of Ireland as it too went through a radical transitional phase. But despite such busyness, it was important for me also to feel that I was actually retired, with more time to myself, to slow down, to look around me, to read and reflect. This was possible because my various new roles were voluntary and part-time, lacking the intensity and time commitment of those that had marked my final years as a full-time academic, giving me time, especially, to become a student again, although one largely self-directed and learning from a variety of practical roles.

* * *

My newly expanded time was used primarily in acquiring a deeper education in art and art history, the lack of which had become evident to me, and no doubt to others, in my attempts to write a number of articles on Irish art and artists in previous years. 'Art history', I had learned, was not simply a subset of 'history' but a distinct discipline, its focus on the visual and the material, on ownership and connoisseurship, on exhibition and attribution – and much more – requiring additional training and knowledge together with new, challenging mindsets. Art galleries became my school and library, and particularly the National in London. Its vast holdings of great paintings, supplemented by the range of art-history books in its shop, could provide the stimulating survey and analysis of art, mainly of the seventeenth to the nineteenth centuries, that I needed for my work.

The apprentice art historian learns to avoid image overload and to focus on a limited number of paintings on each visit. Whereas these sometimes related to my research of the moment, what I came to enjoy most was the time spent in front of paintings that I simply found compelling and could read about afterwards. Such 'time out', time lost in one painting, usually involved for me, with my background in texts, a scene with a story, perhaps a well-known one, like *The Circumcision* of the infant Christ, a wonderful study of calm concentration from the workshop of Giovanni Bellini (*c.*1500), which I spent time with recently. Better still is painting from which the viewer can construct a narrative, such as Nicolas Poussin's *Landscape with a Man Killed by a Snake* (*c.*1640), in which news of the horror spreads to a succession of people as our eye follows the winding path that connects them. T.J. Clark's *The Sight of Death* (2008), a detailed account of hours spent looking at that landscape, together with the same artist's *Landscape with a Calm*, later gave me a master class in how to look closely at, or 'read', a painting.

The excitement of standing before a painting and trying to understand it is, in some ways, akin to that of handling and trying to decipher an original manuscript. In each case you can feel, or imagine at least, a direct connection with the period and the environment from which the painting or document comes. A major apparent difference between the two is that looking at the painting can give the illusion of direct, unmediated communion, a personal rapport with the artist, whereas a manuscript is likely to require an effort to decipher it, often painfully, before trying to understand it. However, you learn that any simple notion of a direct rapport with the artist is an illusion that has to be guarded against; understanding a seventeenth-century painting, for example, also requires deciphering, based on knowledge of the visual culture and the artistic conventions of the time. Yet a direct response to a painting as an attempt to communicate beauty or understanding is equally important for the scholar: developing empathy with the painter and with the ambitions behind the image, rather than seeing them primarily in terms of elements in an academic argument, makes for better art history.

My move into art history was also greatly helped by giving a new undergraduate seminar. Once again new research fed off and contributed to new teaching. But most important was an unexpected, dynamic influence on my academic work, when Peter Murray, the ambitious, transformative director of the Crawford Art Gallery in Cork, invited me onto his curatorial team which was beginning work on a major exhibition featuring the Cork-born history painter James Barry (1741–1806), an exhibition that was to be one of the highlights of Cork's year as European Capital of Culture, 2005. It was the start of one of the most intense and rewarding cultural experiences of my life, extended over the following four years by further large exhibitions, one on Irish genre paintings (scenes of ordinary life) and one on the great Victorian history and genre painter Daniel Maclise. Learning about art in part by working out how best to present and organise it in gallery spaces, so as to share your understanding with those who were to walk through those spaces and engage directly with the work, posed different and more complex challenges than simply talking about the images to a class with the help of slides – just as writing about pictures in an exhibition catalogue demands a different kind of writing than do academic journals.

Mounting the Barry exhibition was a tough apprenticeship; the large number of images posed a bewildering array of challenges, with nearly two hundred items, ranging from very large canvases to small drawings and etchings, filling virtually every room in this charming gallery, many of them suited only to particular items due to various light and humidity issues, among others. Devising to-scale plans for each space was like an elaborate board game, involving not only size and climatic and lighting conditions but also primarily how best to aid viewers to understand what is on the wall before them, both the subject matter of the picture and the mind and training of the artist. Taking on the editing of the complex catalogue and organising the associated international conference involved yet more work, resulting in my missing some family trips, and my younger son marching around the house intoning, 'We hate James Barry.'

My work on this exhibition and conference involved a close collaboration and ultimately great friendship with William (Bill) Pressly, who has been a major influence and encourager in my change to art history, and my ideal of what an art historian should be, both scholarly and empathetic. He had published two key studies on Barry in the 1980s, and having then moved into related fields of research had to be persuaded by Peter Murray to focus on him again as advisor to our exhibition. His fear that he might have nothing new to add on Barry proved very wide of the mark, and it was a great pleasure to be present in London in 2015 when his monumental masterpiece *James Barry's Murals at the Royal Society of Arts: Envisioning a new public art* (a masterpiece also in art history book production by Cork University Press) was awarded the Berger Prize for British Art History. It was a wonderful example of the cross-fertilisation between the work done in mounting exhibitions and that involved in scholarly research, which is such an enriching feature of my new discipline.

After an intense year's preparatory work, I felt very excited and privileged to be a witness as a series of Barry paintings were carefully removed from their climate-controlled crates, some by curators from the galleries that were loaning them, and who would oversee their installation for the Crawford exhibition. The released paintings, many very large and spectacular, were lined up along the walls, where they would soon be hung. Most featured scenes from Greek mythology, from the Bible and Shakespeare, but there were also a number of portraits and, what interested me most, a series of self-portraits in oil paintings, drawings and prints. In some instances the self-portrait was the sole focus, and in others it was integrated into mythological scenes.

Barry was an obvious choice for the Capital of Culture honour, as possibly the only Cork artist of European significance and the standard-bearer in his time for the 'high' art of history painting, dealing mainly with subject matter from antiquity, the Bible and Shakespeare, an art that aimed to educate the ruling elite in the great classical, Christian and national virtues, building on their cultural formation on the Grand Tour. Although long formally considered to be the most important art genre, it was falling out of fashion in the final decades of the eighteenth century. Barry was also a controversial figure, ultimately expelled from the Royal Academy in London where he was professor of painting, mainly for his intemperate attacks on Sir Joshua Reynolds, the academy's president, charging him with, among other things, abandoning history painting for the more fashionable and lucrative art of portrait painting.

My initial academic work on Barry had focused on his politics and sense of identity (strongly influenced by his Catholicism), and this was largely true also of my contributions to the exhibition catalogue. However, I had also developed a wider interest in this driven, moody, solitary artist as an individual from reading his important, if sometimes idiosyncratic, writings on art (the subject of a fine study by my former student Liam Lenihan). This interest was greatly increased by intense acquaintance over several months with the range of self-portraits we had assembled.

As the paintings emerged from their prosaic crates, like butterflies from their chrysalises, the one I was most thrilled to see was the early *Self-Portrait with Paine and Lefèvre* (*c.*1767), painted by Barry in Rome in his mid-twenties and long familiar to me as part of the collection of the National Portrait Gallery in London. Nowadays widely regarded as one of the iconic European self-portraits of the period, it is a remarkably assured, show-off performance, with the highly finished image of the young Barry filling the foreground, leaning, almost arrogantly, into the viewer's space as he paints a canvas within a canvas, depicting his more shadowy companions, one of them painting the Belvedere Torso, a still fainter shadow in the background. This remnant of an ancient Greek statue was for Barry (as it had been for Michelangelo) the ultimate expression of the classical age, considered by him as the basis of all 'high' art. Barry's gaze is direct, challenging, holding the viewer's, a study in confidence and ambition, the first in what became a series of his self-presentations in heroic terms. Yet there is, inevitably, also a hint of vulnerability in the longing to be recognised, and this is reinforced by our knowledge of his modest Cork background, and his later career, during which, while never losing that confidence and ambition, he felt increasingly embattled and isolated.

In the exhibition, this painting was the first in the sequence of his self-portraits, cumulatively tracking his responses to the vicissitudes of his life as an artist. As with Rembrandt's remarkable series of self-presentations from youth to old age (long an obsession in my visits to the National Gallery), the viewer here could get a sense of the artist's development as an individual, as well as how he wanted to represent himself and his work to the world. In several he identifies with Timanthes, the most famous painter of ancient Greece, most dramatically in *Self-Portrait as Timanthes* (National Gallery of Ireland, 1803). Here, in defiant mode, he reasserts the primacy of history painting after his expulsion from the Royal Academy, which he now believed was out to destroy him. This is represented in the painting by the positioning of the head of a serpent, representing envy, threatening his own.

But already at this point he was a well-known eccentric, under siege, as he believed, in his own house, its windows broken by local ruffians and left unrepaired, living a life of Spartan simplicity, though with significant money in the bank. It was the private self-portraits, painted, drawn or engraved at home in these embattled years, that seemed to me the most affecting. They were on show in our exhibition in a small, dimly lit upstairs gallery, and the contrast in mood with the contemporary *Self-Portrait as Timanthes*, prominent in a large gallery downstairs, was striking and haunting. In the small drawings and prints, looking more than his sixty years, Barry, gazing reflectively at his image in a mirror by candlelight, is pensive, the eyes sad, though not defeated. He represents himself as a thinker rather than as a painter, with books on the table before him, referencing his own remarkable output as a writer, the gaze and pose of one thinking deep thoughts. He had achieved his early ambition of creating major history paintings (most notably his series of large murals for the Royal Society of Arts), and was still working in his large home studio on his final masterpiece, *The Birth of Pandora*, despite the changed art environment and his growing sense of alienation and embattlement. On his death he was given the honour of a lying in state in the Great Room of the Society of Arts, surrounded by his murals, and burial in St Paul's beside Reynolds, reflecting perhaps a sense of collective guilt at the manner of his expulsion and the neglect of the much-proclaimed ideal to which Barry, almost alone, had passionately and stubbornly adhered.

The Crawford exhibition and conference were a critical success in drawing fresh attention to Barry; the exhibition was also a surprising popular success, attracting large numbers. Combined, they also proved in time to have a major political impact, important, I am told, in the upgrading of the Crawford Art Gallery from municipal gallery to the status of national cultural institution, the only one outside Dublin – the achievement, above all, of Peter Murray.

Barry was a difficult, increasingly paranoid man, but he is also a sympathetic and truly heroic figure, and for many years now, whenever I pass the National Portrait Gallery in London I call in to say hello to the young Barry and to honour him as one who could say, in the words of St Paul to Timothy, 'I have fought a good fight, I have finished my course, I have kept the faith.'

At the end of my current very short list of future writing projects is a study – or maybe a novel, why not – based on Barry's last years. There has long been a fascination with the 'last works' of writers and composers, in search primarily of their response to intimations of death. My favourite is by Barry's younger contemporary, Beethoven, whose last work, the String Quartet in B Flat, Op. 130, instead of a dying fall, attests to renewed vigour and commitment to innovation, turning many of the beloved – for many musicians sacrosanct – conventions of the quartet form, including his own, on their heads. Most daring was his ending with the boisterous *Grosse Fuge*, especially as it followed what has been called his most lyrical music, in the *Cavatina*. Such was the outcry that his publisher insisted on him substituting a more conventional ending – such was his genius that both endings are used today. My own ambition for late work is more modest, simply to keep writing, seeking new challenges, with that on Barry's 'last work' seeming particularly attractive.

* * *

Semi-retirement has also given me the opportunity of creating my own self-portrait, in the form of this memoir, and indeed Barry's self-portraits, and those of Rembrandt, were to provide valuable reference points. The coincidence that I began these reflections on my life and the approach of death just as the world began to face the threat of the Covid-19 pandemic no doubt added an extra sense of urgency and a deeper level of reflection to the project. It also created a new and strangely enabling writing environment, as government efforts to control the spread of the virus by draconian restrictions on people's movements, known as 'lockdown', enforced extensive social isolation. Clearly, this created profound cultural and psychological as well as social problems for society in general. For the writer, however, isolation not only gave protection against the disease, it also created ideal working conditions, free of distraction and other calls on your time. Recently, looking back, I felt vaguely ashamed by my unguarded response to an old friend, 'I had a very good lockdown actually' – especially as I realised that I had meant that I had enjoyed the peace and quiet, as well as benefiting from it. No doubt it had fitted my already noted attraction to a relatively solitary life. However, even I have belatedly become more aware of the gradual loss of contact with family and friends over the period of successive lockdowns, and the need to repair and restore social networks.

This idea of the pandemic providing optimum writing conditions of course sounds blasé, and wasn't even true. I was very conscious of the pandemic as a time of great suffering by many and a degree of fear for all. I shared that fear, particularly as someone designated as 'vulnerable' in the official response, confining us to our houses and (if privileged enough to have one) gardens in the first 'lockdown'. Even while recognising the value and good intentions of such measures, it was hard not to be annoyed at how extreme and infantilising they appeared, even at the time. But eventually, safely 'cocooned', as the Orwellian term put it, and especially after the vaccines became available, we all, old and young, grew less fearful and adjusted to our new, restricted way of life.

This was made easier by the fact that the pandemic, at least in a wealthy country like Ireland, was invisible to most of us, despite our saturation in information and warnings about it. Few of us actually saw anyone suffering from its appalling symptoms, much less lived among multiple victims or witnessed mass burials, as would have been the case over centuries in cases of the Plague, and was today in many of the poorer countries where Covid has been rampant and accommodation, sanitation and health services rudimentary. The real horror only came through to us – though at the safe remove of news bulletins from far away – with scenes of mass death in public, cremations on the streets of countries like India, while our TV screens showed intensive care wards in Irish hospitals struggling to deal with victims of the virus but (quite properly) not showing the faces of the patients, their bodies shrouded in all-enveloping protective clothing. Only the heroic medical staff in those wards were real witnesses to the destructive course of the disease, and to the distressing deaths; only the grieving family and friends of its victims experienced its devastation first-hand, made worse by the enforced isolation of the dying.

This was already very familiar in our cosy world, where we had long developed ways of hiding death from plain view, even in normal times, as it happened more and more outside the home. Likewise, the brutal realities behind the production of our packaged, tastefully presented supermarket meat has enabled us to avert our gaze from other deaths. 'Cocooned' may have roused the anger of many of my age cohort, but in fact our society as a whole had long been used to living in a 'cocoon', sheltered from the grimmer realities of our lives, not only the certainty of our individual deaths but through a widespread state of individual and communal denial of the very real threats to our planet and our species from nuclear destruction, mass hunger and disease, global warming – and now from a pandemic certain to be followed by others. Even our recent experience of direct, personal threat seems not to be enough to change our overall behaviour sufficiently, especially in relation to climate change.

While it has increased my own awareness of mortality, and my gratitude for a privileged life, the pandemic may also have resonated with the growing sense of helplessness characteristic of old age. Perhaps in learning of the difficulty, indeed near-impossibility, of understanding fully his/her own small life, the memoir-writer is less inclined, even equipped, to think about, much less face up to, the overwhelming, seemingly intractable nature of global problems that threaten us all. This sense of helplessness of course doesn't only affect the old; it is ubiquitous and poses one of the greatest dangers we face as a species. Covid has, indeed, been difficult for us romantic optimists.

The sense of isolation that everyone felt was made more dramatic for my wife Clare and me by the completion of our move (in progress before Covid struck) in the early months of the first 'lockdown' to a town nearly three hundred kilometres away, where we knew no-one. There were major compensations, in living close to the sea and having a much simpler and quieter life, and if we were thrown on our own resources, these were considerable, particularly for our work as historians, with our books and online research tools. For me, this memoir-writing project was indeed a wonderful distraction as well as occupation. We were conscious of being privileged and fortunate compared to so many, having a secure income and good basic health, both helping to reduce our sense of anxiety as we were swept up in the daily news of infections, deaths and economic hardship. But anxiety was also inescapable, given isolation from family and friends and the sense of vulnerability, which ever-stricter restrictions heightened, even as they sought to reassure.

I found that being reminded constantly of my age as a major risk factor was both irritating and distressing; I had the good luck up to then of being able to drift happily into my late seventies without having to think much about my age. Now I began to feel oppressed by the pervasive sense of threat and the judgement of others. This was intensified a few months after our move by a sudden and sustained attack of sciatica, not a life-threatening illness of course but serious enough – and ageing enough – in the reduction of mobility and the experience of intense pain. It also resulted in a series of visits to hospitals, the first in many years and the last place you want to be during a pandemic. Successive tests and procedures all proved reassuring and ultimately successful, at least for now, but the whole sustained experience was also psychologically challenging.

Like many so-called intellectuals, I resorted in those times to the classics of plague literature, Daniel Defoe's *A Journal of the Plague Year*, a realistic account of the Great Plague of London, 1665, and Albert Camus' *The Plague*, a realist/allegorical novel detailing the outbreak of a fictional plague in Oran, Algeria. A feature of both is the visceral, vividly described experience of disease and death, on a large scale, in the midst of communal life, and the sense of panic and despair that resulted from this. The account that has most affected me, however, given his importance to my whole memoir endeavour, was that of Michel de Montaigne, an eyewitness to an outbreak of the plague in the countryside outside his modest chateau, near Bordeaux, in the late sixteenth century.

In 1585, as he finished his second term as mayor of Bordeaux, Montaigne, on hearing that plague was rampant there, decided not to return to the city for the ceremony of investing his successor. He returned instead to his house, and his nowadays-famous library in the tower, and resumed writing his essays. The following year, however, the plague came to the Chateau de Montaigne itself, brought by one of the marauding bands of soldiers that had threatened it throughout the decades of religious wars, in which he had sometimes played a mediating role, making him a target from both sides. He was beset, he wrote, by 'a mighty load of our disturbances', and while he had refused over the years to leave his home in the face of armed threats, had refused even to defend his house, relying on his reputation for hospitality and his ability to talk himself out of trouble, the plague was different; it was not open to negotiation. And so he was forced to flee with his family and household, seeking refuge where he could find it in six months of wandering. When he returned home he found many of the workers on his estate were dead, the crops destroyed, but his tower and library intact. And so he resumed writing the essay he had started before being forced to flee.

'On Physiognomy' is typical of many of Montaigne's essays in that its title has little bearing on his subject matter. This reflects his approach to writing. 'My ideas follow one another,' he wrote elsewhere, 'but sometimes it is from a distance, and look at each other, but with a sideways glance ... The titles of my chapters do not always embrace their matter; often they only denote it by some sign.' 'On Physiognomy' begins with some reflections on the artifice behind the charms of Socrates, but soon gets deflected into Montaigne's reflections on 'monstrous war!', followed by his devastating experience of 'a plague of the utmost virulence', making 'the sight of my house … frightful to me'. After a lifetime of keeping open house, he now had trouble 'finding a retreat for my family', due to widespread fear causing 'a trance of anxiety over that illness'. In terms of his own well-rehearsed views, the plague involved, he wrote, perhaps a little facetiously, 'a kind of death that does not seem to me the worst: it is generally quick, numbed, painless, consoled by the public situation, without ceremony, without mourning, without a crowd around'. But the experience of seeing its destructive powers and its psychological as well as physical effects on his labourers, living all around him, led to a very different tone.

> Each man universally gave up caring for his life. The grapes remained hanging on the vines … as all prepared themselves indifferently and awaited death … I saw some who feared to remain behind, as in a horrible solitude, and found them generally to be concerned only about their burial. It pained them to see the bodies scattered amid the fields, at the mercy of the animals that promptly appeared in swarms.

This devastation is described almost admiringly in terms of how people in these terrible circumstances come to terms with death, and leads to further reflections on philosophy's long obsession with how to do this, as reflected in his early essays. The wealthy and educated, he concluded, are in the end forced to imitate the 'stupid simplicity' of the poor in facing it. His 'peasant neighbours' only reflect on death when dying, and then they do it with 'better grace' than Aristotle. Now, having survived the plague, Montaigne is dismissive of the Stoic obsession with preparing for death, and takes the opportunity to state the philosophy that already marked his later years, that what matters most is learning how to live:

> If you don't know how to die, don't worry; nature will tell you what to do on the spot, fully and adequately … We trouble our life by concern about death, and death by concern about life … If we have known how to live steadfastly and tranquilly, we shall know how to die in the same way.

His stress on making the most of life rather than focusing on death found an echo in the responses of many elderly Irish people who lived in the shadow of Covid. His belief 'that death is indeed the end, but not therefore the goal of life; ... life should be an aim unto itself, a purpose unto itself; its rightful study is to regulate, conduct and suffer itself' summed up the philosophy of his final years. It has also become mine, shaped by reflecting on my life in this memoir but also heightened by a new, more intense awareness of the threat of dying.

* * *

The pandemic transformed my experience of retirement, adding a new sense of threat and vulnerability, but that transformation was already underway with the massive dislocation involved in selling our beloved family home and the imminent move to a very different and unknown, faraway town. This was a pragmatic, shared decision rather than a loss imposed by circumstances, as Montaigne's flight during the plague had been, yet it was, nonetheless, a seismic change, felt very keenly by us all in psychological as much as material terms. We had lived for twenty-six years in a very particular house and place, which had shaped our lives profoundly. It was not only elementally and happily 'home' but also a place apart, one of wonder as well as safety. Now it has gone – it seemed with bewildering speed – from being a lived experience to becoming a site of memory, a time capsule, a place where each of us is likely to continue to partly live at some subconscious but accessible level for the remainder of our lives. Leaving the world of work had offered interesting challenges and expanded my sense of time; leaving this version of home was a different kind of challenge, to remember what it was that we had lost, and how its essentials could be saved and brought with us.

In reflecting on my childhood earlier I wrote about our home, over the shop, as a way into my memory of that long-ago time. While I remember it with affection, I don't think I felt it a great loss when my parents sold it and moved to a new house with a big garden; certainly *they* never did. I have occasionally had dreams featuring some of its scarier aspects, like the dash through the dark shop to the toilet, but not, so far as I know, the happiness of our lives there, real and important though that was to me. But I have already had such dreams of our lost house, high over the river in Cork, and not only because we had been happy there; it was in a magical place and worth celebrating.

The approach is off a narrow, twisting road of fine houses, which originated in a track used in the Middle Ages by lepers on their way to the ships that would bring them to Santiago de Compostela in search of a miracle – hence 'Siubhal na Lobhar' in Irish, 'Lepers' Walk' in English, but gentrified, in keeping with its later prestigious location, as 'Lovers' Walk'. A sharp right turn leads down an even narrower curved lane, plunging precipitously between high walls, on the left a fragile eighteenth-century dry-stone boundary to the garden of an old mansion, on the right a massive early nineteenth-century rampart, which supports the houses and gardens above. Ahead are the piers of an old gate, bringing you through a shadowed arch of sycamore and beech. The house is ahead, a high bank of trees on the right, on the left tree-lined slopes drop down. Looking past the house, a sudden vista of the river and the city below opens up.

The house as we first saw it seemed eccentric, and a challenge. It had been built fifty years earlier on the footprint of an old tennis court, formerly belonging to one of the big houses high above, as did the wild garden that surrounded it. The house was full of light and charm but was badly organised, its rooms connected by cramped twisting corridors and stairs, struggling to make sense of a number of poorly integrated extensions. We could see that it also needed a lot of work, but we had fallen in love with it and its magical location.

The evening we moved in we sat on the terrace, our infant son Oisín on a blanket on the grass beside us. Suddenly, on a lower level, down a short flight of steps, two fox cubs were playing in the last rays of sunlight. That evening, as we tried to assemble a dinner, a family of badgers came to the back door looking for milk, which had often been provided by the previous owners. The following morning we heard and then saw hawks flying overhead, coming from their nests on the cliff in the wilderness beyond our western wall. Below their cliff was the deep sandstone quarry that had provided the familiar red stone used in many Cork city buildings and walls. The quarry was no longer in use, and indeed had been made inaccessible by the building of a railway line to Cobh in front of it in the 1860s – and still snaking around the cliff far below our garden, its sounds regularly competing with our birdsong, as did the road out of the city, which is parallel to it. We had moved from a small, if elegant, Victorian terraced house with a tiny back yard, accessed up and around a series of steps and paths from a busy road. Our sense of wonder at the magic of our new surroundings was never to leave us. This was well captured in the name we inherited with the property, 'Roscúil', which can be translated from the Irish as 'a secluded wooded promontory'. It could not have been better named.

A place of enchantment and privacy for us adults, it became a paradise for our sons, the second one, Fergus, being born in the house three years later, adding to its sense of home. The garden was thronged regularly with their friends, their shouts coming from hides in banks and under bushes, our only anxiety being to police the cliff edge beyond the pampas grass. Years later, when they were tall, strapping adults, I would look up sometimes on hearing the boys' companionable voices as they came in from the garden, surprised not to see them, flushed and muddied, aged six and nine. Do we ever come to terms fully with our children growing up?

As with every paradise, there was a drawback; we were very isolated, for long making it impossible for the boys to walk to the houses of friends, and for their friends to call on them. With no bus route nearby, all had to be ferried in or out by car, also necessary to get to the nearest shops or into town, until the boys were teenagers and great walkers. The location of the house, essentially in a small wood, and four hundred metres from the door of our nearest neighbour yet quite close to the city centre, also raised some concerns. The long, dimly lit lane, out of sight of all houses and of the road above, could make walking it, especially in the dark, somewhat daunting. Every night I locked the high gates, sometimes feeling a little nervous even inside them, walking there and back to the house under the dark shadows of the trees, which could conceal who knew what danger. 'People could be camped down there and you would never know it,' a garda told us, rather unnervingly, early on after searching the bottom of the garden as part of a search for a missing person. But such reminders of our isolation were also part of the romance of living there, and we regarded house and garden as, above all, places of refuge and especially in times of grief or work-related stress. Arriving home then, the drive down between our high walls was like an escape route into another, safer world. It was also a wonderful place to read and to write, my small study looking down on the river, Clare's in the attic above it, the old port still busy with endless distractions, the garden full of birds.

As the boys entered their teens, their maternal grandfather, Jimmy, long a widower, spent more and more time with us, eventually moving in permanently. Loved and enjoyed by us all, his lively, engaged presence added further to our sense of 'Roscúil' as a place apart. He was already in his nineties, and it became clear after a few years that he needed a ground-floor bedroom and bathroom, finding the separate stairs from the kitchen to his room difficult. The obvious solution was to build an extension on the site of the old garage, but that would have introduced yet another badly integrated element into the house, and we had long dreamed about a more radical solution that would make better sense of it. We sold the bottom of the garden as a site and consulted a husband and wife team of architects, Louise Cotter and David Naessens, ultimately committing to a substantial two-storey extension on the side facing the wooded hillside, also allowing for the opening up and proper integration of the whole house. We had to move out for nine months, and saying goodbye to the shabby rooms and crooked corridors of our beloved 'old' home, before the builders got to work, was poignant. Fergus, now a keen photographer, took a series of moody pictures in black-and-white film of the sad emptied rooms; maybe he will make a photo-essay of it someday.

However, any lingering sense of loss evaporated when we returned to a remarkably transformed house, seeming radically new but retaining and refurbishing most of the old rooms on the side facing the river. The architects had managed to keep, embedded in the elegant spaciousness of the new, a powerful sense of the familiar. Their overall achievement and vision were truly remarkable, influenced in part by their working, around the same time, on their brilliant, award-winning Lexicon library in Dún Laoghaire, with its soaring spaces and wonderful light, a vision in oak and polished stone, recreated here in miniature.

Sadly, Jimmy did not live to enjoy his new living quarters for long. When we embarked on the rebuild he was a relatively fit and healthy ninety-four years old, and we all thought he would live at least to get the cheque sent by the president to those reaching a hundred. Instead, his health deteriorated rapidly, and he died in the house, surrounded by all of us. That time of grief, so soon after our return to the house, brought out one of its great qualities, its extraordinary sense of peace. This came, I think, from its use of light, space and proportion, set off by its combination of bright wood and black stone, all done with an eye to beauty as much as function.

We were to enjoy our new 'Roscúil', with its reminders of the old, for only seven years. The idea of selling it seemed perverse initially, given all that it meant to us, but it was something on which, in the end, we were all agreed. It came down to the isolation of the house, and the endless work of managing our still-large wild garden, given that I was in my mid-seventies and fifteen years older than Clare. As well as the work involved, we came to see that our paradise, much as we loved it, would not be a good place to live alone when one of us died and the boys were gone – and the longer we left it to move, the more difficult it would be. It was hard to let it go, particularly for the boys for whom it was the only home they had known, but we knew how privileged we had been to live there all those happy years, and that we are only custodians for a time of any house in which we live. When the house had been emptied I called in for a last look around and, heading for the front door, had a vivid reminder of how integral the house had been to our lives. On my right was the sitting room, where Fergus had been born twenty-three years earlier; on my left was the bedroom where Jimmy had died.

The house by the sea where we live now could hardly be more different in its externals. Built in the long back garden of what was originally a local authority house, it is set well back from a quiet road; going to close the low gate here at night is a walk on well-lit tarmac, between fences, rather than on gravel and between dark high trees. The house is fitted to the site, being also long and narrow, but it has a sense of space and light, not unlike our old house, and we feel very lucky to have found it. We were delighted to learn that it was in the oldest part of Greystones, in a townland called Killincarrig or, in the original Irish, Coillín na Carraige, the little wood on the rock (according to Logainm.ie, the official place-names database), a wonderful echo of 'Roscúil', the secluded wood on a promontory. And, mirroring that sense of continuity, we find ourselves reproducing, as much as possible, the layout of rooms, of pictures on walls, of some of the planting in the garden, as we had long been accustomed to them. Of course, it is only possible to recapture fragments of the past in such small ways, but the sense of continuity seems important – an expansion of time, even as our horizons contract in several ways, not least in the parallel sense of time running out. As Andrew Marvell put it (in a very different context, writing 'To His Coy Mistress'), 'But at my back I always hear/Time's wingèd chariot hurrying near'. Retirement certainly gives space to amplify that sound.

CHAPTER 12

Old Age

Ageing, if you are lucky, is an incremental process, largely unremarked until its progress suddenly surprises. Seeing a recent photograph of myself, taken from behind, my initial reaction was, 'Who is that bald old fellow?' A shaft of sunlight from an unexpected angle can reveal a hitherto unnoticed slackening and creping of the skin on a forearm, or, reflected in a mirror, new liver spots on the face. The surprise is due to the fact that we tend, as we get older, to 'see' ourselves, or rather, visualise ourselves, as much younger than we are. Indeed, men more than women, perhaps, tend not to look closely at body or face until forced to – possibly due to fear of what they might see. I shave every day, but almost never look closely at my face, content to follow the contours to be scraped. Habit, of course, makes you blind, but subconsciously perhaps I may feel that noting the reality would be a bad way to start the day.

If you are lucky with your health, as I have been so far, and stay young in your mind, as my good health has helped me to do, then it might appear that ageing can largely be ignored – for a while. But the reality is different. The *appearance* of ageing may be glided over, but subtle and not so subtle changes in the body register more and more insistently. I notice slight hesitancies in walking, especially coming down steps; a lowering of energy levels, an accumulation of small aches and pains, made more insistent by sciatica, a new care not to fall; climbing out of a car seat can suddenly pose a challenge. But it seems important not to give in to the sense of being old until I have to, and to cling as long as possible to the younger self but in a spirit of acceptance of reality, rather than denial.

As a humanist, my spiritual guides to understanding and coping with ageing and death offer not the consolations of an after-life but those of acceptance and celebration in the only life we will have. Rembrandt's later self-portraits, like Montaigne's late essays, are wonderful, unblinking examinations of ageing, and both have been sources of help and consolation. While the writer attempts to track his mental monitoring and understanding of the process, the painter uses its physical manifestations to also reflect his mental states. Rembrandt records his physical decline almost with curiosity, as a technical challenge, but his real subject, or so it seems to me as to many modern viewers, is his own mortality, the reflections of his internal life in his changing face, responding to his many tragedies, personal and professional, and to the advancing years. The depiction of physical decline is unsparing, both accepting and defiant. Many of these self-portraits are also theatrical presentations, using clothes and other props to emphasise his role as an artist, to celebrate success or reflect setbacks. Cumulatively, as one art historian has called them, they constitute 'an autobiography in paint'.

Rembrandt's work was strongly humanistic. A non-practising member of the relatively liberal Dutch Reformed Church, his focus, even in depicting themes from the Bible, was strongly on the individual, on internal psychological as much as physical states. This was also evident in his particular focus on studies of the head, including of family members, and in his attempts to depict inner life, for example in his use of *chiaroscuro*, light and shade allowing the simultaneous presentation of external and internal states. In 1606, the year of Rembrandt's birth, Shakespeare wrote, in recording the surprise and dismay of King Duncan at the treachery of the Thane of Cawdor (Macbeth, 1.4), 'There's no art/To find the mind's construction in the face'. Especially in his later portraits, Rembrandt was to prove the contrary.

Regular visits over recent decades to the magical room in London's National Gallery that houses so many of Rembrandt's self-portraits have been important in shaping and accepting my own developing sense of ageing. It is impossible not to feel that the painter speaks directly to you, across the centuries and the chasms of cultural change. Of course, my training tells me that this is a fallacy, that these dazzling portraits are complex, not simple, self-explanatory images, produced by a mind and in a culture very different from my own.

Recent scholarship, indeed, has often been dismissive of personal identification with the ageing Rembrandt as naïve, and has viewed the self-portraits not as autobiographical but, for example, as calculating (and largely successful) appeals to the art market, or as connected to developments in history-painting. These and other scholarly interpretations add to our understanding of Rembrandt, but the sense of direct communication between artist and viewer remains a powerful and valid one. Even more powerful is the sense of the artist in dialogue with himself. Rembrandt is not looking at you, the viewer, in his self-portraits but at himself, in a mirror – hence, perhaps, the look of sadness and compassion, but also of equanimity and self-worth in the late studies, in eyes that engage challengingly but calmly, even, it could be said, philosophically.

In dismissing autobiographical explanations, it has been claimed by some scholars that such self-consciousness, such fascination with the interior life and with ageing were unknown in Rembrandt's day. This is to ignore, among other things, the great popularity in the Netherlands of Montaigne's essays, written in the previous century (and an influence also on Shakespeare). Montaigne, inevitably, is philosophical about ageing and, in his later writings, incorrigibly humorous. As part of his rejection of the Stoic principle of 'repentance' in old age, he has no time for clichés like being 'older but wiser', or ridiculous claims of undiminished sexual vigour. We would be doing well if 'we travelled only towards improvement', he writes, believing that this involves, not steady increments, but 'a drunkard's motion, staggering, dizzy and wobbling, or that of reeds that the wind stirs haphazardly as it pleases'. He advocates 'tricking the gloom of old age' with 'the toys and pastimes' as well as the memories of youth. The only benefit of a gradual ageing, he believed, is that it makes death easier to face, quoting Lucretius, 'Death mingles and fuses with our life throughout.' Yet, Montaigne is not as gloomy as this may sound; ageing should be, above all, he believed, a spur to enjoying life. His aim is 'to pass pleasantly and not laboriously what time I have left'. Having few words of wisdom of my own on my experience of ageing, I will share some of those of Montaigne, and how I respond to them.

In what can be read as his great valedictory essay 'Of Experience', he returns to his original ambition 'to study myself more than any other subject', realising 'how much I still have to learn'. But now he disdains reliance on support from philosophers, what he calls 'mounting on stilts', adding characteristically, 'for on stilts we must still walk on our own legs. And on the loftiest throne in the world we are still only sitting on our own rump.' Experience has taught him to be tentative rather than dogmatic, to free his imagination as far a possible from 'all trouble and conflict', to pay less attention to the fame deriving from books and battles. Now, he believes, 'our great and glorious masterpiece is to live appropriately', and that 'it is an absolute perfection and virtually divine to know how to enjoy our being rightfully'. Now his sense of what is 'right' and 'appropriate' involves physical as much as spiritual pleasures, wistfully itemised in his list of what is given back to him on recovering his health after illness; 'the enjoyment of fresh air, and wine, and your wife, and melons'. Advancing years should make us more determined to enjoy what pleasures we can. 'We must hold on, tooth and nail, to our enjoyment of the pleasures of life, which our years tear, one after another, from our hands.' This is not easy, and has to be approached realistically. 'I have made up my mind to my inability to run anymore; it is enough that I crawl. Nor do I complain of the natural decay that has hold of me': indeed, it suits his preference for 'a gliding, obscure and quiet life'. But he is not content to simply 'pass the time'. Instead, 'I savour it, I cling to it ... The shorter my possession of life, the deeper and fuller I must make it'. His continued delight in the physical world in old age, and his sense of its congruence with the life of the mind, marks the distance he has come from the Stoicism of his youth; now he seeks to learn how to live, rather than how to die.

What Montaigne and Rembrandt share – or so it seems to me – is a sense of acceptance of ageing, of facing it with equanimity and without self-recrimination. This involves also an acceptance of the life lived, in Rembrandt's case, it might appear, with a mixture of sadness and defiance, in Montaigne's, with some 'regret', but without need, as he put it, for 'repentance'. Consistently positive and upbeat, Montaigne seems never to have entertained any sense of guilt. This is one of the things that can, at times, make it harder to relate to him – his mainly conventional views of the role of women, or of the glories of war, are others. However, his robust refusal to admit guilt can also seem most attractive, even enviable, especially for those of us with highly developed guilt complexes from our Catholic upbringing. The sadness in Rembrandt's gaze in old age seemed to me to include more mixed feelings. Any such reading being fundamentally subjective, the compassion I see in Rembrandt's late portraits includes self-compassion, self-forgiveness. That is what I see because I need to feel it for myself, as discussed earlier, especially in relation to the failure of my first marriage.

In old age, as well as a tendency to reflect back on what we regret, there is the broader preoccupation with what we have learned from life, what our experience has been. Indeed, there is a tendency to appeal to it as if it contained some accumulated wisdom. 'In my experience' can become a mantra, especially when we cannot find any solid basis for our opinions. However, 'experience', when used to evoke specific precedents to guide our actions, is indistinguishable from 'memory', and thus also shaky ground. Montaigne's magnificent late essay explores this in his characteristic oblique, discursive way, having failed at an attempt at a definition. 'When Reason fails us we use experience,' he wrote, by which is commonly meant 'the inference that we draw from the resemblance of events'. But, like the law, this can be open to a multiplicity of interpretations, leading him to conclude that only 'the experience I have of myself' is reliable. Characteristically, however, he is determined to explore this 'without any system', and instead, 'what I have learned from experience' is presented 'in a general way and tentatively'; it is also focused on his current experiences as an old man, which is my focus as well.

It is tempting to see Montaigne's 'Of Experience' as a concluding statement to the essays overall, the drawing together of his key insights. However, this might infer a systematic approach that would go against his repeated insistence on the randomness of his thought processes, and on his distinctive approach to his writing. Like his life experience, the essays are a jumbled accumulation, a unique kind of palimpsest, its layers reflecting his views at different periods of his life, the original texts still visible, the later insertions (more than a thousand overall) identified only in modern editions, and then unobtrusively; almost nothing was ever deleted. As he described them, the essays were an attempt 'to follow a movement so wandering as that of our mind'. Nowhere is the sense of an ending indicated, much less a conclusion. There are no 'last words'.

More than half of this essay is taken up with his experiences of dealing with illness (ever a common preoccupation of the old), following traditional lines rather than the contradictory and often ignorant advice of the 'domineering' doctors of his day. He deals with illness, he tells us, mainly by ignoring it, following 'habit', 'routine' and the dictates of nature, letting illness take its course, finding a doctor if unavoidable (under family pressure) who agrees with him, trying to 'lull and beguile' his own imagination to help him deal with pain.

While many people, men in particular it seems, still tend to follow Montaigne's approach of ignoring illness, I am driven by worry, and a general belief, or wishful thinking, in relation to modern science, to seek medical advice, particularly when severe pain is involved. Indeed, in my case it is not necessary that the pain be very severe. My doctor of many years, who combines expertise and empathy to an unusual degree, told me early on that I was very lucky to have both low pain tolerance and an over-active imagination – making it more likely that I would seek medical advice early and thus, one day perhaps, put off death or serious illness for a while.

Writing this while coping with a severe attack of sciatica (and with other constraints of a plague year, as Montaigne had been), helped by a sophisticated (and disorientating) cocktail of drugs to manage the pain, I am in awe at the stoicism of Montaigne in bearing routinely in his later years the excruciating pain of passing large kidney stones through his penis (described graphically), and thus, with characteristic humour, 'an affliction that punishes those of your members by which you have most sinned'. He consoles himself that 'the stone' is an affliction of old age, or even 'the tribute due to old age'; that, being associated with a rich diet, it is a disease of 'the great' and is 'essentially noble and dignified'; that 'it detaches you from the world'; that it is intermittent, and 'not ill-suited to my hasty and impetuous disposition'. In these ways, and more, he seeks to 'relieve', 'help' and 'flatter' his 'imagination' in bearing with it. A principal benefit is 'how artfully and gently the stone weans you from life, and detaches you from the world'.

Montaigne's pride in his heroic bearing of pain is strongly male, and in the Stoic tradition. (It was also a major theme of the early art of James Barry.) It is related to his admiration for the military life, both as he experienced it and in many of the examples from classical authors quoted in the early essays. He is proud of the fact that, despite 'the stone', he can stay all day in the saddle. And yet he felt himself to be temperamentally at odds with many related forms of male culture, such as the use of torture, some aspects of blood sports, and the physical abuse of children. I too was characteristically male for my time and culture when younger, partly in terms of a focus on physical prowess but much more in the combination of ignorance, shame and guilt about the body, which Catholic teaching massively reinforced and which Montaigne never seemed to have felt. Being lucky with my health, I could ignore my body for the most part and enjoy it in physical activities, but I never related to it positively.

Ageing and occasional minor illnesses finally brought the male body properly into focus for me, bringing an acceptance of its complexities and ultimately making the experience of it a matter of celebration rather than of guilt. A great help in this was Montaigne's humour and gusto in treating of the ageing male body, making it central to the 'experience' he reflects on in his essay. Believing that 'It is for habit to give form to our life', his central strategy in dealing with ageing is identical to that of dealing with illness, to stick to routines that give pleasure. 'Health, for me,' he wrote, 'is maintaining my accustomed state without disturbance ... I cannot be hurt by the use of things that I have been so long accustomed to.' He defined the happy life in terms of 'ordinary, commonplace, familiar things', which he describes in exuberant detail – the pleasures of food, of sleep, of exercise, of sex, of scratching an itch – even of defecation. His life in retirement, 'obscure and private, enjoys every natural dispensation', and follows 'my urgent appetites'.

He is clear that 'The greatest benefit that good health brings me is sensual pleasure'.

Old age and its illnesses are viewed positively as 'symptoms of the length of years', and part of the fabric of the whole. (My father's invariable response to enquiries about his often-poor health was the quiet boast, 'not bad, for an auld fellow'.) 'Our life,' Montaigne wrote, 'is composed, like the harmony of the world, of contrary things, also of different tones, sweet and harsh, sharp and loud ... our life is impossible without the mixture.' Having celebrated the ageing body, partly in terms of the Stoic tradition of his youth, Montaigne concludes his thoughts on experience with a thrilling statement of the humanist philosophy of his old age – based on respect for both body and mind, and for their interaction. He hates the 'inhuman wisdom', 'the sickly, killjoy mind' that makes an enemy of the body. This anti-body stance was at the core of my own education as a teenager, which went far beyond fear of the body as the enemy of the perfection of the soul; it involved also disgust and shame about bodily functions, and above all about sex. To quote again the seventeenth-century book of meditations that constituted our daily spiritual guide when we were novices:

> This outward man, our flesh and sensuality, is the greatest adversary and enemy that we have, and as such is always at work making mischief for us, lusting against the spirit, against reason and against God.

All of that negativity was buried deep in my subconscious, and was not reflected outwardly in how I lived then, immersed in physical activities, happy, as I believed, in myself. Even when my early experience of sex proved difficult, even traumatic, I did not see it in terms of the wider context of my relationship with my body, and my underlying assumptions about it. Nowadays, ever more conscious, to quote Kurt Weill's 'September Song', that 'the days dwindle down to a precious few', I celebrate, like Montaigne, the simple profundities that we experience through our bodies – the sight of loved ones, the joy of movement, ever-changing skies, a glass of Malbec – felt particularly keenly when, as now for me, they are interrupted by pain. Unlike Montaigne, however, I can anticipate this pain being modified by the miracle of modern medicine and, like him, can also experience it as a particularly insistent intimation of mortality.

At the end of 'Of Experience', Montaigne articulates wonderfully the philosophy that has also come to replace my earlier adherence to religion. This he describes as 'a mixed constitution', combining 'the pleasures of life' with 'pleasures of the imagination'. This is the key to 'how to live appropriately', avoiding the tendency 'to despise our being'. Philosophy is best when 'most human', as the Stoics showed in making nature 'a guide' and in pointing to the folly of attempting to split 'body and soul' (a fine summary of traditional Catholic teaching) rather than marrying 'the divine with the earthly'. He rejects the 'transcendental humours' of those who 'want to get out of themselves and escape from the man'. He ends with a summation of 'experience' as knowing 'how to enjoy our being rightfully', commending 'old age' (which 'needs to be tended a little more tenderly') 'to that god who is the protector of life and wisdom, but gay and sociable wisdom'.

This philosophy also helps him to face his death, which will, he hopes, be normal and natural, allowing him to 'melt and slip away from myself', that is, accepting death as an extension of the experience of ageing. Indeed, dying is part of living; we die little by little over a lifetime, if we are lucky. What he had witnessed at deathbeds, he wrote, did not reflect the general belief in 'the agony of death'. It made no sense that 'with so great a paralysis of the limbs, and so great a failing of the senses, the soul could maintain any force within by which to be conscious of itself'. His near-death experience as a young man, when he was knocked from his horse, freed him, he believed, of his fear of dying, leaving him with the sense that it was merely a more or less pleasurable falling asleep.

These were comforting beliefs, but they were at odds with his moving experience at the deathbed of his great friend Étienne de La Boétie many years earlier. It was a difficult death, marked in Montaigne's detailed account in a letter to his father by stoic fortitude and the acknowledgement of their great friendship. It was also tragically different from the gradual fading away of Montaigne's ideal; La Boétie was only thirty-three years old. Having also witnessed many horrific deaths from war and plague, what Montaigne hopefully envisioned for himself was a 'natural' death, one anticipated and lived with through old age, 'a collected, calm and solitary death all my own, in keeping with my retired and private life'. And so, he would prefer to die away from home, preferably on horseback. 'Dying is not a role for society; it is an act for one single character.'

Of course he also was aware that he would have no say about when and in what circumstances death would come to him, and was, doubtless, little surprised when indeed he did die at home, in the midst of family and retainers, and that, at least by one account, he had mass celebrated in his room, and joined in its rituals. However, 'a local historian' added the detail that he called in his servants 'and paid them the legacies he had left them', which he knew his heirs might find difficult (or inconvenient) to pay – an account the modern reader may find more in keeping with the essays. It is noteworthy, and perhaps significant, that Montaigne had managed skilfully and clearly deliberately to avoid conflict with the Catholic Church (at times even diplomatically endorsing its power in religious matters), despite the secular humanism of his voluminous and widely read essays. Clearly he felt vulnerable to that church's extensive use of censorship, and the essays managed not just to escape censure but also to be used at times as an antidote to Protestant heresy, though his writings show little interest in Catholic doctrine.

Catholicism was also important in his political and social roles, and we shouldn't assume that his religious practice, only adverted to in his travel journals, was *purely* formal. Yet, it seems significant that he never referred to an after-life in his writings, not even to its importance in the idea of the soul, developed by Socrates, one of his greatest influences. This is a reminder that we should not assume that the Montaigne of the essays is the full picture, that there are no deep, private, less rational and more incoherent elements, if only in his subconscious. That would accord with my own experience of second-guessing my rational acceptance of death as final, the end of my existence. As I get nearer to death, I find myself reflecting that my rejection of Catholicism was of the institution's long history of cruelty and corruption, and of the dogmatic nature of its teachings. Does my rejection of the idea of a god necessarily preclude the comfort of Socrates' idea of 'soul' as the core of our nature, or Plato's reimagining of it as 'psyche' – and particularly of their belief that in some way that core survives our individual deaths, that we each possess to some degree an immortal soul, not dependent on religious understanding or belief? I may yet discover that such comforting ideas become more important to me as I age further, as they did for Socrates as he awaited execution.

Today, as we are reminded daily, many die from war, starvation and disease – mainly in the poorest regions on Earth, though even the affluent can experience death as violent, agonising and terrifying. But many of those lucky enough to have lived well-off lives in stable, peaceful societies do experience death today as Montaigne envisioned his own, as a falling asleep, thanks to pain management and sedation through drugs. This marked the deaths of loved ones at which I was present, and it certainly helped the person dying as well as the upset witnesses. More generally, such palliative care can also, I think, reduce the fear of death (or, more particularly, of how you might deal with it) as it gets closer. Being in my eighty-first year ('in the waiting room', as an old friend cheerfully put it lately), I find that I think less about death than I had imagined I would. This is helped by the luck of my good health but also, I think, by the focus I have learned to put on the present, helped immeasurably by Montaigne's writings. The past is beyond recovery, and nearly beyond recall – we cannot change it. The future is unknowable in its details – only the fact of our deaths is certain. We can try to postpone it by avoiding risk and living sensibly, and this will also help us to enjoy what days we have left – and it is on that enjoyment we should focus.

Horace's advice, *Carpe Diem* – make the most of what time you have left – is often quoted as an injunction to the young, but it surely applies even more to the old, especially those who don't believe in an afterlife such as is promised by Catholicism. There is no comfort for us in rehearsing our faults and seeking divine forgiveness for them, no life after death to compensate for the sorrows of this, little to be gained from preparing for a 'good' death, as if it was a passport to eternal life. (An old friend said to me recently that since he stopped believing in God he no longer feared death – 'no prospect of Hell, you see'.) How each individual will die is beyond his/her knowing, but it should not be a contest, the object of which is to 'die well'. The support of loved ones is the greatest possible contribution to our happiness and the greatest consolation in dying, but in the most profound sense each of us lives as well as dies alone. All we have before then is the rich potential of the passing moment, and the opportunity, if we are lucky and understand our nature and needs properly, to enjoy it and benefit from that. Above all, this is what the profound humanism of Montaigne has taught me.

Approaching my recent significant birthday, I resisted all suggestions of a celebration involving more than immediate family – as I had at sixty and seventy. I pointed again to the fact that I have never had a birthday party, even in childhood, and to my dislike of 'fuss' (similar to my father's), but this time I knew there was something more. While it had been relatively easy to ignore being sixty and seventy, I had learned, even in advance, that it would be difficult to ignore being eighty and that the last thing I wanted was a celebration to draw wider attention to it. And so it has proved. I have found that I regularly think of the fact, and sometimes dwell on it. It seems somehow to be quite literally monumental, impossible to ignore, demanding attention. Contributory reasons are not hard to find – the accumulating deaths and serious illnesses of friends my age and younger, the gradual and probably inevitable return of sciatica and a further accumulation of aches and pains (and probably worse), the further loss of energy. More significant is the sense of how much this birthday marks the sense of time running out. After telling an old (and older) friend how relieved I had been to be told by medics after a series of scans and tests that I was in good shape, there was a pregnant pause. 'Of course, some time [in the not-too-distant future clearly implied] a medic will say to you, "Bad news, I'm afraid – you have very little time left."' Such intimations of mortality certainly focus the mind, and it will require fresh resolve to continue to follow the positivity of Montaigne's last essays.

A different kind of positivity can be found in Wordsworth, whose 'Intimations' were of *im*mortality rather than mortality, coming from his sense of childhood as a time when 'Heaven lies about us', and the belief that we are still imbued with a divine sense of wonder, acquired before 'shades of the prison-house begin to close/upon the growing boy'. And so, even as adults we can draw strength from the basic impulses and understandings of childhood, and especially from those intimations that survive through our enduring bond with nature.

> Though nothing can bring back the hour
> Of splendour in the grass, of glory in the flower;
> We will grieve not, rather find
> Strength in what remains behind;
> In the primal sympathy
> Which having been must ever be;
> In the soothing thoughts that spring
> Out of human suffering;
> In the faith that looks through death,
> In years that bring the philosophic mind.
>
> * * *
>
> Thanks to its tenderness, its joys, and fears,
> To me the meanest flower that blows can give
> Thoughts that do often lie too deep for tears.

Old age, with its growing confusion, incomprehension and forgetfulness, is often compared unflatteringly to a second childhood, and the old seen as childish, but what Wordsworth advocates is being child-*like*, which is indeed a worthwhile and not outrageous ambition. Wordsworth's insight is echoed nowadays by those psychologists who stress the importance of recognising, understanding, healing or celebrating 'the inner child' that endures in us all. It can be one path to making old age into 'years that bring the philosophic mind', and became central to what shaped this memoir as it developed, but also no doubt, *pace* Montaigne, with 'a drunkard's motion, staggering, dizzy and wobbling, or that of reeds that the wind stirs haphazardly as it pleases'.

ENVOI

I have had a very privileged and lucky life. My gratitude for that is often nowadays accompanied by a sense of guilt, less in relation to myself (though that persists, in spite of Montaigne) than as part of my generation of well-off Europeans. It becomes increasingly clear that our wealth, coming mainly from the value of our houses, is at the expense of our children's generation, which can't afford the massively inflated prices from which we benefit, and which we did nothing to control. Our wealthy lifestyle owes much to the exploitation of cheap labour in the global economy and of the fossil fuels that are driving climate change and endangering the future of our planet. Ireland, while it still often presents itself as among the victims of colonialism, having a common bond with the world's poor, has long since joined the exploiting nations. Indeed, we have long been beneficiaries, as much as victims, of the British imperial system.

I grew up with certainties – about religion, about our place in history – and with optimism – about an ever-improving future, with each generation having better prospects than the last. Now, in old age, while enjoying the comforts of privilege, however guiltily, I am haunted by insecurities, about the future of the world, about the future of democracy, about the future of my children, and their children. I was born in the shadow of a world war and until recently was happy to think that such devastation would never occur again, at least in Europe; now a European war's obscenities feature nightly in our news programmes. All my life as a historian I pointed, with some optimism as to its ultimate disappearance, to the dangerous distortions of nationalism; today it has risen phoenix-like and is rampant again. The values of academic thought, freedom and autonomy, which I took for granted for most of my working life, are being eroded year by year. I could go on.

Of course, the old have always tended to pessimism about the future they won't live to see, and there are reasons also to be optimistic, especially about the worldwide movement for climate and social justice, driven forward by the young. Our growing sense of insecurity need not be accepted with despair, but fought on an individual as well as a communal level. Understanding what is happening in the world (and our role in it) is key, and must begin at the level of the self. That is part of the value of autobiography; it is social as well as personal. To re-quote Montaigne's justification, 'You can tie up all moral philosophy with a common and private life as well as with a life of richer stuff. Each man bears the entire form of man's estate.' This exercise in writing a memoir of my 'common and private life' has certainly been of value to me, helping me to understand not only my life but also my inner self (my nature) better. It is an understanding that starts with childhood and always brings you back to it. As T.S. Eliot put it in 'Little Gidding', the final poem of *The Four Quartets*, written the year I was born,

> We shall not cease from exploration
> And the end of all our exploring
> Will be to arrive where we started
> And know the place for the first time.

Greystones, December 1, 2023

Index

NOTE: Page locators in **bold** refer to photographs and illustrations.

Abercromby, Gen Ralph, 47
Achebe, Chinua
  Things Fall Apart (novel), 195
Agagianian, Cardinal, 129
All-Ireland hurling finals, the, 50, 74–76, 146
American PhD system, the, 201–202
Apostolic Work Society, the, 71, 72
Aristotle, 99, 240
art history and painting, 231–234, 247
atheism, 114, 176, 177
  (*see also* humanism)
Austen, Jane, 210

Bach, J.S., 112, 173, 180, 181, 182–183
Baily, Tom, 49
Ballymacar farm, New Ross, 15, 21, 30, 43, 45, 53, 165
Baluba babies, 129–130
Banim, John and Michael, 205
Banville, John
  Infinities, The (novel), 188
  Kepler (novel), 188
Barrow river, the, 45, 62, 63
Barry, James, 232–236, 251
  Birth of Pandora, The (painting), 235
  Self-Portrait as Timanthes (painting), 235
  Self-Portrait with Paine and Lefevre (painting), 234
Barthes, Roland, 17, 83
BBC, the, 54, 73, 95, 217
Béaslaí, Piaras
  Michael Collins and the Making of a New Ireland (book), 57–58
Beatles, The, 146
Beethoven, Ludwig von, 180, 182, 226, 236
Bellini, Giovanni
  Circumcision, The (painting), 231
Benedict XVI, Pope, 130
Berger, John, 5
Berger Prize, the, 233
bilingualism and the Irish language, 204, 217, 218–222, 223–224, 226
bird-watching, 228, 229–230
Black Death, the, 65
book-keeping and taxes, 59
books and reading, 54–57, 61, 136, 162, 173, 187–192, 194, 195, 225
  and plague literature, 239–241
  (*see also* Joyce, James; Montaigne, Michel de)
Boylan, Dom Eugene, 119
Bradshaw, Brendan, 86, 168
Breathnach, Máire, 225–226
Breathnach, Páraic, 222
Brennan, Danny, 106
British Merchant Navy, the, 72
Bromell, Tony, 145
Brophy, Annie, 27, 42, 44, 49, 82
Brosnahan, Jackie, 121
brown soda bread, 30, 52
Browne, Aggie, **16**, 32

Browne, Noël, 178
Browne Clayton Monument, the, 47
Butler, Hubert, 186

Cambridge University, 155, 159, 202–203, 216, 220
Camus, Albert
Plague, The (novel), 239
Canon Law and mortal sin, 95
Carroll, Lewis, 199
Casey, Finbarr, 122
Cassin, Barry, 104, 127, 196, 197
Catholic Church, the, 70, 80, 85–87, 114, 118, 129, 177–178, 254
and abuse, 87–88, 112, 117, 130, 135, 140–143, 151, 177
(*see also* Christian Brothers, the)
Catholic Truth Society, the, 85
Chardin, Teilhard de, 119
charity work, 168–169
Charteris, Leslie, 57
chiaroscuro, 247
Children of Mary, the, 71, **79,** 80
Chopin, Frédéric, 181, 182
Christian Brothers, the, 1, 81, 85, 92–97, 100–116, **105, 107, 109, 110,** 151
and abuse, 151–152
and emotional repression, 93, 109, 116–119, 146
and family connection to, 32, 88
and the 'industrial schools,' 89, 98–102, 139–143, **140,** 148
and internal report on, 93
and recruitment to, 88, 89, 106, 122
and thirty-day retreat, 113–114
(*see also* vows of the Christian Brothers)
Christianity and religion, 31, 53–54, 56, 58
(*see also* Catholic Church, the; humanism)
church music, 111
Clare, John, 185
Clark, George Kitson, 216
Clark, T.J.
Sight of Death, The (painting), 231
Clarke, Des
Church and State (book), 178
Clifford, Johnny, 75
Clough, Arthur Hugh
'Easter Day' (poem), 176
Coláiste an Spioraid Naoimh, Cork, 220
Coláiste Chiaráin, Bray, Co. Wicklow, 92
Coláiste Iognáid Rís (Carriglea), Dún Laoghaire, 98–102
Collar of Gold restaurant, Dublin Airport, 76
Collins, Michael, 57
colonialism in Ireland, 217
and scholarly research, 205–206, 210
(*see also* post-colonial Ireland and bilingualism)
comics, 54–55, 74, 77, 131
Confraternity Band, the, 79, 80
Conrad, Joseph
Heart of Darkness, The (novel), 195
Constable, John, 184
Cork University Press, 230, 233
corporal punishment, 83, 85, 118, 126–128, 142–143, 146, 149, 169
Corpus Christi (Catholic feast day), **79,** 80
Cotter, Louise, 244
Counihan, Fr Tom, 113, 114, 115
Courtdale farm, New Ross, Co. Wexford, 21, 23, 24, 25, 26, 27, 29–30, 45–46
Norman tower house, 24, 46, 49, 200
Covid-19, 157, 236–238, 241
Crawford Art Gallery, Cork, the, 156, 232, 233, 235

'Croppy Boy, The' (ballad), 71–72
Crowe, Catriona, 208
Crutched Friars, the, 63
Cullen, Louis, 72
Cullen, Pat, 73
Cullen, Paul, Cardinal, 118

Daly (née Rice), Nancy, 14, **15**, 22
DC Thomson publishers, 55
de Bhaldraithe, Tomás, 219, 220, 224
de Valera, Eamon, 57
Dean Ryan Cup, the, 146
Defoe, Daniel
  Journal of the Plague Year, A (book), 239
Delany, Ronnie, 95–96
Department of Education, the, 122, 137
Descartes, René, 228
Dickens, Charles, 55, 136
Donnycarney National School, Dublin, 121–122
Doran, Johnny, 72
Dublin Review, The (magazine)
  'Seven Years in the Christian Brothers' (essay), 114
Dudley Edwards, Robin, 195
Duff, Frank, 130
Duncannon and summer holidays, 39, 40–41, **41**, 43, 71–72, 77, 155–156
Dunne, Art (father), 14–15, **15**, 19–30, **24**, **26**, **28**, **42**, 43, 53, 56, 155, 252
  and death, 14, 43, 165, 167
  at Duncannon, 40–41, **41**
  and farming, 21, 32–33, 45–46
  and personal qualities, 24, 29, 37, 57
  and politics, 20–21, 57
  and relationship with son, 40, 47–48, 74–75, 76, 89, 148, 167
  and religious beliefs, 21, 58, 117
  and the shoe shop, 27, 29, 58, 59–60
  and social life, 29, 33, 44, 54, 71, 72, 73–75, **74**, 76, 77, **77**
  and visits to son, 97, **110**, 138, **138**, 139, 148
  and wedding, 21–23, **22**
Dunne, Betty (aunt), **34**, 34–35
Dunne, Fergus (son), 243, 244, 245
Dunne, Fr John (cousin), 34, **34**
Dunne, Fr John (uncle), 20, **20**, 21, 22, 53, 58, 76–77, **77**, 96, 131
Dunne, Jim (uncle), 20, 21, 23, 32–33, 34, **34**
Dunne, Mary (sister), 39, **39**, 111
Dunne, Mary (wife), 35, 156, 158–163, 164
Dunne, Nick (uncle), 20, 22
Dunne, Oisín (son), 3, 242
Dunne, Rosaleen (sister), **48**, 49
Dunne, Thomas (grandfather), 19, **19**, 25
Dunne, Tom
  and acrophobia, 166
  on ageing and death, 246–250, 254–257
  and appendix removal, 129
  and art history, 231–232, 233, 234
  and birth and childhood, **24**, 24–26, **27**, 27–29, **28**, 30, 31, 33–35, 37–43, **39**, **41**, **42**, 48–58, 59, 60–61, 69, 77–80, 81, 241
  and books and poetry, 23, 54–57, 61, 62, 132–133, 136, 162, 173, 185, 186, 187–192, 194, 195, 225, 239
  and the Christian Brothers, 85, 88–89, 92–104, 134–135, **135**, 143–144, 148–149, 184, 200, 218–219
    and annual interview with visiting superior, 148, 149
    and departure from, 149–151
    and the novitiate, 102–110, **105**, **107**, **110**, 111–120, 196, 252
    and St Joseph's industrial school, 139–143, 148

Dunne, Tom (*continued*)
and the Christian Brothers (*continued*)
and teaching, 121–129, **125**, 131–134, **132**, **134**, 136–138, 144–148
and education, 81, 83–84, **84**, 85, 99–101, 128
and emotional development, 159–160, 161, 166, 169–170
and First Holy Communion, 81–83, **82**
and health, 37–38, 129, 130–131, 162, 238–239, 246, 250–251, 256
as historian, 69, 71, 155, 178–179, 198–201, 203–209, 210–211
and hobbies, 52, 54–56, 61, 132–133, **143**, 143–144, 146–147
and home in Cork, 241–245
and hurling and sport, 74–76, 81, 83, 84–85, 93–94, 112, 128–129, 132, **132**, 146
and the Irish language, 221–224, 225–226
and marriage to Clare, 96, 134, 156, 157, 164, 165–166, 174, 184, 238, 244
and marriage to Mary, 35, 156, 158–164
and musical tastes, 111–112, 133, 173, 179–183
and nature, 183–186, 228, 229–230
and pessimism about the future, 259–260
and PhD study at Cambridge, 202–203, 216
and political activism, 168
and publications, 65, 114, 199, 203–204, 205, 206, 207–208, 209, 210, 223
Rebellions: Memoir, memory and 1798 (book), 1, 29, 65, 98, 114, 141, 155, 198, 207–208, 209
relationship with father, 40, 47–48, 74–75, 76, 89, 148, 167
relationship with mother, 35–37, 39, 55, 79, 83, 88–89, 96, 97, 138–139, 159, 164–167
and religious beliefs, 85–86, 88, 156, 164, 176, 254
and humanism, 156, 178–179, 181, 190, 246, 252–253, 255
on the role of universities, 211–215
and the Ryan Commission, 141, 148
and self-identity and Irishness, 216–217, 224–225
and semi-retirement, 156–157, 208, 227–228, 230–231, 236–238, 241
and sense of guilt, 168–169, 170–172, 249, 251, 252, 259
and siblings, 42–43, 60, 89, **109**, 111, 155
and study at UCD, 155, 177, 195, 200–201, 219
and teaching, 167–168, 193–197, 203, 204–205, 210, 220
Dunne (née Rice), Johanna (mother), 14–17, **15**, **16**, **17**, 21–27, **22**, **24**, **26**, 32, 40, 56, 57, 67, 87, **110**, 155, 207
and death, 166–167
and leisure and social life, 30–31, 52–53, 71, 72, 79
and life after Art's death, 43–44
and personal qualities, 24, 35–36, 37, 41–42, 164–165
and relationship with son, 35–38, 39, 55, 79, 83, 88–89, 96, 97, 138–139, 159, 164–167
and religious beliefs, 30–31, 53–54, 58, 70, 88, 164–165
and shoe business, 18, **18**, 26, 49, 58–59, 71
and visits to son, 97, 138–139, **139**, 148
Dutch Reformed Church, the, 247

Easter 1916 Rising, the, 201, 206, 209
Economic War, the, 21
Edgeworth, Maria
Castle Rackrent (novel), 205
Einstein, Albert, 210–211
Eliot, T.S., 132–133, 150, 174–175, 177
'Burnt Norton' (poem), 175–176
Four Quartets (collection), 174–175, 260
'Little Gidding' (poem), 174, 260
'Wasteland, The' (poem), 174
English perceptions of the Irish, 216–217
Ernaux, Annie
Years, The (memoir), 4
EU (European Union), the, 225, 226
evening prayer, 31
Evening Press (newspaper), 75
Expert Advisory Group on Centenary Celebrations, the, 208–209

Fanon, Frantz, 206
Far East (magazine), 88
Faulkner, G.T., 93
FCÁ (Fórsa Cosanta Áitiúil), the, 80
Fear Siúil, An (play), 94
Ferrier, Kathleen, 133
Ferritéir, Muiris, 219
Festival of Plain Chant, the, 86
Fianna Fáil, 21
Fiannaíocht poems, the, 100
Field Day movement, the, 207
fiftieth anniversary dinner of Sexton Street CBS hurling victories, 145–146
Fine Gael, 57
flower-arranging, 184–186
flu epidemic (1918–19), the, 19
Foley, Art, 75
Forristals of Courthoyle, the, 29–30
Fossett's Circus, 79
Frame, Donald M., 7
Francis Street school, Dublin, 131
French, Norman, 65
French Revolution, the, 114

GAA, the, 74
and all-Ireland hurling finals, 50, 74–76, 146
Gaelic poetry, 100, 202, 203, 204, 220, 222
Gaelscoileanna, the, 224, 225
Gaeltacht, the, 219, 224
Gall, Fr, 86
Gallagher, Jack, 202
Gantley, Billy, 23–24
Gantley, James, 32
Gantley, May, 14
Gardiner, John Eliot, 180
Gladstone, W.E., 48, 201
'Good Boy syndrome,' 6–7, 35, 36, 37, 61, 81, 92–93, 101, 155, 158, 161, 166, 170, 196, 208
Good Shepherd Convent, New Ross, the, 87, 141
Gough, Viscount, 103
government education policy, 101
Gregorian chant, 86, 111
Grey, Zane, 57
Grimes, Éamonn, 146

Hamill, Claude, 121
Hanrahan, Michael, 81, 97, **97**
Hansen, Peter, 29–30
Harty Cup, the, 146
Hayes, Dick, 133
Heaney, Seamus
'Traditions' (poem), 217
Herrick, Robert, 186
Hickey, John D., 75
Higgins, Michael D., 124
Hood, Thomas, 45
Horgan, Brother, 99–100
Hughes, Kathryn, 55

Hughes, Thomas, 56
humanism, 156, 175–177, 178–179, 181, 190, 192, 246, 252–253, 255
Hyde, Douglas, 222
Hyland, Áine, 126

IADT (Dún Laoghaire Institute of Art, Design and technology), 99
ideologies of empire, 202–203
Immaculata, Sr, 81
Inquisition, the, 113
Investment in Education (report), 101
IRA, the, 21, 33
Irish and the Leaving Certificate, 99–100
Irish Home Rule Bill (1886), the, 202
Irish Independent (newspaper), 57, 75, 76
Irish language, the, 94, 97, 99–100, 218–224, 225–226
Irish Review, The (journal), 206–207
Irish Times, The (newspaper), 222
Irishness and self-identity, 216–217

J. Rice shoe shop, New Ross, 27, **48**, 49–51, 58–60, 62, **63**
J.A. Stanley photography studio, 22
Jansenism, 117–118, 131
Jesuits, the, 113–114, 149
Journal of Scottish and Irish Studies (journal)
  'Voices of the Vanquished' (article), 204
Journal of the Wexford Historical Society, the, 207
Joyce, James, 212–213
  Portrait of an Artist as a Young Man, A (novel), 95, 149, 212, 216, 218
  Ulysses (novel), 28–29, 159, 174, 195, 217–218
Jurassic period, the, 229

Keane, John B.
  Field, The (play), 137
Keegan, Claire
  Small Things Like These (novella), 87
Kennedy, J.F., 73
Kenny, Anthony, 176
Kickham, Charles J.
  Knocknagow or The Homes of Tipperary (novel), 56–57, 96, 150
Killincarrig, Greystones (home), 134, 157, 245

La Boétie, Étienne de, 253
Labour Party, the, 57, 177–178
land annuities, 21
Lawrence, D.H., 136
Leaving Certificate, the, 99–100, 101, 102, 122, 128, 150
Lee, Mrs., 52
Legion of Mary, the, 130
Lenihan, Liam, 234
literary theory, 205
Little Gidding religious community, England, the, 174–175
Longfellow, Henry Wadsworth
  'My Lost Youth' (poem), 62
Longley, Michael, 185
Looking Back: Living and writing history. Oliver MacDonagh 1924–2002 (book), 210
Lucretius, 177, 248
Luddy, Maria, 207
Luftwaffe, the, 23
Luther, Martin, 182

MacDonagh, Oliver, 201, 209–210
  States of Mind: A study of Anglo-Irish conflict, 1780–1980 (book), 209–210
Maclise, Daniel, 232
Macmillan, Harold, 134

Magdalene laundries, the, 87
Mahon, Derek
  'Disused Shed in County Wexford, A' (poem), 130
male body and mortification of the flesh, the, 115–117
Manley Hopkins, Gerard, 132–133, 150, 173
  'Windhover, The' (poem), 173
Marías, Javier, 190
  Your Face Tomorrow (novel), 189–190
Marina, Cork, the, 228, 229
Marshal, William, 65
Marvell, Andrew, 245
Maynooth Mission to China, the, 21
McCormack, John, 52–53, 181
McDonagh, Martin, 217
McGahern, John, 160
McManus, J.P., 145, 146
McQuaid, John Charles, Archbishop, 126
Melbourne Olympics, the, 95–96
memoir writing and authenticity, 2–3, 227–228, 238
Merton, Thomas, 119
monochrome photographs, 14
Montaigne, Michel de, 7–10, 99, 127, 164, 185, 189, 191, 198, 199, 228–229, 239, 252–255, 260
  and ageing, 188, 246, 248, 250, 257
  Essays, 1
  on guilt and repentance, 170, 171–172
  and humanism, 156, 177, 179, 255
  'Of Experience' (essay), 248–250, 252–253
  'On Physiognomy' (essay), 239–241
  'On Repentance' (essay), 7, 170–171
  and Stoicism, 8, 129, 171–172, 250–252
  and teaching, 193–194, 196
Morgan, Lady, 205
mortal sin and Canon Law, 95, 172
Mrs Brown's Boys (TV show), 217
Murphy, John, 81
Murphy, John A., 196, 223
Murray, Peter, 232, 233, 235

Nabokov, Vladimir
  Speak, Memory (memoir), 5
Naessens, David, 244
Nandy, Ashis, 206
Napoleonic Wars, the, 47
National Inventory of Architectural Heritage, The, 49
National Portrait Gallery, London, the, 234, 236, 247
nationalist narratives and the Easter 1916 Rising, 201, 206, 209
Nelson, Ricky, 124
New Ross, 62–64, **63**, **66**, **67**, **68**, 69–70, 73, 78–80, 200
  and the 1798 Rebellion, 65, 66–69, 198, 207
  and annual rowing regatta, 78
  and Corpus Christi celebration, **79**, 80
  Irishtown, **64**, 64–65, 66, 68
  'Murphy's Yard,' 81
  South Street, **48**, 49–51, **74**
  Tholsel (Market House), the, 55, 65, 66–67, **67**, 78
New Ross – Rosponte Ros Mhic Treoin (anthology), 65
New Ross Pipe Band, the, 79–80
Newbawn megalithic dolmen, 15, **16**
Newman, John Henry, 210, 211–212, 213
  Idea of a University, The (book), 211
Nolan, Plunkett, 111, 112
Nowlan, Kevin B., 201
NUI (National University of Ireland), the, 128, 156, 211, 212–213, 230–231

Ó Bruadair, Dáibhí, 222
Ó Cadhain, Máirtín, 218
Ó Criomhthain, Tomás, 218
Ó Direáin, Máirtín
'tEarrach Thiar, An' (poem), 222
Ó Dónallain, Tomás, 126
Ó Dubhshláine, Micheál, 225–226
O Riordan, Michelle, 204
Ó Tuathaigh, Gearóid, 221
obedience and conformity, 6, 92, 101, 155
(*see also* 'Good Boy syndrome')
O'Connell, Daniel, 210
O'Connell, Mick, 129
O'Connor (née Dunne), May (aunt), 54, 57, 76
O'Donnell, Nick, 75
O'Halloran, Clare (wife), 96, 134, 156, 164, 165, 166, 174, 184, 238, 244
O'Halloran, Jimmy, 243, 244, 245
O'Kennedy, Gus, 54, 72–73, **74**
'Old House, The' (ballad), 52–53
Oppermann, Johnny, 76
O'Reilly, Terry, 113, 176, 178

Passion of Christ and *The Spiritual Exercises,* the, 115
Patrician Year and High Mass at Croke Park, the, 129, 130
Penguin Crime books, 57
Peyton, Fr, 31
photography, 4, 14–15, 17, 18, 19, 22, 25, 27, 40, 43, 44, 49, 139, 143, 146, 147, 244
physical and sexual abuse in the Catholic Church, 87–88, 112, 117, 130, 135, 140–143, 151, 177
Piper, Raymond, 185
plagues and literature, 239–241
Poor Law Guardians, 19
post-colonial Ireland and bilingualism, 217, 218–222
Poussin, Nicolas
Landscape with a Man Killed by a Snake (painting), 231
Pressly, William (Bill), 233
James Barry's Murals at the Royal Society of Arts: Envisioning a new public art (book), 233
Primary Certificate, the, 122, 125, 126
Proust, Marcel, 2–3, 62, 112
In Search of Lost Time (novel), 180, 190–192
Provisional IRA, the, 206
pub of Gus O'Kennedy, the, 54, 72–73, **74**
Pugin, Augustus Welby, 131
Pullman, Philip, 56
Purcell, Brother, 99
Puskás, Ferenc, 74

Quigley, John, 73

Rackard, Bobby, 75
radio, the, 53, 54
Radio Éireann, 54
Raftery, Mary, 141
rationing during wartime, 23
Rebellion of 1798, the, 32, 46–47, 49, 52, 64, 65, 66–69, **68**, 88, 198, 200, 207
and the bicentenary of, 207, 208, 209
Rembrandt, 234–235, 246–248, 249
revisionist debate in Irish nationalist history, the, 201, 206–209, 210
Reynolds, Sir Joshua, 234, 235
RIC (Royal Irish Constabulary), the, 32, 33
Rice, Biddy (Bridget) (aunt), 41, **41**, 50, 52, 72
Rice, Edmund, 32, 88, 151
Rice, Jack (uncle), 30, 53, 165, 167
Rice, James (uncle), 26, 45, 46, 50
Rice, John (cousin), 45

Rice, John (grandfather), 15–16, **16, 17,** 18, 23, 24, 32, 35, 43
Rice, John (great-great grandfather), 65, 67–68, 88, 207
Rice, Kathy (aunt), 45, 64, 87
Rice family home, Irishtown, New Ross, the, **64,** 64–65
Richard, Cliff, 143
Richmond Hospital, Dublin, 129, 130
Ring, Christy, 74, 75
'Rock Around the Clock' (song/film), 38
Rodriguez, Fr Alphonsus (Alonso), 104, 119
 Practice of Perfection and Christian Virtues, 116
Roe (née Rice), Maggie (aunt), 30
Rosary, the, 31, 53–54, 100
'Roscúil,' Cork (home), 241–245
Royal Academy, London, the, 234, 235
Royal Hotel, New Ross, the, 64
Royal University, the, 212
Rule of St Benedict, the, 112
rural electrification, 69
Ryan, Justice, 100, 127
Ryan Commission and Report, the, 98, 100, 112, 127, 140, 141, 148

Sacred Heart Messenger, The (magazine), 57
Said, Edward, 36, 37, 206
 Out of Place (memoir), 36
Sebald, W.G., 188–189
 Austerlitz (novel), 23, 187
Second Vatican Council, the, 131
Second World War, the, 23
Sexton Street CBS, Limerick, 144–147
sexual repression and Jansenism, 117–118
Shakespeare, William, 187, 248
 Henry V (play), 217
 Macbeth (play), 147
Sheen, Fulton, Bishop, 130
Sheridan, John D., 57
Sinn Féin, 209
'So Deep is the Night' (song), 181
social change and modernity, 69–71, 80, 103, 146, 158
social status in New Ross, 77–78
Society of African Missions, the, 114
Socrates, 8, 240, 254
St Bernard, 116
St Helen's, Booterstown, Dublin, 103
St Ignatius of Loyola, 114
 Spiritual Exercises, 113–115
St John of the Cross, 108, 175
St Joseph's industrial school, Tralee, 139–143, **140,** 148
St Mary's teacher training college, Marino, Dublin, 121
'Star of the Sea' hostel, the, 130
States of Fear (TV documentary), 141
Stepanova, Maria, 3
Stern, Isaac, 133
Sterne, Laurence
 Life and Times of Tristram Shandy, The (novel), 190
Stoicism, 8, 129, 171–172, 177, 240, 248, 250–251, 253
Studia Hibernica (journal), 204
 'Gaelic Response to Conquest and Colonisation: The evidence of the poetry, The' (article), 203–204
Subaltern Studies (journal), 206
Sullivan, Maureen
 Girl in the Tunnel (memoir), 87
Summer Holiday (film), 143
'Swedish Drill,' the, 83–84
Synge Street School, Dublin, 123–128, **125,** 131, **132,** 132–134

Tauber, Richard, 181
TG4, 221, 222

Tóibín, Colm, 92, 188, 216
Tolstoy, Leo
  Anna Karenina (novel), 43
Tom Brown novels, the, 94, 101
  Tom Brown at Oxford, 55, 56
  Tom Brown's School Days, 55–56
Tone, Theobald Wolfe, 199, 206
tonsillitis and Guinness, 37–38
Tottenhams and New Ross, the, 49, 50, 63–64, 65, 66
traditional folk medicine, 38, 52
Tralee monastery school, 136–137
Travellers, the, 33
Troubles, the, 201, 209
Tunbridge, Laura
  Beethoven: A life in nine pieces (book), 180

UCC (University College Cork), 213–214, 220
UCD (University College Dublin), 85, 106, 212–213, 219, 223
UCG (University College Galway), 221
UN intervention in the Congo, the, 129–130
Universities Act (1997), the, 213
universities and social role, 211–215

VAT (value-added tax), 59
Veale, Fr Joe, 114, 118, 119, 149
voice modulation and audience attention, 196–197
vows of the Christian Brothers
  of chastity, 116–117, 150
  of obedience, 114, 119, 120, 122, 147, 148–149, 150
  of poverty, 119, 149–150

Wall, Maureen, 195, 201
Walton, John, 54
War of Independence, the, 21
wedding photograph, **22,** 22–23
Weill, Kurt
  'September Song' (song), 252
Wexford *vs.* Cork All-Ireland Hurling Finals, 74–76
Whicker, Alan, 73
White, Annie, 72
White, Bob, 72
White, Mrs. Gilbert, 72
wildflowers, 184–185
Williams, John
  Stoner (novel), 194
Wordsworth, William, 108, 183, 184, 186, 256–257
  'Intimations' (poem), 256
Wright, Leo, 105, 106, 122, 123, **123,** 140, 142, 144, 145, 146, 147
writing and Covid-19, 236–237

YouTube, 73